P9-CQP-365

Global Café

Simple, Healthy, and Delicious Meals

52 Complete Menus

Darlene Blaney, MSc, NCP

Conexão Editorial

Gerência Editorial: Sandra D'Alevedo

Criação de projeto gráfico: Alexandre Romão e Dinho Del Puente

Produção Gráfica: Kleber de Messas

Coordenação de edição: Luci Kasai

Edição: Larissa Wostog Ono

Assistência Editorial: Nilce Xavier

Coordenação de revisão: Maya Indra Souarthes Oliveira

Revisão: Daniel Erlich, Diego Rezende, Luciana Martinez, Marcelo Maia, Mariana Munhoz

Coordenação de diagramação: Altemar Dias

Diagramadores: Flavia Y. Boni, Elizabete Pereira, Vinícius Bocato, Flávio Akatuka, Tatiane Coelho, Marcos Masuko

Coordenação de iconografia: Elaine Bueno

Iconógrafos: Ana Carolina Ungersbock, William Guimarães

Published by Autumn House® Publishing, a division of Review and Herald® Publishing, Hagerstown, MD 21741-1119

This book was
Edited by Heather Reseck, R.D.
Copyedited by James Cavil
Cover designed by Ron Pride
"Prepared by Conexão Editorial for Autumn House Publishing"
Typeset: 11/14 Univers 57 Condensed
14 13 12 11 10 5 4 3 2 1

Blaney, Darlene, 1970-

The ultimate vegetarian collection global cafe : simple, healthy, and delicious meals : 52 complete menus / Darlene Blaney.

p. cm. -- (The ultimate vegetarian collection)

Includes bibliographical references and index.

1. Vegan cookery. 2. Cookery, International. 3. Ingredient substitutions (Cookery) I. Title.

TX837.B563 2010

641.5'636--dc22

2009028326

ISBN 978-0-8127-0501-0

Contents

Introduction

It's no secret that what we eat affects our bodies. Elevated cholesterol and triglyceride levels, high blood pressure, diabetes, heart disease, arthritis, and other diseases plague our Western society. Of all the lifestyle factors that play a role in the reversal of these diseases, changing eating habits poses the greatest challenge for most people. It's often easier to find ways to exercise more, drink additional water, get adequate rest, soak up appropriate amounts of sunlight, and breathe plenty of fresh air. How about changing what I eat?

We can easily fall into the rut of eating the same dishes again and again. We may not consider experimenting with foods from other cultures in our own kitchens. Instead we fall into the trap of believing that preparing ethnic food is too time-consuming, complicated, and risky. What if I don't like it?

At one time I was afraid to experiment with cooking international foods. Over the past 15 years I've taught hundreds of vegetarian cooking classes featuring home-style North American foods. I purposely avoided ethnic foods until a friend, Valerie Fitch, who assisted me with most of my cooking classes, coaxed me out of my comfort zone by organizing some international cuisine classes. To my delight, these classes quickly filled, and many times I had to repeat the classes in order to accommodate everyone who registered. I embraced new styles of cooking. Who could resist such a variety of colors, flavors, and aromas?

This cookbook is a compilation of the recipes taught in my international cuisine classes. I have adapted some of the most popular ethnic dishes to a plant-based diet that focuses on more healthful ingredient choices. Most of these recipes use common foods and spices, except a few specialized products that you can find in most large supermarkets or at Adventist Book Centers. I have put the recipes together into menus so you will know how to combine the dishes to make complete meals.

I realize that this cookbook covers only the tip of the iceberg when it comes to representing ethnic diversity. I hope that *Global Café* will give you a taste of the many great foods and cultures in our world, and create a curiosity in you to experiment with other international cuisine recipes.

– Darlene Blaney, M.Sc, N.C.P.

About the Author

Darlene Blaney has a Master of Science degree in nutrition and is currently completing a doctorate in nutrition. She owns and operates a nutrition consulting practice and is the founder of Total Health School of Nutrition, which offers a distance-learning diploma program in nutritional consulting (www.totalhealthschoolofnutrition.com).

Darlene is coauthor of *The Optimal Diet: The Official CHIP Cookbook*, written with Hans Diehl, Dr.H.Sc. (Review and Herald Publishing Association, 2008). Her other cookbooks are *Vegetarian for Life* and *Good Nutrition for Life*.

As health director for the Alberta Conference of Seventh-day Adventists, Darlene enjoys traveling and presenting seminars and workshops. Darlene's passion is to help others enjoy total health of mind, body, and spirit. She desires to help people enjoy quality of life through prevention and reversal of common diseases such as diabetes, cancer, and heart disease. She enjoys teaching nutrition and showing how delicious, healthful food can be simple, fun, and creative.

When she's not teaching workshops or cooking for groups at Foothills Camp, Darlene likes to cook at home in Alberta, Canada, for her husband, Ron, and four sons: Nathan, Reuben, Joseph, and Josiah.

Glossary of Special Ingredients

Most of the ingredients listed in these recipes are available at large supermarkets with ethnic and natural foods sections. However, some special items may need to be purchased at natural food stores or specialty ethnic stores. Here is a list of some of the more unfamiliar ingredients and where to buy them.

To locate the Adventist Book Center serving your area, visit www.adventistbookcenter.com, or, from the United States or Canada, call their toll-free number (1-800-765-6955).

Agar powder: A thickening agent made from seaweed that is used instead of animal gelatin in recipes. The word "agar" comes from the Malay word *agar-agar,* which means "jelly." One teaspoon of agar powder is equivalent to two tablespoons of agar flakes, or one agar stick (*kanten*). The powder is the easiest to work with and is the form used in this cookbook. It is available at natural food stores.

Baking powder (aluminum-free): A baking powder made without aluminum sulfate. Aluminum in foods and cookware has been associated with Alzheimer's disease and other neurological disorders. Rumford is one brand that is commonly available in large supermarkets and in natural foods stores.

Beef-style seasoning: The recipes in this cookbook that contain beef-style seasoning were developed with Blaney's Beef-like Seasoning (www.totalhealthfortoday.com). This seasoning, developed by the author, is vegetable-based, low-sodium, and free of preservatives and artificial colors. The recipes list a wide range in the amount of beef-style seasoning because of variations between brands. If you use Blaney's Beef-like Seasoning, use the higher amount of seasoning and season to taste. If you use a brand that is more concentrated and higher in sodium, such as McKay's Beef Style Seasoning (www.mckays-seasoning.com) or Bill's Best All Vegetable Beaf Seasoning (www.uncledons.com), start with the smaller amount and season to taste. McKay's is available at some large grocery stores and at Adventist Book Centers. Bill's Best is available at Adventist Book Centers, while Blaney's is available at some Adventist Book Centers and by mail order.

Carob chips: These can be used in recipes in place of chocolate chips. Look for carob chips that do not contain dairy or partially hydrogenated fats, and are naturally sweetened (such as with malted barley). Carob chips are available at natural food stores

Carob powder: Carob is a natural chocolate substitute made from the locust bean pod. Unlike chocolate, it does not contain theobromine, methylxanthines, caffeine, or tannins. It is nonaddictive, low-fat, and rich in calcium, phosphorus, magnesium, potassium, and iron. When replacing cocoa powder with carob powder in recipes, use about half the amount of sugar because of carob's natural sweetness. Roasted carob powder has a deeper, richer flavor and color, making it more similar to chocolate. It is available at natural food stores.

Cedar Lake-MGM foods: A line of frozen and canned meat substitutes that are free from preservatives and additives and often considerably lower in fat and sodium compared to other brands of meat substitutes. For more information, access: www.cedarlakefoods.com. It is available at Adventist Book Centers.

Chicken-style seasoning: The recipes in this cookbook that contain chicken-style seasoning were developed with Blaney's Chicken-like Seasoning (www.totalhealthfortoday.com). This seasoning, developed by the author, is vegetable-based, low-sodium, and free of preservatives and artificial colors. The recipes list a wide range in the amount of chicken-style seasoning because of variations between brands. If you opt for Blaney's Chicken-like Seasoning, use the higher amount of seasoning and season to taste. If you use a brand that is more concentrated and higher in sodium, such as McKay's Chicken Style (www.mckays-seasoning.com) or Bill's Best Chik'nish (ww.uncledons.com), start with the smaller amount and season to taste. See beef-style seasoning for availability of these seasonings.

Cinnamon substitute: A combination of ground coriander and ground cardamom may be used as a cinnamon substitute.

Dry unflavored soy protein strips: A high-protein dehydrated product made only from non-genetically modified organism (GMO) soybeans. Soy Curls (www.butlerfoods.com) or Soy Addums (www.soygood.com) can be used in place of chicken. To rehydrate, place soy protein strips in a bowl and cover with boiling water (or broth). Let stand for 10 minutes. Squeeze out any remaining liquid, if desired. They are available at Adventist Book Centers.

Egg replacement powder: A powdered leavening and binding agent made from tapioca flour, potato starch, and leavening. It can be used as an egg substitute, primarily in baked goods. The recipes in this cookbook were developed using Ener-G Egg Replacer. When "egg replacement" is used in recipe directions, it refers to egg replacement powder dissolved in the indicated amount of water.

Eggless mayonnaise: Most commercial brands of eggless mayonnaise are soy-based. Brand names include Nayonaise, Vegenaise, and Nasoya. They are available at large supermarkets and at natural food stores.

Fructose: Referred to as fruit sugar, fructose is the sweetest of all naturally occurring carbohydrates. The primary food sources of fructose are fruits, vegetables, and honey. Because fructose is sweeter than other sugars, you can use about half the amount of sugar called for in a recipe.

Granulated cane sugar: Made by evaporating the water from sugar cane juice, which allows it to solidify and granulate. Compared to regular table sugar, pure cane sugar is not bleached or processed with chemicals, so minerals remain in the final product. Names to look for include: evaporated cane syrup, granulated cane sugar, Sucanat (cane sugar with molasses). Granulated cane sugar is available at large supermarkets and at

natural food stores.

Grape-seed oil: Grape-seed oil is a chef's favorite because of its clean, neutral taste and high smoke point of approximately 320°F. Grape-seed oil is a powerful antioxidant. It helps lower total cholesterol and increases the concentration of beneficial HDLs (high density lipoproteins), which carry excess cholesterol away from body cells and back to the liver, where it is excreted.

Herb-seasoned salt: Spike is the brand most used in developing the recipes in this cookbook. It is a blend of 39 herbs, vegetables, and exotic spices, and is available with salt or salt-free. Other brands include Herbamare, Mrs. Dash, and Vegit.

Kelp powder: Kelp has a salty taste as well as a distinct fishlike odor and flavor, which can be purposeful in some dishes. Some people love it, while others can't stand it. It is high in natural plant iodine, which is absorbed much more slowly and safely than chemical iodine. Iodine is necessary for proper functioning of the thyroid, whose role is essential for growth, energy, and metabolism.

Meatless burger: Brands such as Yves Meatless Ground or Cedar Lake Vegeburger are free of preservatives and low in fat and sodium. They are available in 12-ounce packages that contain about two cups and are equivalent to a pound of hamburger meat. Yves products are available in the refrigerated section of supermarkets. Cedar Lake products are available at Adventist Book Centers.

Nondairy cheese: Sheese is one brand that is 100 percent vegan and free from hydrogenated fats. It is available in block form in flavors such as cheddar and mozzarella at natural food stores.

Nondairy cream cheese: Soy-based alternatives that can be used in place of dairy cream cheese in recipes. Choose brands free of hydrogenated fats, such as Tofutti Nonhydrogenated Cream Cheese or Creamed Sheese. It is available in the natural food sections of supermarkets or at natural food stores.

Nondairy sour cream: Soy-based sour cream substitutes that contain no animal products. Choose a brand free of hydrogenated fats, such as Tofutti Nonhydrogenated Sour Cream. It is available in the natural food sections of supermarkets or at natural food stores.

Nonhydrogenated margarine: Earth Balance is a brand that uses organic cold-pressed oils employed to make a butterlike spread. It is available at supermarkets and natural food stores.

Nutritional yeast flakes: Different from the baker's yeast used in breadmaking, great-tasting nutritional yeast is grown on molasses. It has a cheeselike flavor and is high in B vitamins, particularly B_{12} (in fortified products). It is available at large supermarkets and at natural food stores.

Olive oil: This largely monounsaturated oil is best when used in its extra-virgin form, representing the first pressing at low temperatures, containing higher levels of antioxidants, particularly vitamin E and phenols. Olive oil has a high smoke point of 410°F, which makes it ideal for foods such as stir-fries.

Precooked cornstarch powder: A thickening agent, made from corn, that does not require cooking. Mix it in with other ingredients in a blender or food processor to thicken and prevent lumping. Instant Clear Jel is available at some natural food stores, specialty stores, and at www.kingarthurflour.com.

Pure cane syrup: A natural liquid sweetener, made from concentrated sugar cane juice, that contains all essential minerals and nutrients. Suggested brands include: Roger's Golden Syrup, Lyle's, and Steen's. They are available at natural food stores, specialty stores, and through Web sites.

Sesame oil: Sesame oil is available in two varieties: light (made with untoasted sesame seeds) and dark (made with toasted sesame seeds). Light sesame oil has a nutty flavor and is especially good for frying. Dark (Asian) sesame oil has a stronger flavor. Sesame oil has a high smoke point of 410°F, which makes it ideal for foods such as stir-fries. It is sold at supermarkets, Asian food stores, and natural food stores.

Silken tofu: The most common brand is Mori-Nu, which is a creamy silken tofu made from non-GMO soybeans and is packaged in a convenient long-life package that does not require refrigeration. Reduced-fat tofu is also available. Because of its smooth texture, silken tofu is ideal for making salad dressings and desserts. It is available at most supermarkets and at natural food stores. See also Tofu.

Soy chicken: Canned and frozen products such as Cedar Lake offer great taste and texture. Soy chicken is ideal for casseroles or soups, and it is available at Adventist Book Centers. See also Cedar Lake-MGM foods.

Soy milk powder: Look for brands that are casein-free, such as Soy Good (ww.soygood.com) or Better Than Milk Soy Original. They are available at some natural food stores and at Adventist Book Centers.

Spelt: Part of the wheat family, spelt is a wonderfully nutritious and ancient grain with a deep nutlike flavor. Spelt offers a broader spectrum of nutrients compared to wheat. It can be used in many of the same ways as wheat, including bread and pasta making. Spelt does not seem to cause sensitivities in many people who are intolerant to wheat. It is available at large supermarkets and at natural food stores.

Tahini: A kind of butter made from sesame seeds. There are two types of tahini, light and dark, and the light ivory version is considered to have both the better flavor and texture. Tahini is a source of calcium, protein, essential fatty acids, and vitamins E and B complex. It is available at large supermarkets, ethnic specialty stores, and natural food stores.

Tofu: Fresh soybean curd containing concentrated protein. Water-packed tofu is available in silken, soft, medium, firm, and extra-firm textures. Tofu is available in the refrigerated section of supermarkets, Asian grocery stores, and natural food stores. See also Silken tofu.

TVP (textured vegetable protein): A meat substitute made from defatted soy flour that is compressed until the protein fibers change in structure. TVP is sold in dehydrated granular form. It is available at natural food stores and at Adventist Book Centers.

Unfermented soy sauce substitute: An unfermented liquid seasoning made from organic soybeans and distilled water. It contains 50 percent less sodium than typical soy sauce. Bragg's All Purpose Seasoning (Liquid Aminos) is available at large supermarkets and at natural food stores.

Vegetable broth powder: An excellent flavoring base for soups and stews. Use a vegetable broth powder whenever the stronger flavors of beef or chicken would be too overpowering in a soup or casserole. Use to flavor rice or pasta, or add it to your cooking water. Vegetable broth powder is available at large supermarkets and at natural food stores.

Generic Terms for Brand Names

Blaney's Beef-like Seasoning: beef-style seasoning
Blaney's Chicken-like Seasoning: chicken-style seasoning
Bragg's All Purpose Seasoning: unfermented soy sauce substitute or reduced-sodium soy sauce
Clear Jel: precooked cornstarch powder
Earth Balance Buttery Spread: nonhydrogenated margarine
Ener-G Egg Replacer: egg replacement powder
Minute Tapioca: quick-cooking tapioca
Mori-Nu tofu: silken tofu
Nayonaise: eggless mayonnaise
Roger's Golden Pure Cane Syrup: pure cane syrup
Soy Curls: dry unflavored soy protein strips
Spike Seasoning: herb-seasoned salt
Tofutti Cream Cheese: nondairy cream cheese
Tofutti Sour Cream: nondairy sour cream
Vegenaise: eggless mayonnaise
Yves Ground Round: meatless burger

Cooking Measurement Equivalents

1 tablespoon (tbsp) =	3 teaspoons (tsp)
4 teaspoons =	1 tablespoon + 1 teaspoon
¼ cup =	4 tablespoons
⅓ cup =	5 tablespoons + 1 teaspoon
½ cup =	8 tablespoons
⅔ cup =	10 tablespoons + 2 teaspoons
¾ cup =	12 tablespoons
1 cup =	16 tablespoons
1 cup =	48 teaspoons
1 cup =	8 fluid ounces (fl oz)
1 pint (pt) =	2 cups
1 quart (qt) =	2 pints (4 cups)
1 gallon (gal) =	4 quarts (16 cups)
16 fluid ounces (fl oz) =	1 pound (lb)
1 milliliter (ml) =	1 cubic centimeter (cc)
1 inch =	2.54 centimeters

Source: United States Department of Agriculture (USDA).

About the Nutritional Values

The nutritional values used in the recipes were analyzed with Living Cookbook software and information from food manufacturers. When two ingredient options are listed, the first one was analyzed. Optional ingredients and ingredients without a specified amount were not included in the analysis. When the recipe calls for chicken-style seasoning or beef-style seasoning, Blaney's brand was used in the analysis.

U.S.–Metric Cooking Conversions

U.S. to Metric

Capacity

1 teaspoon =	5 milliliter
1 tablespoon =	15 milliliter
1 fluid ounce =	30 milliliter
1 cup =	240 milliliter
2 cups (1 pint) =	473 milliliter
4 cups (1 quart) =	0.95 liter
4 quarts (1 gallon) =	3.8 liters

Weight

1 ounce =	28 grams
1 pound =	454 grams

Metric to U.S.

Capacity

1 milliliter =	⅕ teaspoon
5 milliliter =	1 teaspoon
15 milliliter =	1 tablespoon
100 milliliter =	3.4 fluid ounces
240 milliliter =	1 cup
1 liter =	34 fluid ounces
1 liter =	4.2 cups
1 liter =	2.1 pints
1 liter =	1.06 quarts
1 liter =	0.26 gallon

Weight

1 gram =	0.035 ounce
100 grams =	3.5 ounces
500 grams =	1.10 pounds
1 kilogram =	2.205 pounds
1 kilogram =	35 ounces

Asian and Pacific

Vegetable Chop Suey

Menu 1

New Peking

Tapioca pudding was a favorite of mine when I was growing up. Now it's a favorite of my children's, too. This recipe fits nicely into a total vegetarian diet without compromising the flavor.

- **Sweet-and-Sour Tofu***
- **Perfect Brown Rice**
- **Chinese Broccoli**
- **Cabbage Noodle Salad**
- **Tapioca Pudding** with **Soy Whipped Cream**

Sweet-and-Sour Tofu

1 package extra-firm tofu, drained (about 12 ounces)
2-3 tablespoons olive oil or ¼ cup water
1 green bell pepper, cut into 1-inch pieces
1 medium onion, cut into 1-inch pieces
2 cups celery, cut diagonally
1 can pineapple tidbits, including juice (14 ounces)
1 can tomato paste (6 ounces)
¼ cup lemon juice
¼ cup unfermented soy sauce substitute or reduced-sodium soy sauce
1 tablespoon honey
¼ teaspoon garlic powder
¼ teaspoon salt
1 tablespoon cornstarch
2 tablespoons water

Cut tofu into ½-inch cubes. Set aside. Heat oil or water in a wok or large skillet. Add the bell pepper, onion, and celery. Cook and stir until tender. Stir in pineapple tidbits, tomato paste, lemon juice, soy sauce substitute, honey, garlic powder, and salt. Dissolve cornstarch in water and stir into skillet. Cook, stirring constantly, until cornstarch thickens and turns translucent. Stir in cubed tofu and simmer about 5 minutes, or until heated through. Serve over brown rice.

Makes 8 servings. 138 calories, 4 g fat, 389 mg sodium.

COOK'S HINTS:

- For **Sweet-and-Sour Sauce**, omit the tofu. Good with **Spring Rolls**. (p. 25)

*Menu items in bold are recipes in this cookbook and are printed following the menu unless a page number is listed.

Perfect Brown Rice

- 4 cups water
- 2 cups brown rice
- 1 teaspoon salt

Heat oven to 350°F. Mix water, brown rice, and salt in a 2-quart baking dish. Cover and bake 1 hour, or until rice is tender and liquid is absorbed.
Makes 12 ½-cup servings. 113 calories, 1 g fat, 195 mg sodium.

VARIATIONS:

- Replace ¼ cup brown rice with ¼ cup wild rice.
- **Perfect Brown Basmati Rice**: Replace brown rice with brown basmati rice.
- **Perfect Steamed Brown Rice**.

Chinese Broccoli

- 2-3 tablespoons olive oil
- 1 medium onion, chopped
- 2 large bunches broccoli, cut into 1-inch florets
- 2 tablespoons unfermented soy sauce substitute or reduced-sodium soy sauce
- 1 teaspoon granulated cane sugar
- 1 cup water
- 2 teaspoons to 2 tablespoons chicken-style seasoning,* or to taste
- 2 teaspoons cornstarch

Heat oil in a skillet over medium-high heat. Add onion. Cook and stir until browned. Stir in broccoli and cook for 3 minutes, stirring constantly. Stir in soy sauce substitute and sugar. Mix water, chicken-style seasoning, and cornstarch; stir into broccoli mixture. Cook and stir 1 minute. Serve immediately.
Makes 8 servings. 70 calories, 4 g fat, 230 mg sodium.

*see glossary

Cabbage Noodle Salad

- 1 3-ounce package ramen noodles
- 3 cups shredded green cabbage
- 1 cup shredded red cabbage
- 2 green onions, sliced
- ½ cup sliced or slivered almonds, lightly toasted
- 2 tablespoons lemon juice
- 1 tablespoon honey
- 2 tablespoons olive or sesame oil
- 1 tablespoon unfermented soy sauce substitute or reduced-sodium soy sauce

Break ramen noodles into smaller pieces and discard seasoning packet. Place noodles in a large salad bowl. Stir in green cabbage, red cabbage, green onions, and almonds. Whisk lemon juice, honey, oil, and soy sauce substitute together in a small bowl. Pour dressing over salad and mix well. Cover and refrigerate about 1 hour.
Makes 8 servings. 106 calories, 8 g fat, 88 mg sodium.

Tapioca Pudding

- 1½ teaspoons egg replacement powder (such as Ener-G)
- 2 tablespoons water
- 2¾ cups soy milk
- ¼ cup granulated cane sugar
- 3 tablespoons quick-cooking tapioca
- 1 teaspoon vanilla extract

Whisk egg replacement powder and water together in a medium saucepan. Whisk in soy milk, sugar, and tapioca. Let stand 5 minutes. Cook over medium heat, whisking constantly until mixture begins to boil; reduce heat and simmer 1 minute. Remove from heat and stir in vanilla. Pour pudding into a serving bowl (or divide between individual bowls). Refrigerate 1-2 hours, or until chilled. Garnish with a dollop of **Soy Whipped Cream**.
Makes 6 ½-cup servings. 96 calories, 2 g fat, 44 mg sodium.

Soy Whipped Cream

¾ cup cold soy milk
2 tablespoons honey
1 teaspoon vanilla extract
¾ cup grape-seed or canola oil
½ teaspoon lemon juice

Process soy milk, honey, and vanilla in a blender or food processor for about 10 seconds. While continuing to process, gradually drizzle in oil. Pour into a bowl. Gently stir in lemon juice until mixed and cream thickens.

Makes 1½ cups; 12 1-tablespoon servings.
69 calories, 7 g fat, 3 mg sodium.

Menu 2

Chopstick Cuisine

When I taught cooking classes for a major grocery store in our city, my friend and cooking class assistant, Valerie Fitch, decided I needed some new class topics. She booked me to teach a Chinese cuisine class. I panicked! I had never cooked much Chinese food, let alone taught a total vegetarian class on it. I prayed that no one would sign up, but to my surprise, the class filled up, and they scheduled another. I am thankful for Valerie's challenge because now we enjoy a variety of Chinese dishes, some of which have become our top family favorites.

- **Wonton Soup with Whole-Grain Buns**
- **Wonton Wrappers**
- **Wonton Filling**
- **Mock Ginger Beef**
- **Perfect Steamed Brown Rice** (p. 16)
- **Chinese Green Beans**
- **Stir-fried Cabbage**
- Sliced Tomatoes and Cucumbers
- **Almond Cookies**
- **Almond Junket**

*see glossary

Wonton Soup

12 cups water
⅓ cup vegetable broth powder or ¼ to ⅓ cup chicken-style seasoning,* or to taste
1-2 tablespoons unfermented soy sauce substitute or reduced-sodium soy sauce
2 tablespoons lemon juice, optional
4 cups finely shredded (or chopped) Swiss chard, spinach, kale, or collard greens
½ cup chopped green onion
50 prepared **Wonton Wrappers**

Stir water, vegetable broth powder and soy sauce substitute together in a 6-quart saucepan. Season to taste. Stir in lemon juice, if desired. Heat to boiling and stir in Swiss chard and green onions; reduce heat and simmer 5-10 minutes, or until greens are softened. Remove from heat. Stir in prepared wontons. Serve immediately.

Makes 10 servings. 257 calories, 1 g fat, 299 mg sodium.

Wonton Wrappers

2 cups unbleached all-purpose flour
½ cup water
2 teaspoons egg replacement powder (such as Ener-G) dissolved in 3 tablespoons water
1 tablespoon olive oil
¼ teaspoon salt
cornstarch, for dusting work surface

Mix flour, water, egg replacement, oil, and salt together. Knead 5 minutes, on a surface that has been lightly dusted with cornstarch, until it is well mixed and forms a soft ball. Place in a plastic bag (or cover with a wet towel) for 30 minutes. Divide dough into two or three sections. Working with one section at a time, roll dough into 1/16-inch-thick sheets on a surface lightly sprinkled with cornstarch. Cut into 3-inch squares.

Makes about 50 wonton wrappers. 21 calories, 0 g fat, 12 mg sodium.

Wonton Filling

2 tablespoons sesame oil
¼ cup thinly sliced green onions
4 fresh mushrooms, chopped
2 teaspoons minced fresh ginger
2 cups meatless burger (such as Yves) or ground **Homemade Gluten** (p. 32) or rehydrated TVP
¾ cup soft tofu
¼ cup finely chopped water chestnuts
1-2 tablespoons seaweed gomasio seasoning
1 tablespoon unfermented soy sauce substitute or reduced-sodium soy sauce
50 **Wonton Wrappers** or 1 14-ounce package 3-inch wonton wrappers

Heat sesame oil in a medium skillet. Cook and stir green onion, mushrooms, and ginger until onions are tender. Mix meatless burger and tofu together; stir into skillet. Mix in water chestnuts, seaweed gomasio, and soy sauce. Remove from heat.

Place 1 teaspoon of filling in the center of each wonton wrapper. Moisten the edges of each wrapper with water. Bring the two opposite corners together by folding over the filling to form a triangle, and seal in the filling by firmly pressing around the edges of the triangle. Pull the two base corners of the triangle together over the filling, then overlap the tips of the two corners and press the ends together.

Fill a large saucepan half full with water and heat to boiling. Drop in wontons. When water returns to a boil, add 2 cups of cold water and cook over medium heat until the water returns to a boil. Remove wontons with a slotted spoon. Use in **Wonton Soup**, or serve hot as dumplings with a sauce.

Makes about 50 wontons. 50 calories, 1 g fat, 86 mg sodium.

*see glossary

COOK'S HINTS:

- You can use rehydrated Chinese black (shiitake) mushrooms.
- Seaweed gomasio (such as Eden Organic) is an Asian mixture of sesame seeds and powdered sea vegetables, which is available at ethnic and natural food stores. You can replace it with 1-2 tablespoons of toasted ground sesame seeds, ½ teaspoon kelp powder, and ¼ teaspoon salt (also available at ethnic and natural food stores).

Mock Ginger Beef

2 cups unbleached all-purpose flour
½ cup cornmeal
2 tablespoons nutritional yeast flakes
1 teaspoon ground ginger
1 teaspoon garlic powder
½ teaspoon paprika
1-2 tablespoons sesame oil
8 large **Homemade Gluten** steaks (p. 32), cut into strips
1 heaping tablespoon minced fresh ginger
3 large cloves garlic, minced
2 cups **Gluten Broth** (p. 32) or 2 cups water plus 2 teaspoons to 2 tablespoons beef-style seasoning,* or to taste
¼ cup cornstarch
¼ cup water
¼ cup unfermented soy sauce substitute or reduced-sodium soy sauce
2 tablespoons granulated cane sugar
¼ teaspoon cayenne pepper, or to taste
1 tablespoon sesame seeds, lightly toasted

Mix flour, cornmeal, nutritional yeast, ginger, garlic powder, and paprika together in a bowl. Heat sesame oil in a skillet. Dip each strip of gluten into flour mixture. Fry gluten steaks until golden brown on each side. Transfer to a baking dish. Cook and stir ginger and garlic in the same skillet, until lightly browned. Stir in broth. Dissolve cornstarch in

water and whisk into broth. Stir in soy sauce, sugar, and cayenne. Simmer, stirring constantly, until thickened. Pour sauce over gluten. Sprinkle with sesame seeds. Serve immediately.
Makes 8 servings. 254 calories, 5 g fat, 461 mg sodium.

COOK'S HINTS:

- Instead of **Homemade Gluten** steaks you can use 3 cups dry unflavored soy protein strips (such as Soy Curls) rehydrated in hot water (or broth) and drained.

Chinese Green Beans

2 tablespoons sesame or olive oil
2 pounds fresh green beans, trimmed
1½ tablespoons minced fresh garlic
1½ tablespoons minced fresh ginger
2 tablespoons sliced green onions (white part only)
1-2 tablespoons bean sauce, or to taste
2 tablespoons unfermented soy sauce substitute or reduced-sodium soy sauce
2-3 teaspoons granulated cane sugar
½ teaspoon cayenne pepper, or to taste

Heat oil in a skillet over medium-high heat. Add green beans and stir-fry 7 minutes. Stir in minced garlic, ginger, and green onions. Stir-fry until green beans are crisp-tender. Stir in bean sauce, soy sauce substitute, sugar, and cayenne; cook 1 minute. Remove from heat and serve immediately.
Makes 8 servings. 76 calories, 4 g fat, 158 mg sodium.

COOK'S HINTS:

- **Bean sauce**, also called **bean paste**, is a salty brown sauce made from fermented soybeans or black beans. Chinese bean sauce isn't as salty as Thai bean sauce. Some are more spicy than others.

*see glossary

Stir-fried Cabbage

2 tablespoons sesame oil
6 cups shredded Chinese cabbage
1-3 tablespoons chicken-style seasoning,* or to taste
2 cups shredded carrots

Heat sesame oil in a large skillet. Add cabbage and chicken-style seasoning. Stir-fry for a few minutes. Stir in carrots and continue to cook until cabbage is crisp-tender. Serve immediately.
Makes 6 servings. 72 calories, 5 g fat, 72 mg sodium.

COOK'S HINTS:

- For a different flavor, replace the chicken-style seasoning with some of your favorite herbs and seasonings, such as dill, garlic powder, onion powder, or seasoned salt.

Almond Cookies

3 cups all-purpose spelt flour or unbleached all-purpose flour
½ cup olive oil
½ cup honey
2 teaspoons egg replacement powder (such as Ener-G) mixed with 2 tablespoons water
2 teaspoons almond extract
1 teaspoon baking powder (preferably aluminum-free)
¼ teaspoon salt
1 tablespoon water (optional)
cooking spray
¼ cup blanched almonds

Heat oven to 350°F. Mix flour, oil, honey, egg replacement, almond extract, baking powder, and salt together in a mixing bowl. If dough is too dry, stir in 1 tablespoon water. Roll dough into 1-inch diameter balls and place on a baking sheet coated with cooking spray. Flatten balls with a glass. Press a blanched almond in the center of each cookie. Bake 10 minutes, or until golden brown around the edges.
Makes 2½ dozen. 80 calories, 4 g fat, 20 mg sodium.

Almond Junket

- ½ cup water
- ¼ cup agar powder
- 1¼ cups soy milk
- ¼ cup fructose or granulated cane sugar, to taste
- 1 teaspoon almond extract
- cooking spray
- 1 28-ounce can fruit cocktail (in fruit juice, without added sugar), drained

Heat water to boiling. Add agar; stir until dissolved. Stir in soy milk, fructose, and almond extract. Pour into a 9-inch square baking dish coated with cooking spray. Refrigerate 2 hours, or until set. Cut into ½-inch squares and mix with fruit cocktail in a serving bowl. Cover and refrigerate.

Makes 10 ½-cup servings. 69 calories, 1 g fat, 15 mg sodium.

Menu 3

East Meets West

This delicious pumpkin cake recipe gives you a wonderful alternative to pumpkin pie. Moist and flavorful, the pumpkin flavor shines through. My husband, Ron, and our boys especially enjoy this for a dessert, or eaten with fruit for a light supper.

Most people are usually surprised when I use pumpkin in Chinese cooking. Originally brought from South America, pumpkin is now a very common ingredient in China, most commonly found in southern Chinese cooking. It is used to make soup, stew, sweet dishes, and of course stir-fry dishes. There are many varieties of Asian hybrid pumpkins, but only one, the Kabocha pumpkin, is commonly found in North America. In China one can find other varieties, such as papaya-shaped pumpkins or smooth green round pumpkins with a net pattern.

- **Chinese Noodle Casserole**
- **Perfect Steamed Brown Rice** (p. 16)
- **Stir-fried Vegetables**
- **Edamame Bean Salad**
- **Pumpkin Cake**

Chinese Noodle Casserole

- 1 cup raw cashews
- 2 cups cubed soy chicken (such as Cedar Lake Turkettes), or **Homemade Gluten** (p. 32)
- olive oil or water, for cooking onions and celery
- 2 medium onions, chopped
- 3 stalks celery, chopped
- 1 8-ounce can sliced mushrooms, including liquid (do not drain)
- 1¼ cups **Condensed Mushroom Soup** (p. 145) mixed with 1 cup water
- 3 cups crispy chow mein noodles (egg-free)
- cooking spray

Heat oven to 300°F. Toast cashews on a baking sheet, stirring occasionally, for about 15 minutes or until lightly toasted; set aside. Increase oven temperature to 350°F. Drain soy chicken and cut into ½-inch cubes. Heat a little oil (or water) in a large skillet. Add onions and celery; cook and stir until onions are tender. Remove from heat. Stir in cashews, soy chicken, mushrooms and liquid, condensed soup, and chow mein noodles. Transfer to a 2-quart baking dish coated with cooking spray. Bake 45 to 60 minutes, or until hot and bubbling.

Makes 8 servings. 398 calories, 19 g fat, 324 mg sodium.

COOK'S HINTS:

- Instead of the **Condensed Mushroom Soup**, you can use 2 cups prepared brown gravy mix or **Beef-style Gravy** (p. 34).

Stir-fried Vegetables

- 1-2 tablespoons olive or sesame oil
- 1 12-ounce package extra firm tofu, drained and cut into ½-inch cubes
- 2 cloves garlic, minced
- 2 carrots, sliced diagonally
- ⅓ cup water, as needed
- 2 cups baby bok choy sliced into 1-inch pieces
- 2 stalks celery, sliced into 1-inch diagonal pieces
- 1½ cups fresh broccoli florets
- 1½ cups cauliflower florets
- 1 medium onion, chopped into 1-inch cubes
- ½ green bell pepper, cut into 1-inch cubes
- ½ red bell pepper, cut into 1-inch cubes
- 1 cup baby corn, frozen or canned
- 1 8-ounce can sliced water chestnuts, drained
- 1 8-ounce can bamboo shoots, drained and cut, if desired
- ½ cup fresh pods of snow peas
- 6 mushrooms, cut in quarters
- ¼ cup unfermented soy sauce substitute or reduced-sodium soy sauce
- 2 teaspoons to 2 tablespoons chicken-style seasoning,* or to taste
- 1 16-ounce package thick fresh Chinese noodles or 2 cups cooked brown rice spaghetti, optional

Heat oil in a large skillet or wok over medium heat. Add cubed tofu and garlic; stir-fry until tofu is golden brown. Add sliced carrots and water as needed to keep from sticking. Stir-fry 5 minutes. Add bok choy, celery, broccoli, cauliflower, onion, bell peppers, baby corn, water chestnuts, bamboo shoots, pea pods, mushrooms, soy sauce substitute, and chicken-style seasoning. Stir-fry until moisture evaporates and vegetables are crisp-tender. (If using noodles, rinse and separate noodles; add to skillet and heat through.) Season to taste with additional soy sauce substitute and chicken-style seasoning, if desired. Serve immediately.

Makes 14 1-cup servings. 82 calories, 3 g fat, 216 mg sodium.

COOK'S HINTS:

- Look for fresh Chinese noodles, such as Shanghai noodles, in the produce section.

Edamame Bean Salad

- 2 cups frozen edamame
- 1 red bell pepper, chopped
- 1 small sweet onion or red onion, minced
- 2 tablespoons olive oil
- 1 tablespoon lemon juice
- 2 tablespoons minced fresh basil
- ¼ teaspoon salt, or to taste

Cook edamame according to the package directions until crisp-tender. Drain and let cool. Stir bell peppers, onion, and edamame together in a salad bowl. Whisk oil, lemon juice, basil, and salt together in a small bowl. Pour dressing over salad. Toss until mixed.

Makes 8 servings. 100 calories, 6 g fat, 80 mg sodium.

COOK'S HINTS:

- Frozen edamame beans (green soybeans) can be found in the frozen vegetable section of the grocery store.

*see glossary

Pumpkin Cake

- 2 cups mashed and cooked pumpkin
- 1 cup raisins
- ⅓ cup olive oil
- 2 tablespoons egg replacement powder (such as Ener-G) dissolved in ½ cup water
- 1 cup whole-wheat flour
- 1 cup unbleached all-purpose flour
- 1 cup granulated cane sugar
- 2 teaspoons baking powder (preferably aluminum-free)
- 1 teaspoon baking soda
- 1 teaspoon ground cinnamon or substitute
- ¾ teaspoon salt
- ½ teaspoon ground allspice
- ½ teaspoon ground nutmeg
- cooking spray

Heat oven to 350°F. Mix pumpkin, raisins, oil, and egg replacement together in a mixing bowl. Mix in whole-wheat flour, all-purpose flour, sugar, baking powder, baking soda, cinnamon, salt, allspice, and nutmeg. Divide between two 5"x9"x3" loaf pans coated with cooking spray. Bake 50 minutes, or until a toothpick inserted near the center comes out clean. Transfer to a wire rack, and cool to room temperature before removing from pans.

Makes 2 loaves; 32 ½-inch slices. 90 calories, 2 g fat, 95 mg sodium.

COOK'S HINTS:

- This cake freezes well.
- Pumpkin Cake is also good with **Mock Cream Cheese Frosting** (p. 45). It's a favorite birthday cake in our family.

About Edamame

Edamame beans (pronounced ed-ah-ma-may) are young, green soybeans. They have a nutty, sweet flavor and have been used by the Japanese as part of their staple diet for many years. Edamame contain high amounts of iron, fiber, and protein, and are valued for their healthy omega-3 fat content.

Menu 4

Chinese Flair

My son Reuben presented a home school project on China in the sixth grade. Together we had fun adapting traditional Chinese recipes into total vegetarian recipes. The Lemon "Chicken" turned out to be one of our favorites. It even impressed his teacher, who was not a vegetarian.

- **Lemon "Chicken"**
- **Vegetable Chop Suey**
- **Perfect Steamed Brown Rice** (p. 16)
- **Bok Choy Salad**
- Edamame Beans, cooked in olive oil and sprinkled with salt
- Jasmine Tea
- **Rhubarb Tofu Pie**

Lemon "Chicken"

¾ cup soy milk
½ cup cornstarch
½ teaspoon salt
2 pounds frozen soy chicken, thawed (such as Cedar Lake)
1-4 tablespoons olive oil for frying, as needed
shredded lettuce
Lemon Sauce, as desired
lemon wedges

Whisk soy milk, cornstarch, and salt together in a small bowl. Slice soy chicken into ¼- to ½-inch rounds. Cut each round in half (or tear off small chunks for a more chickenlike look) and dip in batter. Heat 1 tablespoon oil in a large skillet; add soy chicken and fry on both sides until golden brown.

To serve: Place shredded lettuce on a platter. Arrange soy chicken pieces slightly overlapping each other on top of lettuce. Drizzle with **Lemon Sauce**. Garnish with fresh lemon wedges.
Makes 10 servings. 281 calories, 11 g fat, 750 mg sodium.

*see glossary

Lemon Sauce

2 cups water
½ cup granulated cane sugar
⅓ cup cornstarch
⅓ cup lemon juice
2 teaspoons to 2 tablespoons chicken-style seasoning,* or to taste
½ teaspoon ground ginger
shredded lettuce, for garnish
lemon wedges, for garnish

Mix water, sugar, cornstarch, lemon juice, chicken-style seasoning, and ginger together in a saucepan. Heat to boiling, stirring constantly; reduce heat and simmer until thickened.

Vegetable Chop Suey

2 cups hot water
1½ cups chopped onion
1½ cups chopped celery
2 tablespoons unfermented soy sauce substitute or reduced-sodium soy sauce
2 teaspoons to 2 tablespoons beef-style seasoning,* or to taste
2 cups fresh mung bean sprouts
1 cup chopped baby bok choy
1 10-ounce can sliced water chestnuts, drained
2 tablespoons cornstarch
½ cup water

Heat water, onion, celery, soy sauce substitute, and beef-style seasoning to boiling in a skillet or wok; reduce heat and simmer until onions and celery begin to soften. Stir in bean sprouts, bok choy, and water chestnuts. Simmer for another couple of minutes until bok choy begins to wilt slightly. Dissolve cornstarch in water; stir into skillet. Cook, stirring frequently, until the mixture thickens.
Makes 8 servings. 53 calories, 0 g fat, 189 mg sodium.

VARIATION:

- Replace beef-style seasoning with ½ teaspoon yeast spread (such as Marmite).

Bok Choy Salad

- 1 large bok choy, finely chopped (about 8 cups)
- 2 cups fresh mung bean sprouts, rinsed and drained
- 1 cup fresh snow peas or sugar snap peas, cut into thirds
- 1 cup raw sunflower seeds
- ⅓ cup olive oil
- 2 tablespoons lemon juice
- 1 tablespoon pure maple syrup
- ½ teaspoon garlic powder

Gently mix bok choy, bean sprouts, peas, and sunflower seeds in a large salad bowl. Whisk oil, lemon juice, maple syrup, and garlic powder together in a small bowl. Pour over salad and toss well.
Makes 8 servings. 146 calories, 12 g fat, 10 mg sodium.

Rhubarb Tofu Pie

- ¼ cup whole-wheat flour
- 4 teaspoons granulated cane sugar cooking spray
- 1 12-ounce package firm silken tofu (preferably reduced-fat)
- ½ cup granulated cane sugar
- ¼ cup whole-wheat flour
- 2 tablespoons lemon juice
- 4 cups rhubarb, cut into ½-inch pieces
- 1 large sweet apple, peeled, cored, and chopped
- ½ cup water
- 3 cups sliced frozen strawberries
- ¼ cup water
- ¼ cup cornstarch

Heat oven to 400°F. Mix ¼ cup whole-wheat flour and 4 teaspoons sugar together. Sprinkle evenly on the bottom and sides of a 10-inch pie plate coated with cooking spray. Process tofu, sugar, flour, and lemon juice in a blender or food processor until smooth. Pour into the prepared pie plate. Bake 20 minutes. Cool to room temperature.

Heat rhubarb, apples, and ½ cup water to boiling in a medium saucepan; reduce heat and simmer, covered, 10-15 minutes, until rhubarb and apples are tender. Stir in strawberries. Dissolve cornstarch in water and stir into rhubarb mixture. Cook, stirring constantly, until thickened. Pour over baked tofu mixture. Refrigerate 3-4 hours, or until set.
Makes 8 servings. 163 calories, 1 g fat, 41 mg sodium.

Menu 5

Bamboo Garden

Good news for spring roll lovers everywhere! Instead of being deep-fat fried, these spring rolls are baked with a little oil brushed on the outside to crisp them up. Plus, they are easy to make.

- **Rice Noodles With Vegetables**
- **Spring Rolls** with Plum Sauce or **Sweet-and-Sour Sauce** (p. 15)
- **Fried Rice**
- **Vegetable Salad**
- **Pumpkin Pie** with **Coconut Cream** (p. 54) or **Soy Whipped Cream** (p. 17)

Rice Noodles With Vegetables

- 1 16-ounce package rice noodles
- 1 16-ounce package frozen stir-fry vegetables
- 2 tablespoons sesame oil
- ¼ cup unfermented soy sauce substitute or reduced-sodium soy sauce
- 4 teaspoons to ¼ cup beef-style seasoning,* or to taste

Heat a large saucepan of water to boiling. Turn off heat and stir in rice noodles. Cover and let stand 5 minutes, or until noodles are tender. Drain noodles.

Heat sesame oil in a skillet or wok. Add vegetables and stir-fry until crisp-tender. Stir in noodles, soy sauce substitute, and beef-style seasoning. Stir-fry until heated through. Transfer to a serving dish.
Makes 8 servings. 379 calories, 5 g fat, 418 mg sodium.

*see glossary

COOK'S HINTS:

- Replace the frozen stir-fry vegetables with 4 cups fresh vegetables, such as carrots, mushrooms, baby corn, water chestnuts, green beans, and broccoli, cut into bite-size pieces.

Spring Rolls

2-3 tablespoons sesame oil
3 clove garlic, minced
¼-½ inch fresh ginger, minced
6 cups shredded Chinese cabbage
1 cup sliced fresh mushrooms
⅔ cup thinly sliced green onions
1 8-ounce can sliced water chestnuts, drained and chopped
½ cup unfermented soy sauce substitute or reduced-sodium soy sauce
4 cups fresh mung bean sprouts
1 16-ounce package spring roll wrappers (24 large or 48 small)
⅓ cup olive oil, as needed
cooking spray

Heat sesame oil in a wok or large skillet. Add garlic and ginger; cook and stir 3 minutes. Add cabbage, mushrooms, green onions, water chestnuts, and soy sauce substitute; cook and stir until vegetables are tender. Add bean sprouts. Cook and stir until bean sprouts are crisp-tender. Remove from heat.

*see glossary

Heat oven to 350°F. Using a pastry brush, lightly brush one side of the spring roll wrappers with oil. Turn wrappers over and arrange with one corner pointed toward you. Place about ½ cup filling on large wrappers (about ¼ cup on small wrappers) toward the front corner. (Use a slotted spoon to remove excess moisture.) Fold corner up over filling, then fold in sides. Roll up tightly. Place seam side down on a baking sheet coated with cooking spray. Bake 20 minutes, or until golden brown. Serve warm with **Sweet-and-Sour Sauce** or plum sauce.

Makes 24 large spring rolls (or 48 small).
54 calories, 4 g fat, 181 mg sodium.

COOK'S HINTS:

- **Spring Rolls** keep up to a week in the refrigerator or can be frozen. Reheat them in the oven to crisp up before serving.

Fried Rice

4 cups water
2 cups brown rice
4 teaspoons to ¼ cup chicken-style seasoning,* or to taste
1 cup reduced-fat silken firm tofu
6 fresh mushrooms, sliced
½ cup shredded carrots
½ cup sliced green onions
½ cup frozen peas
2-3 tablespoons unfermented soy sauce substitute or reduced-sodium soy sauce

Heat oven to 350°F. Mix water, rice and chicken-style seasoning together in a 2-quart baking dish. Cover and bake 1 hour, or until rice is tender and liquid is absorbed.

Place tofu in a large nonstick skillet and mash with a fork (or the back of spoon). Cook over medium heat, stirring occasionally, until most of the moisture has evaporated. Stir in cooked rice, mushrooms, carrots, green onions, and peas. Season to taste with soy sauce substitute. Cook and stir until the vegetables are crisp-tender.

Makes 8 servings. 198 calories, 2 g fat, 194 mg sodium.

Vegetable Salad

½ pound green beans, trimmed (about 2 cups)
4 cups water
salt, for blanching
1 pound mung bean sprouts, rinsed
1 large red bell pepper, cut into julienne strips
2 tablespoons olive oil
2 tablespoons lemon juice
2 tablespoons unfermented soy sauce substitute or reduced-sodium soy sauce
2 teaspoons sesame oil
1 teaspoon honey
½ teaspoon garlic powder
½ teaspoon ground ginger

Snap or cut green beans in half (or leave whole if they are small). Bring water and a small amount of salt to boiling in a saucepan. Add green beans. Cook 1 minute to blanch. Drain in a colander and rinse with cold water to stop the cooking process. Mix green beans, bean sprouts and red pepper together in a serving bowl. Whisk olive oil, lemon juice, soy sauce substitute, sesame oil, honey, garlic powder, and ginger together; pour over salad and mix well.
Makes 8 servings. 103 calories, 7 g fat, 157 mg sodium.

Pumpkin Pie

1 unbaked **Whole-Wheat Piecrust** (9-inch)
1 15-ounce can mashed pumpkin (about 2 cups)
1½ cups soy milk
¾ cup brown sugar
1 tablespoon cornstarch
1 tablespoon egg replacement powder (such as Ener-G) dissolved in ¼ cup water
½ teaspoon salt
1 teaspoon ground cinnamon or substitute

Heat oven to 425°F. Prepare 1 **Whole-Wheat Piecrust**; set aside. Mix pumpkin, soy milk, brown sugar, cornstarch, egg replacement, salt, and cinnamon together in a mixing bowl. Pour into pie crust. Bake 15 minutes; decrease oven temperature to 350°F and bake 45 minutes. Cool to room temperature. Refrigerate until chilled. Serve with **Coconut Cream** (p. 54) or **Soy Whipped Cream** (p. 17).
Makes 8 servings. 209 calories, 8 g fat, 413 mg sodium.

Whole-Wheat Piecrust

2 cups whole-wheat pastry flour
2 tablespoons wheat germ
¾ teaspoon salt
½ cup boiling water
½ cup olive oil

Heat water to boiling. Mix flour, wheat germ, and salt together in a mixing bowl. Make a well in the center; pour in water and oil. Stir vigorously with a fork and gradually mix into flour mixture. Form dough into a ball and divide into two pieces.

Roll one piece of dough between two sheets of waxed paper and fit into a 9-inch pie plate. (Or press into the pie plate with your hands). Roll out the remaining dough.
Makes 2 single 9-inch crusts or 1 double crust; 16 servings. 114 calories, 7 g fat, 110 mg sodium.

COOK'S HINTS:

- For a double-crust pie: Add filling and top with crust. Seal the edges and trim. Cut slits in the top crust with a sharp knife, forming steam vents. Bake according to pie filling instructions.
- For **Baked Piecrust**: Prick bottom and sides of crust with a fork to prevent air bubbles. Bake at 350°F about 10-15 minutes, or until golden brown.
- For **Spelt Piecrust**: Replace whole-wheat pastry flour with spelt flour.
- For **Wheat-free Piecrust**: Omit the wheat germ.
- For **Tart Shells**: Divide dough into 18 portions. Form each portion into a ball and press into a tart or muffin tin.

Menu 6

Picture-perfect Thai

A friend and I celebrated our birthdays at a restaurant where we ordered a Thai salad. I enjoyed it so much that I went home and experimented until I could duplicate it. The variety of colors, flavors, and textures are outstandingly attractive. This meal is light, yet satisfyingly filling.

- **Thai Noodle Salad** with **Mango Salsa** and **Thai Salad Dressing**
- Flat Bread of choice
- **Mango Sorbet**
- **Iced Watermelon Drink**

Thai Noodle Salad

1 recipe **Mango Salsa**
1 recipe **Thai Salad Dressing**
1 13.25-ounce package whole-wheat spaghettini or vermicelli
1-2 tablespoons sesame oil
1 large head green leaf lettuce, chopped
½ medium red onion, thinly sliced
1 large carrot, shredded
4 large mushrooms, thinly sliced
2 ripe avocados, mashed
½ red bell pepper, sliced into thin rings
½ yellow bell pepper, sliced into thin rings
1 14-ounce can water-packed artichoke hearts, drained and cut into thirds

Prepare Mango Salsa and Thai Salad Dressing, and refrigerate. Cook pasta according to package directions. Drain and rinse with cold water. Toss pasta with 1 or 2 tablespoons of sesame oil. Prepare vegetables and place in separate bowls.

Arrange the ingredients in the following order, dividing each equally between eight plates. Arrange pasta in the center of the plate. Place a handful of lettuce on top of the pasta, allowing it to fall down and around the pasta, filling out the plate. On top of the lettuce, arrange groupings of red onion slices, shredded carrots, sliced mushrooms, Mango Salsa, and mashed avocado. Place several red and yellow pepper rings on the center of each salad. Arrange the artichoke hearts in the center of the pepper rings. Drizzle about 3 tablespoons **Thai Salad Dressing** over each salad. Serve immediately.

Makes 8 servings. 468 calories, 24 g fat, 221 mg sodium.

Mango Salsa

1 medium or large ripe mango, cut into ½-inch cubes (see p. 29)
1 small red bell pepper, finely chopped
2 tablespoons minced fresh cilantro or parsley
1½ tablespoons lime juice
pinch cayenne, or to taste
pinch salt, or to taste

Stir mango, bell pepper, cilantro, lime juice, cayenne, and salt together in bowl. Cover and refrigerate at least 1 hour.

Makes 8 servings. 20 calories, 0 g fat, 29 mg sodium.

Thai Salad Dressing

½ cup lime juice
½ cup olive oil
3 tablespoons sesame oil
3 tablespoons chopped cilantro
2 tablespoons unfermented soy sauce substitute or reduced-sodium soy sauce
2 tablespoons minced fresh ginger
1 tablespoon brown sugar
1 large clove garlic, minced or peeled

Process all ingredients in a blender or food processor until smooth. Refrigerate 1 hour before serving to allow flavors to blend. Keeps up to 1 week in the refrigerator.

Makes 1¾ cups; 28 1-tablespoon servings. 51 calories, 5 g fat, 44 mg sodium.

Mango Sorbet

1 14-ounce can coconut milk
2 tablespoons pure maple syrup
1 tablespoon vanilla extract
2-3 tablespoons precooked cornstarch powder (such as Instant Clear Jel)
2 ripe mangos, peeled, pitted, and cubed (see p. 29)
2 teaspoons lemon juice

Process coconut milk, maple syrup, and vanilla extract in a blender or food processor for a few seconds. While processing, gradually add enough precooked cornstarch powder to make it slightly thickened. Pour into a bowl. Process mangos and lemon juice in a blender or food processor until smooth. Add thickened coconut mixture and process until well mixed. Pour into a freezerproof container. Cover and freeze for a minimum of 6-8 hours. Remove from freezer and thaw slightly. Scoop into individual bowls.

Makes 8 servings. 120 calories, 10 g fat, 7 mg sodium.

VARIATIONS:

- Replace fresh mangos with 24 ounces of frozen mango cubes.
- Replace mangos with 24 ounces of frozen berries.
- Replace coconut milk with reduced-fat coconut milk for a lower fat sorbet.

Iced Watermelon Drink

12 ice cubes, divided
4 cups cubed watermelon, seeded

Process six ice cubes in a blender for a few seconds to break up ice. Add watermelon and process another few seconds. Add the remaining six ice cubes. Continue to process until it becomes smooth and slushy. Pour into glasses and serve immediately with a straw.

Makes 4 servings. 46 calories, 0 g fat, 3 mg sodium.

COOK'S HINTS:

- Melon ice drinks are popular in Thailand. Most are made with artificially flavored syrups. This is a natural, fresh approach.
- Replace watermelon with other fresh fruits, such as pineapple, mango, strawberries, or peaches.

The Art of Thai Cuisine

Thai cuisine reflects the people who created it. The beauty takes colorful shape in fruits and vegetables exquisitely carved to entice the eye. Served on china plates, they seem like precision-cut gems in a perfect setting.

The balance comes through the skillful combination of spices, herbs, and seasonings to orchestrate the flavors in each dish or the overall meal: spicy, sour, sweet, and salty.

Contrary to the popular misconception that Thai dishes are spicy, far more Thai foods are pleasantly mild. The heat in spicy dishes usually comes from red or green chili peppers.

How to Cut a Mango

METHOD

The mango has a flat oblong pit in the center of it. Cut along the sides of the pit, separating the flesh from the pit. Holding the mango with one hand, stand it on its end, stem side down.

With a sharp knife, cut from the top of the mango down one side of the pit. Repeat on other side. (You should end up with three pieces—two halves, and a middle section that includes the pit.)

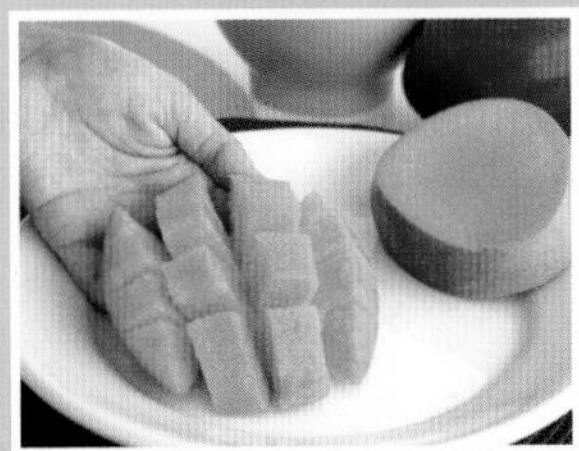

Cut each mango half to make lengthwise and crosswise cuts in it, but try not to cut through the peel.

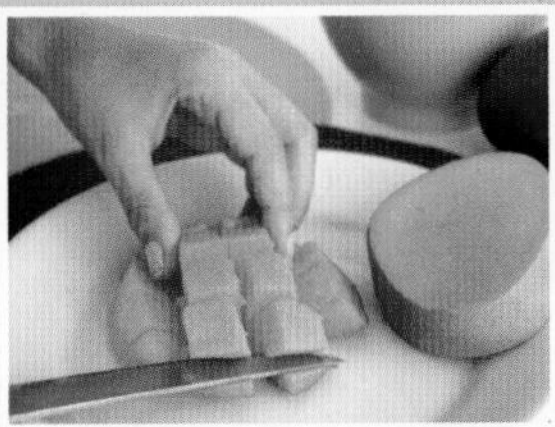

Peel with your fingers; or, using a knife, thinly slice the segments of mango off of the peel. Remove the peel from around the mango piece that has the pit. Carefully cut off any mango around the pit. (Or enjoy eating it straight off the pit.)

Menu 7

Taste of Thailand

Jasmine rice is a long-grain variety of rice grown primarily in Thailand, although other nations cultivate the long grain, aromatic rice as well. It is popular in Asian cooking, especially with Thai and Chinese dishes, since the subtle, nutty flavor and rich aroma are very pleasing to the palate. The trick to cooking jasmine rice well is using minimal water, so that the rice is steamed, rather than boiled. Thai cooks wrap bundles of rinsed rice in muslin and suspend them in a steamer so that the rice cooks by steaming, and never touches the water at all.

- **Thai Jasmine Rice**
- **Thai Wraps With Peanut Sauce**
- **Fruit Salad**
- Dried Tamarind
- **Strawberry Limeade**

Thai Jasmine Rice

7 cups water
4 cups white jasmine rice
1½ tablespoons to ⅓ cup chicken-style seasoning,* or to taste
1 teaspoon salt, or to taste
½ teaspoon turmeric
1 teaspoon saffron filaments

Heat water to boiling in a large saucepan. Stir in rice, chicken-style seasoning, salt, turmeric, and saffron. Reduce heat and simmer, partly covered, 15-20 minutes, or until rice is tender and water is absorbed. Remove from heat. Cover and let stand at least 5 minutes, or until ready to serve. Fluff with a fork.

Makes 12 1-cup servings. 227 calories, 2 g fat, 292 mg sodium.

*see glossary

COOK'S HINTS:

- While the rice is cooking, tilt the lid so that about three fourths of the saucepan is covered.
- If you can find brown jasmine rice, increase the water to 8 cups and the cooking time to about 45 minutes.

Thai Wraps With Peanut Sauce

1 tablespoon olive or sesame oil
4 cups thinly sliced **Homemade Gluten** (p. 32) or soy chicken
4 cups shredded leaf lettuce
2 cups thinly sliced cucumber
2 cups fresh mung bean sprouts
1 cup shredded carrots
3 green onions, sliced
8 large whole-wheat tortillas

Heat oil in a large skillet. Stir in gluten and cook until browned. Stir lettuce, cucumbers, bean spouts, carrots, and green onions together in a bowl; set aside.

Warm tortillas. Place ½ cup gluten and about 1 cup salad in the center of each tortilla. Drizzle with 2 tablespoons of **Peanut Sauce**. Roll up tightly. Slice each wrap in half with a crosswise diagonal cut.
Makes 8 servings. 310 calories, 17 g fat, 325 mg sodium.

Peanut Sauce

½ cup natural peanut butter
¼ cup sesame oil
¼ cup water
3 tablespoons unfermented soy sauce substitute or reduced-sodium soy sauce
3 tablespoons lime juice
2 teaspoons brown sugar
1 teaspoon garlic powder
½ teaspoon cayenne, or to taste

Whisk peanut butter, sesame oil, water, soy sauce substitute, lime juice, brown sugar, garlic powder, and cayenne together until smooth. (Or process in a blender or food processor.)

VARIATION:

- Replace gluten with rehydrated unflavored soy protein strips (such as Soy Curls).

Fruit Salad

1 20-ounce can lychee fruit, with juice
1 20-ounce can pineapple tidbits, with juice
1 cup fresh berries, such as raspberries, blackberries, or strawberries
1 cup seedless grapes
3 large bananas, sliced
2 mandarin oranges, peeled and separated into sections or 1 11-ounce can, drained
1 cup pomegranate seeds (from 1 large pomegranate)
1 star fruit

Stir lychee, pineapple, berries, grapes, bananas, oranges, and pomegranate seeds together in a salad bowl. Slice star fruit crosswise to make ¼-inch thick stars and arrange on the top of the fruit salad. Garnish with a pomegranate seed (or a berry) in the center of each star.
Makes 12 1-cup servings. 120 calories, 0 g fat, 2 mg sodium.

Strawberry Limeade

2 cups fresh or frozen strawberries
2 cups cold water
½ cup fresh lime juice (from about 1½ limes)
¼ cup fructose or granulated cane sugar, or to taste
6 ice cubes
1 12-ounce can natural lemon-lime carbonated drink

Process strawberries, water, lime juice, and fructose in a blender until smooth. While blending, add one ice cube at a time and process until smooth after each ice cube. Pour into a pitcher. Stir in lemon-lime drink. Serve immediately.

Makes 6 servings. 63 calories, 0 g fat, 13 mg sodium.

COOK'S HINTS:

- Look for a carbonated drink that is sweetened with fruit juice or cane sugar (not high fructose corn syrup), and does not contain phosphoric acid, artificial flavors, or colors (such as Blue Sky or Knudsen Spritzer).
- Replace carbonated drink with 2 cups sparkling water and a little more fructose to taste.

About Tamarind

The tart tamarind fruit pulp is edible and used as a base for a sweet-and-sour sauce in central Thailand. It is also used as a spice in both Asian and Latin American cuisines. A carefully cultivated sweet variety of tamarind is grown specifically to be eaten as a fresh fruit.Tamarind is available in specialty food stores in pod form or as a paste or concentrate.

In Mexico, it is sold in various snack forms, where it is dried and salted, or candied. It is a traditional food plant in Africa. It is well known in Malaysia, Africa, Sudan, Madagascar, Indonesia, the Philippines, India, Vietnam, Puerto Rico, and many other areas.

Menu 8

Polynesian Palate

As a teenager, I thoroughly enjoyed making shish kebabs with my sister Carolyn (Good), who would grill them in the oven or on the grill. Dishes such as these are not only pleasing to the taste buds, but can create fond memories when you make them with your family and friends.

- **Shish Kebabs**
- **Homemade Gluten**
- **Hawaiian Haystacks**
- **Chicken-style Gravy**
- **Spinach Dip** with Fresh Vegetables and Hawaiian Bread or Round French Bread
- **Carrot and Pineapple Cake** with **Mock Cream Cheese Frosting** (p. 45)
- **Tropical Punch**

Shish Kebabs

½ cup unfermented soy sauce substitute or reduced-sodium soy sauce
½ cup water
¼ cup olive oil
1 tablespoon honey or granulated cane sugar
1 teaspoon garlic powder
¼ teaspoon ground ginger
¼ teaspoon onion powder
6 large **Homemade Gluten** steaks, cut into 1-inch cubes
24 cherry tomatoes
6 canned pineapple rings, cut into 1-inch pieces
2 large green bell peppers, cut into 1-inch pieces
2 large yellow bell peppers, cut into 1-inch pieces
24 medium-sized mushrooms

Whisk soy sauce substitute, water, oil, honey, garlic powder, ground ginger, and onion powder together in a medium bowl. Stir in gluten cubes: cover and refrigerate 2 hours to marinate.

Heat oven to 400°F. Thread ingredients onto 12 skewers in the following order: cherry tomato, pineapple, green bell pepper, marinated gluten, yellow pepper, and mushroom. Repeat until skewer is full. Transfer filled skewers to a baking sheet. Brush a small amount of marinade over each skewer. (Not too much or it will burn on the baking sheet.) Bake 10-15 minutes, or until vegetables are tender. Serve immediately.

Makes 12 large skewers. 157 calories, 5 g fat, 366 mg sodium.

COOK'S HINTS:

- Replace gluten with firm tofu cubes that have been frozen and thawed.
- You can buy gluten steaks, or *seitan* (pronounced SAY-tahn), in the refrigerated section at natural food stores.

Homemade Gluten

Gluten Broth:

14 cups water
¼ cup unfermented soy sauce substitute or reduced-sodium soy sauce
4 teaspoons to ¼ cup beef-style seasoning,* or to taste
1 teaspoon instant coffee substitute, optional
1 teaspoon garlic powder
1 teaspoon onion powder
2 tablespoons olive oil, optional

Gluten:

3 cups vital wheat gluten
⅓ cup whole-wheat flour
⅓ cup quick-cooking tapioca
2 tablespoons nutritional yeast flakes
1-3 tablespoons beef-style seasoning,* or to taste

*see glossary

2¼ cups water
¼ cup unfermented soy sauce substitute or reduced-sodium soy sauce

Gluten Broth: Heat water, soy sauce substitute, beef-style seasoning, coffee substitute, garlic powder, onion powder, and oil, if desired, to boiling in a 6-quart saucepan; reduce heat and simmer, covered.

Gluten: Thoroughly mix vital wheat gluten, whole-wheat flour, tapioca, nutritional yeast, and beef-style seasoning together in a mixing bowl. Make a well in the center. Stir in water and soy sauce substitute. Using your hands, mix well, but do not knead. (Kneading the dough will make the gluten tough.) Do not force extra flour to mix in. (If too wet, roll the dough in a towel and pat dry.) Form dough into a log about 12 inches long. Cut dough into ½-inch thick slices. Drop slices one at a time into the simmering broth. Simmer, covered, for 1- to1½ hours. (The gluten will be softer the longer it cooks.) Remove from heat. If time allows, let cool for 1 hour. Drain, reserving broth for making gravy or soup.
Makes about 16 large gluten steaks (or 16 cups of ground burger). 182 calories, 9 g fat, 156 mg sodium. (Analysis does not include broth.)

COOK'S HINTS:

- Vital wheat gluten is a flour made from the protein (gluten) of the wheat kernel. It can be used to make meat substitutes, as a binder in recipes, and in bread recipes to promote elasticity to enhance the rising of bread.
- Instant coffee substitutes, such as Caf Lib or Krakus, are made from roasted grains. Look for them at Adventist Book Centers and natural food stores.
- To serve gluten steaks, bread each slice of gluten and fry in a little oil until golden brown on each side.
- Cut gluten steaks into cubes and use in stir-fry, shish kebabs, or stew.
- For **Ground Gluten**: Grind gluten steaks in a food processor and use as a meatless burger in recipes.
- Gluten may be frozen before or after cooking. The broth may be frozen and reused to make gluten.

Hawaiian Haystacks

8 cups hot cooked **Perfect Brown Rice** (p. 16)
3 cups dry unflavored soy protein strips (such as Soy Curls) or soy chicken
1 recipe **Chicken-style Gravy** (4 cups)
6 cups crispy chow mein noodles (eggless)
2 8-ounce cans water chestnuts, drained and sliced (or chopped)
4 cups chopped tomatoes
4 cups chopped celery
4 cups chopped green bell pepper
2 cups chopped green onions
2 20-ounce cans pineapple tidbits, drained
1 cup sliced almonds, lightly toasted

Prepare **Perfect Brown Rice**. Cover soy protein strips with hot water (or broth) and let them rehydrate for about 10 minutes, or until soft; drain. Prepare **Chicken-style Gravy**. Prepare each ingredient and place in separate serving bowls in the order listed. Let each person assemble his or her own plate by layering (stacking) each ingredient as desired.
Makes 12 servings. 518 calories, 18 g fat, 248 mg sodium.

VARIATION:

- Try adding other varieties of fresh vegetables to your haystack.

Chicken-style Gravy

- 3 tablespoons olive oil, or to taste
- ¾ cup unbleached all-purpose or whole-wheat flour
- 4 cups water
- 1-3 tablespoons chicken-style seasoning,* or to taste
- 2 tablespoons unfermented soy sauce substitute or reduced-sodium soy sauce
- Salt

Mix oil and flour together in a medium saucepan. Gradually whisk in water. Whisk in chicken-style seasoning and soy sauce substitute. Heat to boiling; reduce heat and simmer until thickened. Season to taste with salt.

Makes 4 cups; 8 ½-cup servings. 90 calories, 5 g fat, 153 mg sodium.

VARIATIONS:

- For less fat, omit or reduce the oil.
- For **Beef-style Gravy**: replace the chicken-style seasoning with beef-style seasoning.

Spinach Dip

- 1 10-ounce package frozen chopped spinach, thawed and drained
- 2 cups nondairy sour cream (such as Tofutti)
- 1½ cups eggless mayonnaise (such as Nasoya)
- 1 8-ounce can sliced water chestnuts, drained and chopped
- 1 4-ounce package dehydrated soup mix (such as Knorr)
- 3 green onions, chopped
- 1 loaf Hawaiian bread or round French bread, optional

Mix spinach, sour cream, mayonnaise, water chestnuts, soup mix, and green onions together in a bowl. Cover and refrigerate at least 1 hour. Serve in a hollowed out loaf of Hawaiian bread or round French bread, if desired. Pull chunks of bread from out of the center. Arrange with fresh vegetables around the loaf for dipping.

Makes about 5½ cups; 88 1-tablespoon servings. 32 calories, 2 g fat, 65 mg sodium.

*see glossary

Carrot and Pineapple Cake

- ¾ cup granulated cane sugar
- ½ cup olive or grape-seed oil
- 4 teaspoons egg replacement powder (such as Ener-G) dissolved in ¼ cup water
- 2 cups shredded carrots
- 1 14-ounce can crushed pineapple, drained (not too dry)
- 2 cups unbleached all-purpose flour
- 1½ teaspoons baking powder (preferably aluminum-free)
- 1½ teaspoons baking soda
- ½ teaspoon salt
- cooking spray
- **Mock Cream Cheese Frosting** (p. 45), optional

Heat oven to 325°F. Mix sugar, oil, egg replacement, carrots, and pineapple together in a mixing bowl. Stir in flour, baking powder, baking soda, and salt. (Do not overmix.) Spread batter evenly in a 9"x13" baking dish coated with cooking spray. Bake 50 minutes, or until a toothpick inserted near the center comes out clean. Let cool in the pan on a wire rack. Frost cake with **Mock Cream Cheese Frosting**, if desired. Refrigerate cake until frosting is set.

Makes 16 servings. 175 calories, 7 g fat, 203 mg sodium.

Tropical Punch

- 1 12-ounce can frozen orange juice concentrate, thawed
- 4 cups cold water
- 2 frozen bananas
- 1 12-ounce can frozen pineapple juice concentrate, thawed
- 2 liters sparkling water
- 1 fresh orange, cut into thin rings, for garnish

Process orange juice concentrate, cold water, and bananas in a blender and blend until smooth. Pour into a punch bowl. Stir in pineapple juice concentrate and sparkling water. Float orange rings on top of punch to garnish.

Makes 18 1-cup servings. 94 calories, 0 g fat, 5 mg sodium.

COOK'S HINTS:

- If you have a small blender, add 2 cups water to the blender and the remaining 2 cups water to the punch bowl.

Curried Pasta Stir-Fry

Menu 9

Jewel of India

Juliette (Clarke) Fuentmann and I have been best friends since second grade. We always loved to tease each other. When we got older, I teased Juliette about her lack of cooking skills and that it showed in the way many of her dishes turned out. But things have changed over the years, and Juliette has evolved into a fabulous cook. I was thrilled when she gave me permission to refine and share a recipe she created — Juliette's Vegetable Curried Cream Sauce. Everybody agrees that Juliette can cook now. And the teasing has stopped — at least about her cooking!

- **Vegetables With Curried Cream Sauce**
- **Perfect Brown Basmati Rice** (p. 16)
- **Samosas**
- **Naan**
- Fresh Bell Pepper Platter (assorted colors of bell peppers cut into strips)
- Herbal Tea
- **Rice Pudding**

Vegetables With Curried Cream Sauce

2 cups raw cashews
oil or water, for cooking onion
1 medium onion, chopped
3 cloves garlic, minced
¼ cup unfermented soy sauce substitute or reduced-sodium soy sauce
2 cups chopped fresh tomatoes
2 cups chopped zucchini
2 cups broccoli florets
2 cups cauliflower florets
2 cups chopped carrots
3 cups soy milk or rice milk
1 19-ounce can chickpeas, drained and rinsed
3 tablespoons curry powder
1 teaspoon ground ginger
salt
cayenne

Heat oven to 300°F. Place cashews on a baking dish and toast for 15-30 minutes, stirring every 10 minutes or until golden brown. Heat a little oil or water in a large skillet. Add onion and garlic; cook and stir until onion is tender. Add soy sauce, tomatoes, zucchini, broccoli, cauliflower, and carrots. Cook, stirring occasionally, until vegetables are crisp-tender. Stir in cashews, soy milk, chickpeas, curry powder, and ginger. Heat to boiling; reduce heat and simmer 5-10 minutes, or until vegetables are tender and sauce thickens slightly. Season to taste with salt and cayenne. Serve over **Perfect Brown Basmati Rice**.

Makes 10 servings. 417 calories, 24 g fat, 283 mg sodium.

Samosas

1-2 tablespoons olive oil
1 cup chopped onion
2 teaspoons minced garlic
½-1 teaspoon minced fresh ginger, optional
3 large potatoes, peeled, boiled, and finely chopped
½ cup fresh or frozen peas
1 tablespoon curry powder
1 teaspoon salt
⅛ teaspoon cayenne
water, for moistening
28 samosa wraps or 1 recipe of **Homemade Samosa Wraps**
olive oil, for brushing

Heat oil in a large skillet. Add onion, garlic, and ginger, if desired; cook and stir until light brown in color. Stir in potatoes and cook for 2 minutes. Add peas, curry powder, salt, and cayenne; cook and stir for 2 minutes. Remove from heat; set aside.

Heat oven to 400°F. Place a small amount of water in a small bowl. Dip a finger in the water and use it to moisten the edges of one half-circle samosa wrap. Put the ends of the straight edge together to make a cone shape. Fill the dough cone with 2 tablespoons of the cooled filling and push it down with your finger. Fold one of the top ends down toward the center and the other end over the top of that. (If necessary, moisten the ends with water so they will seal.) With a pastry brush, lightly brush both sides of the dough with oil. Place filled samosa on a baking sheet coated with cooking spray. Repeat with remaining samosa wraps and filling. Bake samosas 10-15 minutes, or until golden brown. If desired, turn them over to brown both sides evenly. Serve immediately.
Makes 28 servings. 60 calories, 2 g fat, 129 mg sodium.

COOK'S HINTS:

- Look for samosa wraps in the supermarket's freezer section.
- You can replace the curry powder with ½ teaspoon masala, 1 teaspoon ground coriander, and ½ teaspoon cumin seeds.
- If made ahead, heat samosas briefly in the oven to crisp them up.

Homemade Samosa Wraps

1½ cups unbleached all-purpose flour
2 tablespoons olive, canola, or grape-seed oil
½ teaspoon salt
½ cup water, as needed
cooking spray, as needed

Mix flour, oil, and salt together in a medium bowl. Add water, 1 tablespoon at a time, until mixture becomes crumbly. Keep adding water, 1 tablespoon at a time, and kneading, until dough becomes soft and pliable. Cover with a moist cloth and let rest for 20 minutes. Knead dough on a lightly floured surface for about 5 minutes. Divide dough into 14 equal portions. Roll each portion into a ball. Roll out each ball until it is a 6-inch circle. (Coat counter with cooking spray, if necessary, to keep dough from sticking, but do not add flour.) Cut each circle in half. If desired, stack samosa wraps with waxed paper between layers to keep them from sticking together. Cover; set aside.
Makes 28 wraps. Per wrap: 33 calories, 1 g fat, 42 mg sodium.

Naan

1 cup warm water
1 teaspoon instant dry active yeast
1 teaspoon granulated cane sugar
1 cup whole-wheat flour
1-2 cups unbleached all-purpose flour, as needed
¼ cup olive oil
1 teaspoon salt
2 large cloves garlic, minced, optional
olive oil or nonhydrogenated margarine, for brushing

Mix water, yeast, and sugar together in a mixing bowl. Stir in whole-wheat flour, 1 cup all-purpose flour, oil, salt, and garlic, if desired. Mix well. (Dough

should be soft and slightly sticky. If too sticky, add a little more all-purpose flour.) Cover dough; let stand 15-20 minutes. Divide dough into eight pieces. Roll each piece of dough into a ball, generously coating with flour as needed to keep from sticking to your hands. Let dough rest 20 minutes. Heat oven to 500°F. Flatten one ball of dough with hands by tossing dough back and forth and stretching the edges out until it is about an 6"x8" oval, about ¼-inch thick. Place on a nonstick baking sheet (or one coated with cooking spray). Repeat with the remaining dough. Bake 2½ minutes, or until golden brown on top. Turn naan over and bake another 30 seconds. Remove from oven. Lightly brush the top with oil. Stack on a plate. Serve immediately.
Makes 8 servings. 199 calories, 7 g fat, 293 mg sodium.

COOK'S HINTS:

- If made ahead, bake naan in a covered dish to warm up slightly.

Rice Pudding

cooking spray
2 cups soy milk
1 tablespoon egg replacement powder (such as Ener-G)
½ cup raisins
6 tablespoons brown sugar
1 teaspoon vanilla extract
¼ teaspoon salt
½ teaspoon ground cinnamon or substitute, optional
4 cups cooked **Perfect Brown Rice** (p. 16)
soy milk, optional

Heat oven to 350°F. Lightly coat a large baking dish with cooking spray. Whisk soy milk and egg replacement powder together in the baking dish. Stir in raisins, brown sugar, vanilla, salt, and cinnamon, if desired. Gradually stir in rice. Cover and bake 1 hour, until heated through. Serve hot, warm, or cold, with additional soy milk, if desired.
Makes 8 servings. 82 calories, 1 g fat, 49 mg sodium.

Menu 10
Punjab Veggie Cuisine

Before I taught an East Indian cuisine cooking class, several people asked me if I could demonstrate how to make a vegetarian version of Butter Chicken. At first it stumped me because I had never tasted Butter Chicken, and after 18 years as a vegetarian I wasn't going to! I researched a number of recipes and eventually decided to try it. I substituted cashew cream for the dairy cream, a natural butter flavoring for the dairy butter, and Soy Curls for the chicken. It turned out amazing! When one of the women who requested this recipe tasted Butter "Chicken," she was impressed and excited.

- **Butter "Chicken"**
- **Perfect Brown Basmati Rice** (p. 16)
- **Phool Gobi Rassa**
- **White Chickpea Chutney**
- **Roti (Chappati)**
- Fresh Salad Plate
- **Lemongrass Tea**
- Fresh Fruit Platter with Raw Sugar Cane (cut into 1-inch pieces)

Butter "Chicken"

- 3 cups dry unflavored soy protein strips (such as Soy Curls)
- 1 cup water
- ½ cup raw cashews
- 2 tablespoons tomato paste
- 5 cloves fresh garlic
- 2 teaspoons ground ginger
- 2 teaspoons ground coriander
- 1 teaspoon ground cumin
- 1 teaspoon salt
- ¼ teaspoon cayenne, or to taste
- 1 tablespoon fenugreek, optional
- 2 tablespoons chopped fresh cilantro
- 2 tablespoons olive or grape-seed oil
- 1 teaspoon natural butter flavoring
- 1½ teaspoons chopped canned green chilies

Cover soy protein strips with hot water (or broth) and let rehydrate for 10 minutes, or until soft. Process water, cashews, tomato paste, garlic, ginger, coriander, cumin, salt, cayenne, and fenugreek in a blender or food processor until smooth. Add cilantro and process briefly. Pour over rehydrated soy protein strips and mix well. Cover and refrigerate 2 hours to marinate. Heat oil and butter flavoring in a large skillet over medium heat. Add marinated soy protein strips and green chilies; cook and stir until heated through and slightly browned. Serve with **Perfect Brown Basmati Rice**.

Makes 8 servings. 171 calories, 12 g fat, 331 mg sodium.

COOK'S HINTS:

- Look for natural butter flavoring in supermarkets with a natural foods section or at natural foods stores.
- Fenugreek is a yellow seed used in Indian dishes, especially in curry powders and pastes. Look for it in the ethnic food section at supermarkets, or in bulk at natural food stores. Fenugreek is also available in capsule form for use as a supplement because of its reputation as a digestive aid and because it contains properties to lower high cholesterol and triglycerides. Because of its flavor, fenugreek is also used as a substitute for maple syrup flavoring.

Phool Gobi Rassa

Masala:

- 1 tablespoon olive or grape-seed oil
- 1 1-inch stick cinnamon
- 6 whole cloves
- 2 teaspoons coriander seeds
- 1 large onion, sliced fine
- 3 cups shredded fresh coconut
- water, as needed

Sauce:

- 2 teaspoons olive or grape-seed oil
- 2 teaspoons cumin seeds
- 1 medium head cauliflower, cut into small florets (about 1¼ pounds)
- 1 cup peas
- ¼ cup dry-roasted unsalted cashews
- 1 medium tomato, chopped
- 1 teaspoon turmeric powder
- ½-1 teaspoon cayenne, or to taste
- water, for cooking vegetables
- salt

Masala: Heat oil in a wok or skillet. Add cinnamon stick, cloves, and coriander seeds; cook and stir for 1 minute. Add onion; cook and stir until golden in color. Add coconut; cook and stir until lightly browned. Remove from the heat and let cool. Transfer to a blender or food processor and process, adding water 1 tablespoon at a time until a coarse paste is formed.

Sauce: Heat oil in a skillet. Add cumin seeds; cook, stirring constantly, until they change color and become fragrant. Stir in cauliflower, peas, and cashews. Stir in tomato, turmeric, and cayenne. Stir in a little water, cover, and cook for 5 minutes or until cauliflower is almost tender. Gently stir in the masala. Season to taste with salt. Simmer for 3 minutes. Serve with **Roti** and **White Chickpea Chutney**.

Makes 10 cups; 20 ½-cup servings. 86 calories, 6 g fat, 6g, 21 mg sodium.

COOK'S HINTS:

- Look for coriander seeds and cumin seeds where bulk herbs are sold in ethnic markets and natural food stores.
- This dish is usually made with peppercorns and is very spicy. Since black peppercorns irritate the stomach lining, they are not included in this recipe.

White Chickpea Chutney

2 teaspoons olive oil
1 teaspoon anise seeds
1 large onion, chopped
1 teaspoon minced fresh garlic
1 teaspoon mango powder or lemon juice
1 teaspoon granulated cane sugar or fructose
½-1 teaspoon cayenne, or to taste
1 15-ounce can chickpeas, drained (reserve liquid)
salt

Heat oil in a skillet; cook and stir anise seeds until they pop. Add onion; cook and stir until golden. Stir in garlic, mango powder, sugar, and cayenne; cook, stirring constantly, for 3 minutes, allowing flavors to blend together. Stir in chickpeas. Remove from the heat. Transfer to a blender or food processor and process, adding a small amount of the reserved chickpea liquid if needed, to form a thick, smooth paste. Season to taste with salt. Serve with Roti and as a complement to other Indian dishes.

Makes about 2¼ cups; 36 1-tablespoon servings. 14 calories, 0 g fat, 1 mg sodium.

COOK'S HINTS:

- Look for anise seeds where bulk herbs are sold in ethnic markets and natural food stores.

Roti (Chappati)

4 cups whole-wheat flour
2 teaspoons olive or grape-seed oil
1¼-1½ cups warm water, or as needed
whole-wheat flour, as needed
oil, for brushing

Mix flour and oil together in a mixing bowl. Stir in enough warm water to make into a soft, pliable ball. Knead about 5 minutes. (The more you knead, the softer the dough will become.) Divide dough into 24 golf ball-sized pieces. Lightly coat each piece of dough with flour and shape into a ball. With the palm of your hand, flatten slightly. On a lightly floured surface, use a rolling pin to roll out each piece to about a 4-inch circle. Heat a skillet over medium heat. Cook the roti until the surface becomes bubbling and golden brown spots appear on the bottom. Turn roti over with a spatula. When it begins to puff up, press it down with the spatula to help it cook evenly. As soon as golden brown spots appear on the bottom, remove roti from the heat. Brush with a little oil on each side of the roti. Keep it warm by wrapping in a towel or piece of aluminum foil. Repeat the process with the remaining dough. Serve warm or reheat in a hot skillet, taking care not to let roti dry out or burn.

Makes 24 servings. 17 calories, 1 g fat, 1 mg sodium.

COOK'S HINTS:

- Roti means *everyday bread.*
- You can replace whole-wheat flour with roti flour, which contains extra fiber.

About Sugarcane

About 200 countries grow sugarcane crops, producing 1.3 billion tons. This is more than six times the amount of sugar beets produced. The world's largest producer of sugarcane is Brazil, followed by India. Uses of sugarcane include the production of sugar, molasses, and ethanol for fuel. The tissue that remains after sugarcane crushing may be burned to provide both heat used in the mill and electricity (typically sold to the consumer power grid). It may also, because of its high cellulose content, be used as raw material for paper and cardboard, and is branded as environmentally friendly, as it is made from a by-product of sugar production. The leftover fiber is used to make mats, screens, or baskets in some countries.

Sugarcane field in India

The thick stalk stores energy as sucrose in the sap. From this juice, sugar is extracted by evaporating the water, turning it into crystallized sugar.

Extraction of juice from sugarcane

Cut sugarcane

Sugarcane was, and still is, grown extensively in the Caribbean, where it was first brought by Christopher Columbus during his second voyage to the Americas.

In India, sugarcane is sold as "jaggery," traditional unrefined sugar, and also refined into sugar, primarily for consumption in tea and sweets, and for the production of alcoholic beverages. ***Interesting Fact***: It takes 50 feet of sugarcane to produce ½ cup of sugar.

Lemongrass Tea

- 8-9 lemongrass blades, cut crosswise into 1½-inch pieces
- 2½ cups water
- 2 caffeine-free herbal tea bags
- soy milk, optional
- granulated cane sugar or other sweetener, optional

Heat lemongrass and water to boiling; reduce heat and simmer 3 minutes. Stir in tea bags. Remove from heat. Cover and steep 3 minutes. Strain. Serve with soy milk and sugar.

Makes 4 servings. 5 calories, 0 g fat, 1 mg sodium.

Menu 11

Tandoori Kitchen

Lentils in cake? Sounds strange! When my oldest son, Nathan, was small, he did not like beans. I thought, What a terrible vegetarian he will be if he doesn't like beans. *So I began to sneak puréed beans and lentils into some of his favorite foods, such as waffles, cakes, and cookies. I liked knowing he was getting more protein and minerals. And he didn't have a clue! The lentils in this cake help to make it a rich dark-brown color.*

- **Lentil Patties**
- **Perfect Brown Rice** (p. 16)
- **Chickpea Salad**
- **Tomato-Onion Salad**
- **Potatoes and Peas**
- **Sweet Potato Biscuits** with Margarine
- **Vegetable-Lentil Spice Cake** with **Mock Cream Cheese Frosting**

Lentil Patties

1 cup lentils, sorted and rinsed
2 cups water
¾ cup raw sunflower seeds, ground
¼ cup raw pecans or walnuts, ground
1 medium onion, finely chopped
1 cup soy milk
½ cup quick-cooking oats
1 tablespoon dried parsley
½ teaspoon garlic powder
½ teaspoon ground cumin
½ teaspoon salt
cooking spray

Cook lentils in water 20-30 minutes, or until tender, adding more water if needed to keep from drying out. Process sunflower seeds and pecans in a food processor or blender until ground; transfer to a mixing bowl. Process cooked lentils in a food processor or blender until smooth. Add to mixing bowl. Mix in onion, soy milk, oats, parsley, garlic powder, cumin, and salt; let stand 5-10 minutes.

Heat oven to 350°F. Shape mixture into patties using hands and place on a baking sheet coated with cooking spray (or cook in a nonstick skillet on both sides until golden brown). Bake 15 minutes. Turn patties over and bake 15 minutes, or until lightly browned on the bottom.
Makes about 20 patties. 119 calories, 4 g fat, 96 mg sodium.

COOK'S HINTS:

- These patties are soft, but will stiffen after cooling.
- If desired, cover patties with **Beef-style Gravy** (p. 34) or tomato sauce and bake 20-30 minutes, or until heated through.
- Variation: serve on whole-wheat burger buns with lettuce, tomatoes, onions, and your favorite condiments.

Chickpea Salad

3 15-ounce cans chickpeas, drained and rinsed
½ green bell pepper, finely chopped
3 green onions, sliced
2 tablespoons lemon juice
2 tablespoons minced fresh cilantro or parsley
¾ teaspoon salt
¼ teaspoon cayenne, or to taste

Mix chickpeas, bell pepper, green onions, lemon juice, cilantro, salt, and cayenne together in a salad bowl. Serve cold or at room temperature.
Makes 8 servings. 196 calories, 2 g fat, 332 mg sodium.

COOK'S HINTS:

- This is a very simple version of a traditional Indian chickpea salad.

Tomato-Onion Salad

4 large tomatoes, cut into wedges
1 sweet onion, cut into rings
3 tablespoons olive oil
2 tablespoons lemon juice
½ teaspoon seasoned salt, or to taste

Mix tomatoes and onion rings together in a salad bowl. Stir oil and lemon juice together and pour over salad. Sprinkle with seasoned salt. Mix well.
Makes 8 servings. 70 calories, 5 g fat, 78 mg sodium.

Potatoes and Peas

- 3 medium red potatoes, peeled, cooked, and cut into 2-inch cubes (about 2 cups)
- 1 tablespoon olive oil
- 1 teaspoon cumin seeds
- ½ cup finely chopped red onion
- 2 medium tomatoes, cut into 1-inch pieces
- 1 teaspoon salt
- ¼ teaspoon turmeric
- ½ teaspoon cayenne, or to taste
- 1 cup water
- 1 cup frozen peas, thawed
- 2 tablespoons minced fresh cilantro

Prepare potatoes. Heat oil in a 2-quart saucepan over medium-high heat. Add cumin seeds and toast 15-30 seconds, or until fragrant. Add onion; cook, stirring, 1-2 minutes, or until golden brown. Add tomatoes, salt, turmeric, and cayenne; cook and stir 1-2 minutes, or until tomatoes are softened. Stir in water and peas. Heat to boiling; reduce heat to medium and simmer, covered, 5 minutes. Uncover and simmer 5 minutes longer, or until sauce thickens slightly. Stir in cilantro.

Makes 6 servings. 101 calories, 3 g fat, 423 mg sodium.

Sweet Potato Biscuits

- ⅓ cup dates
- 3 tablespoons water, as needed
- 2 cups whole-wheat flour
- 1 cup unbleached all-purpose flour
- ½ cup cornmeal
- 3 tablespoons granulated cane sugar
- 1 tablespoon baking powder (preferably aluminum-free)
- 1 teaspoon baking soda
- 1 teaspoon ground allspice
- ½ teaspoon salt
- 1 cup mashed sweet potato
- ⅓ cup soy milk
- ¼ cup olive oil
- 2 tablespoons egg replacement powder (such as Ener-G), dissolved in ½ cup water
- unbleached all-purpose flour, if needed
- cooking spray

Heat oven to 375°F. Cook dates in water, adding more water if needed, until dates are soft and start to lose their shape. Mash and measure ⅓ cup; set aside. Mix whole-wheat flour, all-purpose flour, cornmeal, sugar, baking powder, baking soda, allspice, and salt together in a mixing bowl. Make a well in the center. Add sweet potato, date puree, soy milk, oil, and egg replacement; mix well. Add additional flour if necessary so dough is not sticky. Roll dough out on a lightly floured surface to about ½-inch thick.
Cut it into 24 squares. Place about 2 inches apart on two baking sheets coated with cooking spray. Bake 20 minutes, or until golden brown. Serve warm.

Makes 2 dozen biscuits. 105 calories, 3 g fat, 107 mg sodium.

Vegetable-Lentil Spice Cake

- 1 cup whole-wheat flour
- 1 cup unbleached all-purpose flour
- 2 teaspoons baking powder (preferably aluminum-free)
- 1 teaspoon baking soda
- 2 teaspoons ground cinnamon or substitute
- 1 teaspoon ground allspice
- ¼ teaspoon salt
- 1½ cups shredded apple
- 1½ cups peeled and shredded carrot
- 1 cup peeled and shredded potato
- 1 cup mashed cooked lentils
- 1 cup raisins
- ½ cup chopped pecans
- 1 cup brown or granulated cane sugar
- ¾ cup nonhydrogenated margarine (such as Earth Balance), softened
- 1½ tablespoons egg replacement powder (such as Ener-G), dissolved in 6 tablespoons water
- 2 tablespoons blackstrap molasses
- cooking spray
- 3 tablespoons chopped walnuts, optional

Heat oven to 350°F. Mix whole-wheat flour, all-purpose flour, baking powder, baking soda, cinnamon, allspice, and salt together in a bowl.

Mix apple, carrot, potato, lentils, raisins, and pecans together in a separate bowl. Beat sugar and margarine with an electric mixer on medium speed in a large mixing bowl until light and fluffy. Beat in egg replacement and molasses. Beat in flour mixture until dry ingredients are moistened. Gradually beat in lentil mixture on low speed. Scrape the batter into a 9"x13" glass baking dish coated with cooking spray. Bake 45 minutes, or until a toothpick inserted near the center comes out clean. Let cake cool before frosting with **Mock Cream Cheese Frosting**. Sprinkle with walnuts, if desired.
Makes 16 servings. 267 calories, 11 g fat, 262 mg sodium.

COOK'S HINTS:

- Bake in a fluted tube pan and drizzle with icing.

Mock Cream Cheese Frosting

⅓ cup nondairy cream cheese (such as Tofutti)
1 tablespoon lemon juice
1 teaspoon vanilla extract
1½-2 cups confectioners' sugar, as needed

Process cream cheese, lemon juice, and vanilla in a food processor until smooth. Add 1½ cups confectioners' sugar and process until smooth. Add additional confectioners' sugar as needed to make frosting a spreadable consistency. Spread frosting on top of cake. Refrigerate cake until frosting is set.
Makes 16 servings. 85 calories, 1 g fat, 15 mg sodium.

Menu 12

Flavors of India

Stir-fries hold amazing mealtime potential. Changing the vegetables and seasonings will make it a completely different dish. My husband, Ron, could eat stir-fry every day. Sometimes it's easy to forget that such a simple dish can be one of the most healthful, colorful, and tasty meals.

- **Black Bean Soup**
- **Curried Pasta Stir-fry**
- **Perfect Brown Basmati Rice** (p. 16)
- **Naan** (p. 38)
- Mint Tea
- **Gluton-free Banana Bread**

Black Bean Soup

8 cups water
2 cups black beans, sorted and rinsed
1 28-ounce can diced tomatoes
2 cups chopped onions
2 cups chopped celery
2 cups chopped green bell pepper
½ cup minced fresh parsley
½ cup quinoa, thoroughly rinsed
2 large cloves garlic, minced
1 teaspoon ground cumin
1 teaspoon dried basil
1 teaspoon salt

Heat water and black beans to boiling in a large saucepan; reduce heat and simmer 1½-2 hours, or until beans are tender. Stir in tomatoes, onions, celery, bell pepper, parsley, quinoa, garlic, cumin, basil, and salt; simmer 15-20 minutes, or until vegetables and quinoa are tender.
Makes 20 1-cup servings. 115 calories, 1 g fat, 187 mg sodium.

Curried Pasta Stir-fry

8 ounces brown rice pasta
2 cups dry unflavored soy protein strips (such as Soy Curls)
1 tablespoon olive or sesame oil
1 large onion, cut in half and sliced
3 cloves garlic, minced
2 cups fresh green beans, trimmed and cut into 1-inch pieces
2 cups cauliflower florets
2 cups cooked chickpeas
1 cup red bell pepper cut into thin strips
1 tablespoon curry powder
¼ cup unfermented soy sauce substitute or reduced-sodium soy sauce, or to taste

Cook pasta according to package directions; drain. Cover soy protein strips with hot water (or broth) and let rehydrate for about 10 minutes, or until soft; drain. Heat oil in a large skillet or wok over medium-high heat. Stir-fry onion and garlic for 2 minutes. Add green beans and cauliflower, adding a little water if needed to keep from sticking; stir-fry until green beans and cauliflower are crisp-tender. Stir in chickpeas, bell pepper, and cooked pasta. Stir in rehydrated soy protein, curry powder, and soy sauce substitute; heat through. Serve immediately over cooked **Perfect Brown Basmati Rice** or quinoa.
Makes 15 1-cup servings. 140 calories, 2 g fat, 125 mg sodium.

COOK'S HINTS:

- If using long pasta such as spaghetti, break it in half before cooking.

Banana Bread

1½ cups whole-wheat flour
1½ cups unbleached all-purpose flour
1 cup granulated cane sugar
2 teaspoons baking powder (preferably aluminum-free)
1 teaspoon baking soda
1 10-ounce package soft tofu, preferably reduced-fat (1¼ cups)
2 tablespoons lemon juice
1¾ cups mashed banana
⅓ cup chopped walnuts, optional
cooking spray

Heat oven to 350°F. Mix whole-wheat flour, all-purpose flour, sugar, baking powder, and baking soda together in a mixing bowl. Process tofu and lemon juice in a blender or food processor until smooth. Add tofu mixture, mashed banana, and walnuts, if desired, to the flour mixture; mix until flour is moistened. (Do not overmix.) Divide dough between two 5"x9"x3" loaf pans coated with cooking spray. Bake 40 minutes, or until a toothpick inserted near the center comes out clean.
Makes 2 loaves; 32 ½-inch slices. 80 calories, 0 g fat, 48 mg sodium.

Gluten-free Banana Bread

¾ cup potato flour (not potato starch)
½ cup millet flour
½ cup sorghum flour
½ cup granulated cane sugar
1½ teaspoons gluten-free baking powder
½ teaspoon salt
1 cup mashed ripe banana
⅓ cup olive oil
1 tablespoon lemon juice
1 tablespoon egg replacement powder (such as Ener-G) dissolved in ¼ cup water
1 teaspoon vanilla extract
cooking spray

Heat oven to 350°F. Mix potato flour, millet flour, sorghum flour, sugar, baking powder, and salt together in a mixing bowl. Stir in banana, oil, lemon

uice, egg replacement, and vanilla. (Do not overmix, or bread will turn out heavy.) Spread mixture in a 5"x9"x3" loaf pan coated with cooking spray. Bake 40 minutes, or until a toothpick inserted near the center comes out clean. Cool before slicing. Store in a sealed bag or container in the refrigerator.
Makes 1 loaf; 16 ½-inch slices. 109 calories, 5 g fat, 74 mg sodium.

COOK'S HINTS:

- This is a heavier bread, but a good option for those who cannot eat gluten.

Menu 13

Spice Road Specialties

The word "curry" is usually understood to mean "gravy" in India, rather than "spices."

Essentially, the word "curry" was invented by the English administrators of the East India Trading Company and later continued by British government employees. In India, Sri Lanka, Malaysia, and the Maldives, practically all curries (called garam masala*) are mixed just before use. Some of the spices are dry-roasted, blended and ground, or pounded in a mortar with a pestle.*

Contrary to common Western belief, curries are not always hot. They may be mild, medium, or hot. To tone down a hot curry, add coconut milk.

- **Sweet Curried Lentil Pastries**
- **Tomato Chutney**
- **Coconut Rice *(Narial Ke Chaaval)***
- **Vegetable Curry**
- **Lentil Hermit Cookies**

Sweet Curried Lentil Pastries

Filling:

1 cup cooked sweet potato cut into small cubes
1½ cups cooked brown lentils
1 tablespoon olive oil
1 cup finely chopped onion
¼ cup tomato paste
1½ tablespoons curry powder
1 tablespoon unfermented soy sauce substitute or reduced-sodium soy sauce
½ teaspoon garlic powder

Pastry:

1 cup water
4 cups whole-wheat pastry flour
¼ cup wheat germ
¾ teaspoon salt
1 cup olive oil
cooking spray

Filling: Prepare sweet potato and lentils. Heat oil in a large skillet. Add onion; cook and stir until onion is tender. Add sweet potatoes and lentils, tomato paste, curry powder, soy sauce substitute, and garlic powder. Cook for several minutes, stirring occasionally, until heated through and flavors are blended.

Pastry: Heat oven to 350°F. Heat water to boiling. Mix flour, wheat germ, and salt together in a mixing bowl. Make a well in the center. Pour in boiling water and oil and mix with a fork or spoon. Form dough into a ball with hands. Roll dough into a rectangle about ¼-inch thick on a lightly floured surface. Cut dough into 3-inch-diameter circles with a biscuit cutter or drinking glass. Place a small spoonful of the curried mixture in the center of each circle and fold dough in half over the mixture. Pinch the dough around the edges to seal. Place on a baking sheet coated with cooking spray. Repeat with remaining filling and dough, rerolling dough as needed. Bake 10-15 minutes, or until golden brown.
Makes 54 pastries. 79 calories, 4 g fat, 53 mg sodium.

Tomato Chutney

4 tomatoes, finely chopped
½ medium onion, finely chopped
½ green bell pepper, finely chopped
½ red bell pepper, finely chopped
½ cup minced fresh parsley or cilantro
¼ cup olive or canola oil
2 tablespoons lemon juice

Mix tomatoes, onion, bell peppers, and parsley together in a serving bowl. Season to taste with oil and lemon juice. Serve as a condiment for other dishes.

Makes 6 cups; 96 1-tablespoon servings.
8 calories, 1 g fat, 1 mg sodium.

Coconut Rice *(Narial Ke Chaaval)*

1½ cups red rice or brown basmati rice
3 cups water
1½ teaspoons olive or canola oil
1 teaspoon black mustard seeds
1 teaspoon chopped green chilies (fresh or canned)
2 teaspoons split black lentils *(urad dal)*
⅛-¼ teaspoon asafetida, optional
2 cups shredded fresh coconut
salt
1½ teaspoons olive or canola oil
2 tablespoons raw cashews
10 fresh curry leaves (more if using dried leaves)

Cook rice in the water at least 40 minutes, or until tender. Drain. Heat oil in a skillet. Add mustard seeds; cook and stir until they pop. Stir in chilies, lentils, and asafetida and cook for 1 minute. Stir in coconut and cook until the color begins to change to golden. Stir in cooked rice; cook until heated through. Season to taste with salt. Heat oil in a small skillet. Add cashews; cook and stir until lightly browned. Stir in curry leaves. Spoon on top of coconut rice. Serve hot with **Vegetable Curry**.

Makes 6 servings. 311 calories, 15 g fat, 10 mg sodium.

COOK'S HINTS:

- **Red rice** is high in the same nutrients as brown rice, but contains more potassium. Try adding red rice to brown rice for added nutrients, color, and flavor.
- If you can't find split black lentils, try red lentils or another type of small lentils.
- Asafetida is commonly used in Indian vegetarian and lentil dishes to add flavor and aroma, and to reduce flatulence. Because of its aroma, reminiscent of cooked onion and garlic, asafetida is especially used by the Hindus, who do not eat onions or garlic. Its strong odor requires that it be stored in an airtight container to avoid overpowering other spices stored nearby. The odor and flavor become much milder and more pleasant when heated in oil. However, most people agree that asafetida's taste needs to be acquired.
- To use dried coconut instead of fresh, soak 1½ cups unsweetened dried coconut in 1½ cups water for 20 minutes and drain.
- Curry leaves are highly aromatic, used mainly in southern Indian cooking as an essential ingredient of curry powder, green chutneys, and marinade pastes. Curry leaves are to south Indian cuisine the equivalent of coriander leaves in north Indian cuisine. Because curry leaves lose much of their flavor when dried, use generously when substituting dried leaves for fresh leaves. Indian dishes are usually served with curry leaves, but they should be picked out and not eaten (similar to bay leaves).

Vegetable Curry

- 2 tablespoons olive or canola oil
- ½ large onion, finely chopped
- 2 large carrots, sliced
- 2 large potatoes, peeled and cubed
- 1 head cauliflower, broken into small florets
- 2 tablespoons curry powder, or to taste
- ½ teaspoon ground turmeric
- 1 pinch red, or cayenne, pepper flakes
- 1 cup water
- 1 teaspoon to 1 tablespoon chicken-style seasoning,* or to taste
- 1 cup frozen peas
- salt

Heat oil in a large skillet over medium heat. Add onion, carrots, potatoes, and cauliflower. Mix in curry powder, turmeric, and red pepper flakes. Add water and chicken-style seasoning; reduce heat to medium-low and simmer, covered, stirring occasionally, 20 minutes, or until vegetables are tender. Stir in peas. Season to taste with salt. Simmer, uncovered, 5 minutes.

Makes 8 servings. 109 calories, 4 g fat, 68 mg sodium.

VARIATION:

- Replace potato with sweet potato.

Lentil Hermit Cookies

- 1 cup brown sugar
- 1 cup slivered almonds
- ½ cup mashed cooked lentils
- ½ cup grape-seed or olive oil
- ½ cup soy milk
- 1 tablespoon egg replacement powder (such as Ener-G) dissolved in ¼ cup of water
- 1 teaspoon vanilla extract
- 1 teaspoon ground cinnamon or substitute
- ½ teaspoon nutmeg
- 1 cup whole-wheat flour
- 1 cup unbleached all-purpose flour
- 1 teaspoon baking powder (preferably aluminum-free)
- ½ teaspoon salt
- cooking spray

Heat oven to 350°F. Mix brown sugar, almonds, lentils, oil, soy milk, egg replacement, vanilla, cinnamon, and nutmeg together in a large mixing bowl. Stir in whole-wheat flour, all-purpose flour, baking powder, and salt; mix well. Drop by spoonfuls onto a baking sheet coated with cooking spray. Bake 10 minutes, or until the bottoms of the cookies are lightly browned.

Makes 36 cookies. 94 calories, 5 g fat, 37 mg sodium.

*see glossary

Mexican

Vegetable Quesadilla

Menu 14

Veggie Mex

This is one of my favorite menus to prepare. It is an ideal menu to serve people with gluten intolerance. The ***Quinoa Salad*** *can be a meal in itself. It is colorful, simple to make, high in calcium, and especially fun to serve people who have never tasted this fabulous grain!*

- **Mexican Tortilla Casserole**
- **Quinoa Salad**
- **Mexican Black Bean Salad**
- Fresh Vegetable Platter of Sliced Cucumbers, Sliced Tomatoes, and Olives
- Tortilla Chips with **Chunky Salsa** or **Mild Salsa**
- **Coconut Cream Squares With Coconut Cream**
- Pineapple Juice

Mexican Tortilla Casserole

Cheeze Sauce:

1 cup raw cashews
¼ cup nutritional yeast flakes
1 tablespoon unfermented soy sauce substitute or reduced-sodium soy sauce
1 small clove garlic, peeled
¼ cup **Roasted Red Bell Peppers**
½ cup water, as needed
3 tablespoons fresh lemon juice
2 tablespoons finely chopped onion
1 teaspoon salt

Casserole:

water or olive oil, for cooking vegetables
1 small onion, minced
1 red or green bell pepper, chopped
1 large bunch fresh spinach, chopped
2 small zucchini, chopped
4 cups thick tomato sauce (such as Hunt's Zesty Tomato Sauce)
1½ cups cooked kidney beans
1 cup **Mild Salsa**
2 tablespoons **Chili Powder Substitute** or mild chili powder
1 teaspoon salt
1 teaspoon dried basil
12 corn tortillas

Cheeze Sauce: Process cashews, nutritional yeast, soy sauce substitute, garlic, **Roasted Red Bell Peppers**, water, lemon juice, onion, and salt in a blender or food processor until very smooth.

Casserole: Heat a little water or oil in a large skillet; add onion, bell pepper, spinach, and zucchini. Cook and stir until vegetables are tender. Spread about ½ cup tomato sauce on the bottom of a 9"x13" glass baking dish. Stir remaining tomato sauce, kidney beans, **Mild Salsa**, **Chili Powder Substitute**, salt, and basil into skillet. Remove from heat and set aside.

Heat oven to 350°F. Place six tortillas in the baking dish, slightly overlapping to cover the bottom of the dish. Spread half of tomato and vegetable sauce over tortillas. Drizzle with half of the Cheeze Sauce. Repeat with remaining tortillas, tomato and vegetable sauce, and Cheeze Sauce. Bake 25 minutes, or until heated through. Let stand 10 minutes. Cut into squares and serve.

Makes 10 servings. 220 calories, 5 g fat, 183 mg sodium.

- Replace **Mild Salsa** with tomato salsa made with black beans and corn.
- This is an excellent gluten-free dish.

Chili Powder Substitute

- 2 tablespoons paprika
- 1 tablespoon dried parsley
- 1 tablespoon dried red bell pepper
- 1 tablespoon dried basil
- 1 tablespoon onion powder
- 1 teaspoon ground cumin
- 1 teaspoon dried oregano leaves
- ½ teaspoon dried dill
- ½ teaspoon dried savory
- ¼ teaspoon garlic powder
- ½ teaspoon cayenne

Process all ingredients in a food processor or blender until fine and powdery. Store in an airtight container.

Makes ½ cup; 24 1-teaspoon servings. 4 calories, 0 g fat, 1 mg sodium.

Roasted Red Bell Peppers (Pimento)

Red bell peppers, as desired

Position oven rack in the top position. Heat oven to broil. Place whole peppers in a single layer in a baking dish. Place under broiler and roast peppers about 8-9 minutes, until the skins are blackened but flesh is still firm. Remove peppers from the oven and let cool for about 15 minutes. Remove the skins by peeling them off with your fingers. Slice each pepper open and remove the seeds from the inside. Cut peppers into strips. Refrigerate up to one week.

Per ¼-cup serving. 10 calories, 0 g fat, 1 mg sodium.

COOK'S HINTS:

- Roast extra peppers during the summer, when their price is low, and freeze or can them.

Quinoa Salad

- 1½ cups quinoa
- 2½ cups water
- ½ teaspoon salt
- 1 medium tomato, chopped
- ½ cup sliced green onions
- ½ cup sliced ripe olives
- ½ cup chopped English cucumber
- 1 cup chopped orange or yellow bell pepper

Dressing:

- 3 tablespoons olive oil
- 2 tablespoons fresh lemon juice
- 1 teaspoon garlic powder
- ½ teaspoon salt

Rinse quinoa thoroughly in a fine-mesh strainer under running water. Drain well. Heat water to boiling in a medium saucepan. Stir in quinoa and salt; reduce heat and simmer, covered, 15 minutes or until water is absorbed. Remove from heat. Cool to room temperature. Cover and refrigerate at least 1 hour.

Mix tomato, green onions, olives, cucumber, and bell pepper together in a bowl. Stir in chilled quinoa.

Whisk oil, lemon juice, garlic powder, and salt in a small bowl. Pour dressing over salad; mix well. Refrigerate 30 minutes before serving.
Makes 8 servings. 188 calories, 8 g fat, 375 mg sodium.

- Can be served as a complete meal with whole-wheat pita bread, or served as a side dish.

Mexican Black Bean Salad

- 2 15- to 19-ounce cans black beans, drained and rinsed
- 1 cup fresh or frozen corn
- 1 cup finely chopped, peeled jicama
- ½ cup finely chopped red onion
- ½ red bell pepper, finely chopped
- 3 tablespoons minced fresh cilantro
- ¼ cup olive oil
- 2 tablespoons lemon juice
- 1 tablespoon pure maple syrup
- 1 teaspoon garlic powder
- 1 teaspoon ground cumin
- ¼ teaspoon salt

Mix black beans, corn, jicama, red onion, bell pepper, and cilantro together in a salad bowl. Whisk oil, lemon juice, maple syrup, garlic powder, cumin, and salt together in a separate bowl. Pour dressing over salad and mix well. Refrigerate at least 1 hour before serving.
Makes 8 servings. 278 calories, 8 g fat, 77 mg sodium.

Chunky Salsa

- 1 16.5-ounce can Mexican-style stewed tomatoes
- 1 4-ounce can chopped green chilies
- 1 cup chopped onion
- Cooking spray
- 1 cup chopped fresh tomatoes, drained
- ½ cup tomato sauce
- 1 tablespoon minced fresh cilantro or parsley
- salt, or to taste

Process canned tomatoes in a blender or food processor until smooth. Pour into a bowl. Stir in green chilies. Cook and stir the onion over medium heat in a nonstick skillet coated with cooking spray. Cook 1-2 minutes, stirring constantly, or until lightly browned. Stir into tomato mixture. Stir in fresh tomatoes, tomato sauce, and cilantro. Season to taste with salt. Refrigerate at least 30 minutes before serving. Keeps about 1 week in the refrigerator.
Makes 5 cups; 40 2-tablespoon servings.
8 calories, 0 g fat, 54 mg sodium.

Mild Salsa

- 1½ cups finely chopped, peeled fresh tomatoes
- 1 4-ounce can chopped green chilies
- ⅓ cup finely chopped green onions
- 2 tablespoons minced fresh cilantro or parsley
- 2 tablespoons fresh lemon juice
- 1 clove garlic, minced
- ¼ teaspoon salt

Mix tomatoes, green chilies, green onions, cilantro, lemon juice, garlic, and salt together in a small mixing bowl. Remove half of the mixture and process in a blender or food processor until smooth. Stir into remaining tomato mixture. Cover and refrigerate at least 4 hours. Keeps about 1 week in the refrigerator.
Makes about 2½ cups; 12 2-tablespoon servings.
4 calories, 0 g fat, 52 mg sodium.

Coconut Cream Squares

Coconut Crust:

3 cups shredded, unsweetened coconut
2 tablespoons unbleached all-purpose flour
½ cup soy milk
cooking spray

Coconut Filling:

6 cups hot water
⅔ cup soy milk powder
1½ cups dried pineapple pieces
1 cup cornstarch
1 teaspoon vanilla extract
1 teaspoon coconut extract
1 recipe **Coconut Cream**, optional
fresh banana slices, optional

Coconut Crust: Heat oven to 350°F. Mix coconut and flour together in a medium bowl. Stir in soy milk with a fork. Press mixture evenly on the bottom of a 9"x13" glass baking dish coated with cooking spray. Bake 10 minutes or until golden brown. Cool on a wire rack.

Coconut Filling: Process hot water, soy milk powder, dried pineapple, cornstarch, vanilla, and coconut extract in a blender or food processor until very smooth. Pour into a medium saucepan and heat to boiling; reduce heat and simmer until thickened, whisking often. Be careful not to let it stick to the bottom of the saucepan. Pour filling over coconut crust. Refrigerate 2-3 hours or until firm. Cut into squares. Serve with a dollop of **Coconut Cream** and fresh banana slices, if desired.

Makes 12 servings. 450 calories, 37 g fat, 44 mg sodium.

COOK'S HINTS:

- The coconut crust in this recipe is what drives the fat content up. If you are concerned about the amount of fat or calories in this recipe, replace the coconut crust with one of your favorite crusts, or serve the filling as pudding and garnish with shredded coconut.

Coconut Cream

1 14-ounce can coconut milk
1 tablespoon vanilla extract
1 tablespoon pure maple syrup
2 tablespoons precooked cornstarch powder (such as Instant Clear Jel), as needed

Process coconut milk, vanilla, and maple syrup in a blender or food processor a few seconds. While processing, gradually add precooked cornstarch powder until a thick whipped cream consistency is reached. Refrigerate until chilled.

Makes about 1¾ cups; 28 1-tablespoon servings. 32 calories, 3 g fat, 2 mg sodium.

COOK'S HINTS:

- Coconut milk with a thicker consistency works best for this recipe.
- I use this recipe for special occasions.

About Quinoa

Quinoa, pronounced *keen-wah*, is not a true cereal grain, but rather the botanical fruit of an herb plant. It is treated as a grain in cooking. The grains are small yellow flattened spheres, about 1.5 to 2 millimeters in diameter. When cooked, the germ coils into a small "tail." Quinoa is known as the Mother Grain. Quinoa contains more protein than any other grain (an average of 16 percent, compared with 7.5 percent for rice, 10 percent for millet and 14 percent for wheat). It is also a good source of dietary fiber and is high in magnesium, potassium, and iron and is a good source of phosphorous, calcium, vitamin E, and several B vitamins. Quinoa is also gluten-free and is easy to digest, making it an excellent food for infants, seniors, and gluten-free diets. It contains an almost perfect balance of all eight essential amino acids needed for tissue development in humans, making it a complete protein food.

There are almost 2,000 varieties of quinoa, ranging in color from ivory to pink, brown to red or almost black. The larger, whiter varieties are the most common.

Quinoa cooks in about 15 minutes and can be added to stews, soups, stir-fries, and salads to add bulk, flavor, and nutrients. It can also, be eaten as an alternative to oatmeal and is good with honey, nuts, or berries. Quinoa flour can be added to breads, muffins, bagels, cookies, and pancakes.

In its natural state, quinoa has a coating of bitter-tasting saponins, making it unappetizing. Most quinoa sold commercially has been processed to remove this coating. But it is still a good idea to place quinoa in a fine-mesh strainer and thoroughly rinse until the water runs clear.

When prepared, quinoa has a light, fluffy texture and a mild, slightly nutty flavor that makes it an excellent alternative to rice or couscous. For a roasted flavor, toast quinoa in a dry skillet for about five minutes. To cook quinoa, heat one part quinoa and slightly less than two parts liquid to boiling; cover and reduce to a simmer for about 15 minutes, or until the grains are translucent and the water is absorbed.

Store quinoa in a glass or plastic container, in a cool, dry, dark place. Stored properly, it should stay fresh for up to one year.

Quinoa cultivation

Quinoa grains

Nutrition Facts	
Serving Size:	¼ cup (43 g)
Calories:	160
Total Fat:	2.5 g (4%)
Sodium:	10 mg (0%)
Total Carbohydrates:	30 g (10%)
Dietary Fiber:	3 g (12%)
Sugars:	0 g (0%)
Protein:	6 g (11%)
Calcium:	25.5 g (2%)
Iron:	3.9 mg (20%)

Cooked quinoa

Menu 15

Mexican Fiesta

The birthplace of chocolate lies in present-day Mexico, so this is a perfect place to put my recipe for Eat-More Bars. I have demonstrated this recipe so many times on cookbook tours that people started calling me the Eat-More Lady! Many people express surprise at how close these bars taste to the real Eat-More Chocolate Bars! I love to say that the only difference between the two recipes is that you can enjoy these Eat-More Bars guilt-free.

- **Quesadillas** with **Guacamole** (p. 66), **Salsa** (p. 53), and Nondairy Sour Cream
- **Refried Beans**
- **Spanish Rice**
- **Mexican Salad With Honey-Lime Dressing**
- **Eat-More Bars**

Quesadillas

cooking spray or olive oil
16 small wheat or corn tortillas or 2 recipes **Homemade Corn Tortillas**
1 cup salsa
4 teaspoons minced fresh cilantro, optional
½ cup cooked black beans, drained
½ cup fresh or frozen corn
¼ cup minced red onion
½ cup sliced ripe olives
1-1½ cup shredded nondairy cheese or **Almond Cheese** (p. 132)

Heat a medium-sized nonstick skillet over medium-low heat. Coat pan with cooking spray or a drop of oil. Place one tortilla into the skillet. Spread 2 tablespoons salsa and sprinkle ½ teaspoon minced cilantro, if desired. Sprinkle with 1 tablespoon black beans, 1 tablespoon corn, 1 teaspoon minced red onion, 1 tablespoon olives, and 2–3 tablespoons cheese. Cover with another tortilla and press down gently. Cook until the bottom tortilla browns lightly. Carefully turn over and brown the other tortilla. Transfer to a plate and cut into wedges. Repeat with remaining ingredients. Serve with **Guacamole, Salsa**, and nondairy sour cream for dipping.

Makes 8 servings. 169 calories, 4 g fat, 291 mg sodium.

Homemade Corn Tortillas

1 cup *masa harina* (corn flour)
½ cup warm water
¼ teaspoon salt

Mix the *masa harina*, warm water, and salt together in a mixing bowl. Press together by hand to form a moist, smooth ball of dough. Divide the dough into eight equal pieces. Roll each piece between moistened palms to form small balls and cover with plastic wrap to prevent drying. Roll out one tortilla at a time between two layers of waxed paper into a 6-inch circle. Repeat with remaining dough.

Heat a skillet over high heat. Place one tortilla in the skillet and cook about 20 seconds, or until the edges begin to darken. Turn over with a spatula and cook the second side about 40 seconds, pressing with the spatula once or twice, until the tortilla begins to puff. Turn over and cook 10 seconds longer. Wrap the finished tortillas in a towel to keep warm.

Makes 8 servings. 52 calories, 1 g fat, 74 mg sodium.

Refried Beans

3 cups pinto beans, sorted and rinsed
6-12 cups water, as needed
2 teaspoons salt
2 tablespoons olive oil
1 medium onion, minced
3 cloves garlic, minced
2 tablespoons chopped canned green chilies, optional

Cook beans in water according to one of the following methods:

- Stove: Place beans in a large saucepan and cover with at least 3 inches of water above the bean level (about 10-12 cups). Heat to boiling; reduce heat and simmer, covered, 2 hours, or until beans are tender.
- Slow Cooker: Place beans and 7-8 cups of water in a medium or large slow cooker. Cook on high for about 6-8 hours (or overnight) or until beans are tender. (Most of the water will be absorbed.)
- Pressure Cooker: Place beans in a 4-quart pressure cooker with 8-10 cups of water. Heat to high pressure and cook for 30-35 minutes. Release pressure. If beans are not tender, return them to heat and simmer until soft.

Drain cooked beans in a colander. Return beans to the cooking pan and add ¼-½ cup of hot water to keep beans from drying out. Mash beans with a potato masher until most of the beans are mashed. Stir in salt. Heat oil in a large skillet. Add onion and garlic. Cook and stir until onion is tender. Stir in mashed beans. Stir in green chilies, if desired. Cook, stirring frequently, until heated through.

Makes 7 cups; 14 ½-cup servings. 165 calories, 2 g fat, 340 mg sodium.

COOK'S HINTS:

- The cooking time may vary depending on the freshness of the beans. As the beans age, they take longer to cook.
- Don't add salt to beans until they are fully cooked, because the salt will keep the beans from cooking.

Spanish Rice

2 tablespoons olive oil
2 cups long grain brown rice
1 onion, chopped fine
1 clove garlic, minced
4 cups water
4 teaspoons to ¼ cup chicken-style seasoning,* or to taste
1 cup chopped fresh tomato
1 teaspoon salt
¼ teaspoon dried oregano leaves

Heat oil in a large skillet; stir in brown rice. Add onion and garlic; cook and stir until onion is tender. Heat water and chicken-style seasoning to boiling in a 2-quart saucepan. Stir in tomatoes, salt, and oregano. Stir in rice mixture. Cover and simmer for 1 hour or until rice is done. Turn off heat and let stand 5 minutes.

Makes 6 servings, 288 calories, 7 g fat, 446 mg sodium.

*see glossary

Mexican Salad With Honey-Lime Dressing

- 1 head romaine lettuce, chopped
- 2 15-ounce cans black beans, drained and rinsed
- 2 cups chopped tomato
- 1½ cups shredded jicama
- 1½ cups fresh corn (or frozen corn, thawed)
- 1 cup sliced green onions
- 1 ripe avocado, peeled, pitted, and chopped
- 1 red bell pepper, cut in half and sliced into thin strips
- ¼ cup olive oil
- ¼ cup honey
- ¼ cup lime juice
- 2 cloves garlic, minced
- ¼ cup minced fresh cilantro or parsley
- ½ teaspoon cayenne, or to taste
- ¼ teaspoon salt

Mix romaine lettuce, black beans, tomato, jicama, corn, green onions, avocado, and bell pepper together in a large bowl. Stir together oil, honey, lime juice, garlic, cilantro, cayenne, and salt. Pour over the salad and toss. Serve immediately.

Makes 8 servings. 300 calories, 11 g fat, 281 mg sodium.

Eat-More Bars

- 1 cup carob chips
- ½ cup pure cane syrup (such as Roger's) or honey
- ½ cup natural peanut butter
- 1 cup wheat germ
- 1 cup dry roasted peanuts, chopped
- ½ cup raw sunflower seeds

Stir carob chips, cane syrup, and peanut butter together in a medium saucepan. Cook over medium heat, stirring frequently, until carob chips melt. Remove from heat. Stir in wheat germ, peanuts, and sunflower seeds. Press into a 9-inch square baking pan. Refrigerate at least 2 hours, or until firm. Cut into 1-inch squares. Serve chilled.

Makes 32 servings. 117 calories, 7 g fat, 20 mg sodium.

COOK'S HINTS:

- These freeze well.

Menu 16

Vegetarian Verde

Taco salad is a modern variation on the traditional Tex-Mex dish, which first appeared in America in the 1960s. The traditional taco salad is served in a deep-fried flour tortilla shell lined with refried beans, stuffed with shredded iceberg lettuce, and topped with diced tomato, shredded cheddar cheese, sour cream, guacamole, and salsa. The salad is then topped with ground beef. No wonder taco salad was mocked in a radio advertisement as being a very high-calory dish made into a salad.

*Our family enjoys vegetarian **Taco Salad**. Instead of the rich original ingredients, we use the opportunity to showcase a variety of fresh, raw foods. Use your imagination when making this salad. Add some extra veggies, such as colored bell peppers, raw diced zucchini, or corn. We like to sprinkle our salad with hemp hearts for additional omega fats. My son Joseph likes to say, "Taco salad isn't taco salad without the hemp hearts."*

- **Taco Salad**
- **Guacamole** (p. 66)
- Nondairy Sour Cream or **Soy Sour Cream** (p. 66)
- **Salsa** (p. 53)
- Raw Vegetable Platter and Dip
- **Garlic Toast** (p. 131)
- Fruit Punch
- **Carob Brownies**

Taco Salad

½ cup textured vegetable protein (TVP) granules
2 tablespoons taco seasoning
8 cups chopped green leaf lettuce
2 cups chopped tomatoes
2 cups cooked kidney beans
1 cup sliced ripe olives, optional
1 cup shredded nondairy cheese, optional
¼ cup finely chopped red onion
½ cup olive oil
2 tablespoons lemon juice
1 tablespoon dried parsley
1 teaspoon garlic powder
½ teaspoon onion powder
4 cups corn or tortilla chips, or to taste

Cover the TVP with hot water. Stir in the taco seasoning and let stand 10 minutes or until water is absorbed. Toss lettuce, tomatoes, kidney beans, rehydrated TVP, olives, nondairy cheese, and red onion together in a large salad bowl. Whisk oil, lemon juice, parsley, garlic powder, and onion powder together in a small bowl. Pour over salad and mix well. Mix in tortilla chips. Serve immediately. Serve with **Guacamole**, nondairy sour cream, and **Salsa**, if desired.

Makes 16 servings. 196 calories, 12 g fat, 205 mg sodium.

COOK'S HINTS:

- Hemp hearts are seeds containing a concentrated and balanced source of protein, essential fats (omega 3 and 6), and vitamins, including vitamin D and particularly the B-complex vitamins, providing a great source of energy!
- Replace lettuce with spinach.
- Replace kidney beans with black beans.
- Omit TVP and taco seasoning; add 1 tablespoon taco seasoning to the dressing.
- Sprinkle with hemp hearts.

Carob Brownies

- 2 cups unbleached all-purpose or spelt flour
- 1 cup chopped walnuts or pecans
- 1 cup pure cane syrup (such as Roger's) or honey
- ⅓ cup carob powder
- ¼ cup olive or grape-seed oil
- 2 tablespoons egg replacement powder (such as Ener-G) dissolved in ½ cup water
- 1 tablespoon vanilla extract
- ½ teaspoon salt
- cooking spray
- ⅓ cup carob chips, or to taste

Heat oven to 350°F. Mix flour, walnuts, cane syrup, carob powder, oil, egg replacement, vanilla, and salt together in a mixing bowl. Press into a 9-inch square baking dish coated with cooking spray. Bake 20 minutes. Remove from oven and sprinkle with carob chips. Return to oven and bake 5 minutes, or until carob chips melt. Remove from oven. Spread melted carob chips evenly across the top with a knife. Cool to room temperature. Refrigerate 1-2 hours, or until frosting is set. Cut into squares.

Makes 24 servings. 149 calories, 6 g fat, 50 mg sodium.

Menu 17

South of the Border

This vegan version of nachos gives you fun, flavor, and nutritional value all at the same time. Nachos work well for party food or for a light supper.

- **Cream of Spinach Soup**
- **Nachos** with **Cheeze Sauce**
- Raw Vegetable Platter
- **Dried Fruit Candies**
- **Iced Herbal Tea**

Cream of Spinach Soup

- 2 tablespoons olive oil, optional
- 2 medium onions, chopped
- 6 cups water
- 6 tablespoons whole-wheat pastry flour or unbleached all-purpose flour
- 2-6 tablespoons chicken-style seasoning,* or to taste
- 1 teaspoon salt
- 2 bunches fresh spinach, chopped
- 1 cup water
- ½ cup raw cashews

Heat oil or a little water in a large saucepan. Add onions; cook and stir until tender. Stir in water, flour, chicken-style seasoning, and salt. Heat to boiling over medium heat; reduce heat and simmer 2-3 minutes, or until thickened. Steam spinach, covered, for 5 minutes, or until spinach wilts; drain. Process 1 cup water and cashews in a blender or food processor until smooth. Add steamed spinach and process a few seconds to mix. Stir spinach mixture into saucepan. Simmer until heated through, but do not boil.

Makes 12 1-cup servings. 97 calories, 5 g fat, 283 mg sodium.

VARIATION:

- For added texture, process half of the spinach and add the remaining spinach to the soup.

*see glossary

Nachos

Tortilla chips
Cheeze Sauce, heated
Chopped fresh tomatoes
Sliced green onions
Sliced ripe olives

Place ingredients in separate serving bowls based on the number of people being served. Let each person assemble his or her own nachos.

COOK'S HINTS:

- Additional ideas for toppings: heated **Refried Beans, Salsa, Guacamole, Soy Sour Cream** or nondairy sour cream, or canned green chilies.

Cheeze Sauce

2 cups water
1 cup raw cashews
¼ cup **Roasted Red Bell Peppers** (p. 52) or
1 2-ounce jar pimentos (not pickled)
3 tablespoons cornstarch
1½ tablespoons lemon juice
2 tablespoons nutritional yeast flakes
1 teaspoon salt, or to taste
½ teaspoon onion powder
½ teaspoon garlic powder
1 4-ounce can chopped green chilies, optional

Process water, cashews, roasted red peppers, cornstarch, lemon juice, nutritional yeast, salt, onion powder, and garlic powder in a blender or food processor until smooth. Pour mixture into a saucepan and heat over medium heat, stirring constantly with a whisk, until mixture thickens. Stir in green chilies, if desired. Keeps about 1 week in the refrigerator. Also freezes well.
Makes 3½ cups; 56 1-tablespoon servings.
25 calories, 2 g fat, 42 mg sodium.

COOK'S HINTS:

- Replace green chilies with finely chopped fresh jalapeño peppers, or cayenne, to taste.
- Serving ideas: Serve sauce warm over tortilla chips for nachos, or use as a cheeze sauce on baked potatoes, steamed vegetables, or pasta.

Dried Fruit Candies

½ cup golden raisins
½ cup dates
½ cup prunes
½ cup dried apricots
¼ cup slivered almonds
orange or pineapple juice, as needed
¼ cup unsweetened shredded coconut

Process raisins, dates, prunes, apricots, and almonds in a food processor until finely ground, adding a small amount of juice, if necessary, to process mixture. (Mixture should be dry and sticky, not overly moist.) Form mixture into

*see glossary

1-inch balls with your hands. Roll each ball in coconut. Place balls in covered container. Refrigerate until firm.

Makes 22 servings. 65 calories, 2 g fat, 1 mg sodium.

Iced Herbal Tea

- 10 cups water
- 8 fruit-flavored herbal tea bags
- 1 tablespoon honey or granulated cane sugar, or to taste
- 12 ice cubes

Heat water to boiling in a large saucepan. Add tea bags. Simmer for 5 minutes. Remove tea bags, and gently squeeze to release any remaining flavor. Stir in honey until dissolved. Season to taste with additional honey, if desired. Refrigerate at least 3 hours, or until chilled. Serve with ice cubes in a large pitcher or individual glasses.

Makes 10 1-cup servings. 6 calories, 0 g fat, 5 mg sodium.

Menu 18

Meatless Mexican

Serve this festive menu for Cinco de Mayo (Spanish for May 5), a Mexican holiday celebrated around the world in honor of Mexican heritage and culture. Contrary to what many North Americans believe, Mexico's national Independence Day celebration is September 16, not Cinco de Mayo.

- **Mexican Rice**
- **Veggie Fajitas** with **Soy Sour Cream** (p. 66) and **Guacamole** (p. 66)
- Tortilla Chips with **Salsa** (p. 53)
- **Agua Fresca**
- **Sesame Bars**

Mexican Rice

- 1¾ cups water
- ¾ cup stewed tomatoes
- ½ cup chopped onion
- 1 large clove garlic, peeled
- ¼-1 teaspoon chicken-style seasoning,* or to taste
- 1 teaspoon dried parsley
- ¾ teaspoon salt
- ¼ teaspoon dried basil
- ¼ teaspoon paprika
- ¼ teaspoon ground cumin
- 1 cup chopped carrots
- ¼ cup chopped green bell peppers
- ¼ cup chopped red bell peppers
- 1½ cups converted brown rice
- 1 tablespoon chopped canned green chilies
- 1 tablespoon minced fresh parsley

Process water, tomatoes, onion, garlic, chicken-style seasoning, parsley, salt, basil, paprika, and cumin in a blender or food processor until smooth. Pour into a large skillet over medium heat. Stir in carrots and bell peppers; cook, covered, for 20 minutes. Stir in rice and cook, covered, for 10 minutes, or until the liquid is absorbed and the rice is tender. Stir in chilies and fresh parsley.

Makes 6 1-cup servings. 198 calories, 2 g fat, 384 mg sodium.

Veggie Fajitas

2 cups dry unflavored soy protein strips (such as Soy Curls)
1-2 tablespoons olive oil
1 small red bell pepper, sliced into thin strips
1 small green bell pepper, sliced into thin strips
1 small yellow bell pepper, sliced into thin strips
1 small orange bell pepper, sliced into thin strips
1 small red onion, cut in half and sliced into thin strips
1 small onion, cut in half and sliced into thin strips
¼ cup unfermented soy sauce substitute or reduced-sodium soy sauce
¼ cup plum sauce, or to taste
1 teaspoon garlic powder, or to taste
8 large (or 16 small) whole-wheat tortillas
chopped fresh cilantro or parsley, optional
fancy toothpicks
Soy Sour Cream (p. 66), optional
Salsa (p. 53), optional
Guacamole (p. 66), optional

Heat oven to 300°F. Cover the soy protein strips with hot water (or broth) to rehydrate for 10 minutes, or until soft; drain. Heat oil in a large skillet; cook and stir rehydrated soy protein strips, bell peppers, and onions. Stir soy sauce substitute, plum sauce, and garlic powder together and pour into the skillet with the vegetables. Simmer until vegetables are nearly tender.

To heat tortillas: Wrap tortillas in a damp towel, then wrap in aluminum foil. Bake about 15 minutes, or until hot and pliable. Keep covered.

To serve: Using a slotted spoon (to drain off excess liquid), place about ½-1 cup (depending on tortilla size) vegetable mixture in the center of a warm tortilla. Sprinkle with cilantro or parsley, if desired. Fold in the sides of the tortilla and roll it up. Fasten it closed using a fancy toothpick. Place fajitas on a serving platter. Serve with nondairy sour cream or **Soy Sour Cream**, **Salsa**, and **Guacamole**, if desired.

Makes 8 large (or 16 small) fajitas. 99 calories, 4 g fat, 319 mg sodium.

- The plum sauce may seem unusual, but give it a try. I think you'll like it.
- For a different flavor, replace the plum sauce with taco sauce.
- You can replace whole-wheat tortillas with corn tortillas or **Homemade Corn Tortillas** (p. 56).
- You can also let each person assemble his or her own fajita.

Agua Fresca

3 cups cold water
2 cups watermelon chunks, seeded
1-2 teaspoons honey, fructose, or sugar, or to taste

Process water and fruit in a blender or food processor until smooth. Pour through a fine-mesh strainer to remove seeds and pulp. Stir in honey. Sweeten to taste with additional honey, if desired. Add additional fruit or water, if desired (since fruits vary in sweetness and flavor).

Makes 5 1-cup servings. 23 calories, 0 g fat, 4 mg sodium.

COOK'S HINTS:

- *Agua Fresca* means "fresh water" in Spanish and is a very popular beverage in Mexico. It is similar to lemonade, but can be made with other fruits, such as pineapple, papaya, mango, strawberries, or raspberries.
- For an extra-special treat, try replacing water with sparkling water.

Sesame Bars

2 cups sesame seeds
1½ cups carob chips
½ cup natural peanut butter
½ cup honey
1½ cups unsweetened shredded coconut

½ cup finely ground pecans or walnuts
1 teaspoon vanilla extract
½ teaspoon salt

Heat oven to 300°F. Toast sesame seeds on a baking sheet for about 30 minutes, or until lightly browned. Heat carob chips, peanut butter, and honey in a saucepan over medium heat until carob chips melt. Remove from heat. Mix in toasted sesame seeds, coconut, ground pecans, vanilla, and salt. Press into a 9-inch square baking dish. Refrigerate (or freeze) 1-2 hours, or until firm. Cut into squares.

Makes 24 servings. 280 calories, 22 g fat, 81 mg sodium.

Menu 19

Meal for Amigos

*The **Oatmeal-Date Cake** has become a popular birthday cake in my family. Originally my dad's favorite, it now has become a top choice for my husband, Ron, too.*

- **Taco Soup** with **Soy Sour Cream** (p. 66)
- Vegetable Platter (Jicama sticks, Baby Carrots, Assorted Bell Peppers, Zucchini Sticks)
- **Savory Mexican Muffins** with Margarine
- **Oatmeal-Date Cake**

Taco Soup

1 15- to 19-ounce can black beans, drained
1 15- to 19-ounce can kidney or pinto beans, drained
1 28-ounce can diced tomatoes
1½ cups water
1 cup corn
½ cup chopped onion
2 tablespoons taco seasoning
¼ cup minced fresh cilantro or parsley
7 ounces tortilla chips (about 8 cups), crushed
Soy Sour Cream (p. 66), optional

Heat beans, tomatoes, water, corn, onion, and taco seasoning to boiling in a 3-quart saucepan; reduce heat and simmer 15 minutes or longer, until onion is tender and flavors are blended. Stir in cilantro. Ladle into soup bowls. Top with crushed tortilla chips, and a dollop of **Soy Sour Cream**, if desired.

Makes 8 servings. 310 calories, 9 g fat, 577 mg sodium.

Savory Mexican Muffins

2 cups nine-grain flaked cereal
1½ cups soy milk
1 cup **Salsa** (p. 53)
¾ cup olive oil
1 cup shredded nondairy cheese
2 tablespoons chopped fresh cilantro
2 tablespoons chopped, canned green chilies

1 tablespoon egg replacement powder (such as Ener-G) dissolved in ¼ cup water
1½ cups whole-wheat flour
1½ cups unbleached all-purpose flour
⅓ cup cornmeal
2 tablespoons baking powder (preferably aluminum-free)
½ teaspoon salt
cooking spray

Stir flaked cereal, soy milk, and salsa together in a mixing bowl; let stand 1 hour. Heat oven to 375°F. Stir in oil, nondairy cheese, cilantro, green chilies, and egg replacement. Stir whole-wheat flour, all-purpose flour, cornmeal, baking powder, and salt together in a separate bowl. Stir flour mixture into cereal mixture until just mixed. Spoon into muffin pans coated with cooking spray. Bake 15-20 minutes or until golden brown. Serve warm with margarine.

Makes 1½ dozen. 222 calories, 2 g fat, 169 mg sodium.

Oatmeal-Date Cake

1½ cups boiling water
1 cup quick-cooking oats
1 cup chopped dates
1½ cups whole-wheat pastry flour or unbleached all-purpose flour
¾ cup granulated cane sugar or ½ cup honey
2 teaspoons baking powder (preferably aluminum-free)
1 teaspoon ground cinnamon or substitute
½ teaspoon salt
¼ cup olive or grape-seed oil
1 tablespoon egg replacement powder (such as Ener-G) dissolved in ¼ cup water
1 teaspoon vanilla extract
cooking spray

Topping:

¾ cup unsweetened shredded coconut
½ cup brown sugar
¼ cup soy milk
2 tablespoons olive or grape-seed oil
8 pecan halves

Pour boiling water over oats and dates in a mixing bowl. Let cool to room temperature. Mix flour, sugar, baking powder, cinnamon, and salt together; set aside. Heat oven to 350°F. When date mixture has cooled, stir in oil, egg replacement, and vanilla. Stir in flour mixture until well mixed. Spoon batter into a 9-inch springform pan (or a 9-inch square baking pan) coated with cooking spray. Bake 35-40 minutes until done, when a toothpick inserted near the center comes out clean.

Topping: Stir coconut, brown sugar, soy milk, and oil together in a small saucepan. Heat to boiling; boil for 1 minute. Spread topping on cake. Position oven rack in top position. Heat oven to broil. Broil cake 1-2 minutes or until topping is golden brown. Remove from oven and quickly arrange and gently press pecan halves on the top of the cake. Let cool before removing the sides of the springform pan.

Makes 9 servings. 522 calories, 23 g fat, 216 mg sodium.

Menu 20

Hacienda Homestyle

This is a simple menu to prepare when you have a sudden craving for Mexican food, but are limited for time. Jicama is probably one of the most unique foods I have been introduced to. Our family (yes, even the children!) enjoys raw jicama sticks on our vegetable platters. One of the homework assignments I always give my cooking class students is to taste jicama. My students always come back to the next class excited about this interesting food!

- **Mexican Skillet Nachos**
- **Guacamole**
- **Soy Sour Cream**, **Tofu Sour Cream**, or **Almond Sour Cream**
- **Sliced Jicama**
- Fresh Baby Carrots
- Nondairy Ice Cream with **Pineapple Topping**

Mexican Skillet Nachos

water or oil, for cooking vegetables
1 medium onion, chopped
1 medium green bell pepper, chopped
1 package or 13-ounce can meatless frankfurters, sliced
½ cup unbleached all-purpose flour
1 28-32-ounce can herb-seasoned tomatoes, mashed
1 28-32-ounce can diced tomatoes
4 cups cooked pinto beans
tortilla chips
shredded nondairy cheese, optional

Heat a small amount of water or oil in large skillet or saucepan. Cook and stir onion and bell pepper until onion is tender. Stir in frankfurters and cook until lightly browned, stirring occasionally. Stir in flour and mix well. Stir in herb-seasoned tomatoes, diced tomatoes, and pinto beans. Simmer for 20-30 minutes, stirring occasionally. Serve over tortilla chips. Sprinkle with nondairy cheese, if desired. Serve with **Guacamole** and **Soy Sour Cream**, **Tofu Sour Cream**, or **Almond Sour Cream**.
Makes 10 servings. 198 calories, 3 g fat, 489 mg sodium. (Analysis does not include tortilla chips.)

Guacamole

2 large ripe avocados
3 tablespoons lemon juice
2 teaspoons garlic powder
1 teaspoon onion powder
¾ teaspoon salt

Cut avocados in half and remove the pits. Scoop avocado from peel with a spoon. Transfer to a food processor and process until smooth. (Or mash with a fork.) Stir in lemon juice, garlic powder, onion powder, and salt.
Makes about 2½ cups; 40 1-tablespoon servings. 15 calories, 1 g fat, 44 mg sodium.

COOK'S HINTS:

- Serve with nachos, taco salad, tacos, burritos, or haystacks.
- When making guacamole ahead, place an avocado pit in the center before covering and refrigerating. This keeps the guacamole from turning brown. When storing an avocado half, leave the pit in to minimize browning.

Soy Sour Cream

1 cup soy milk
½ teaspoon salt
½ teaspoon onion powder
1 cup grape-seed or canola oil
2½ tablespoons lemon juice

Process soy milk, salt, and onion powder in a blender or food processor for 1 minute. While processing, gradually drizzle in oil. Remove from blender or food processor. Gently stir in lemon juice. Cover and refrigerate.
Makes 2 cups; 32 1-tablespoon servings.
64 calories, 7 g fat, 39 mg sodium.

Tofu Sour Cream

1 12.3-ounce package firm silken tofu (preferably reduced-fat)
½ cup raw cashews
2 tablespoons lemon juice
1½ teaspoons seasoned salt
¼ teaspoon garlic powder
¼ teaspoon onion powder

Process tofu, cashews, lemon juice, seasoned salt, garlic powder, and onion powder in a blender or food processor until smooth. Refrigerate several hours.
Makes 1½ cups; 24 1-tablespoon servings.
33 calories, 2 g fat, 110 mg sodium.

Almond Sour Cream

1 cup water
½ cup blanched slivered almonds
¼ cup grape-seed or canola oil
2 tablespoons lemon juice
½ teaspoon salt
½ teaspoon onion powder
1½ tablespoons precooked cornstarch powder (such as Instant Clear Jel)

Process water, almonds, oil, lemon juice, salt, and onion powder in a blender or food processor until very smooth. While processing, add precooked cornstarch powder; continue to process until slightly thickened. Refrigerate before serving.
Makes 1½ cups; 24 1-tablespoon servings.
40 calories, 4 g fat, 50 mg sodium.

COOK'S HINTS:

- Cornstarch may be substituted for the precooked cornstarch powder, but requires heating in order to thicken. Cook, stirring constantly, in a small saucepan until thickened.

Sliced Jicama

1 large jicama
1 fresh lemon or lime
salt, optional

Cut a jicama in half vertically and snip off the ends. Cut each half into ½-inch wedges. Peel each wedge using a paring knife. Slice each wedge into ½-inch sticks. Place jicama sticks on a platter or festive-looking plate. Squeeze fresh lemon or lime juice over the jicama sticks. Season to taste with salt, if desired.
Makes 8 servings. 57 calories, 0 g fat, 6 mg sodium.

Pineapple Topping

2 cups crushed pineapple
1 tablespoon cornstarch
1 tablespoon granulated cane sugar, optional, or to taste
ice cream
unsweetened shredded coconut, for garnish, optional

Stir crushed pineapple, cornstarch, and sugar, if desired, together in a small saucepan. Cook over medium heat, stirring frequently, until slightly thickened. Refrigerate until chilled. Serve over ice cream. Garnish with coconut, if desired.
Makes 2 cups; 32 1-tablespoon servings.
12 calories, 0 g fat, 0 mg sodium.

About Jicama

Jicama (Spanish: *hee*-kah-mah), also known as "Mexican potato" and "Mexican turnip," is the name of a native Mexican vine, most commonly used referring to the plant's edible tuberous root. "Yam bean" is sometimes another known name for jicama.

The jicama vine can reach a height of 13-16 feet (4-5 meters) if given suitable support. Its root can spread to lengths of up to 6½ feet (2 meters) and weigh up to 44 pounds (20 kilograms). The root's exterior is yellow and papery, while its inside is creamy white with a crisp texture that resembles a raw potato or pear. The flavor is sweet and starchy, similar to some apples, and it is usually eaten raw in Mexico, often with salt, lemon or lime juice, and sometimes chili powder. In Mexico it is very popular in salads, fresh fruit combos, fruit bars, soups, and other cooked dishes. It can also be cooked in stir-fried dishes to resemble water chestnuts.

Because of its growing popularity, cultivation of jicama has recently spread from Mexico to other parts of Central America, and to China and Southeast Asia, where raw jicama is included in salads. Jicama has also become popular in Vietnamese food.

In contrast to the root, the remainder of the jicama plant is very poisonous; the seeds contain the toxin rotenone, which is used to poison insects and fish.

Jicama is high in carbohydrates in the form of dietary fiber. It is composed of 86-90 percent water; it contains only trace amounts of protein and fats. Its sweet flavor is just amazing. It comes from the plant's inulin and oligofructose, which are completely soluble and are not digested in the upper gastrointestinal tract, and therefore have a reduced caloric value. It does not lead to a rise in serum glucose or stimulated insulin secretion, and stimulates the growth of good intestinal bifidobacteria.

Jicama should be stored dry, between 53°F and 60°F (12°C and 16°C) and not in the refrigerator, since colder temperatures will damage the root. A fresh root stored at an appropriate temperature will keep for a month or two.

See page 67 for **Sliced Jicama**, a simple and tasty way to enjoy jicama.

Menu 21

Tex-Mex, the Meatless Way

*Tamales have become a favorite autumn food in Mexico and many parts of the United States. The Hispanic women in the community would gather in the fall to make tamales. Tamale making was a social event—a time to renew old friendships and make new ones. Often, young women would return home to make tamales with their mothers. **Tamale Pie** can spice up any supper with the flair of a fiesta!*

- **Tamale Pie**
- Tossed Salad with **Lemon Oil Dressing**
- Tortilla chips with **Salsa** (p. 53)
- **Pineapple Whip** with **Soy Whipped Cream** (p. 17)

Tamale Pie

water or olive oil, for cooking
1 cup chopped onion
2 fresh cloves garlic, minced
1 12-ounce package meatless burger (such as Yves) or 2 cups **Ground Gluten** (p. 33)
2 cups cooked kidney, pinto, or black beans, drained
2 small fresh tomatoes, chopped (or 1 large)
1 8-ounce can tomato sauce (1 cup)
1 teaspoon **Chili Powder Substitute** (p. 52) or chili powder
½-1 teaspoon salt
½ cup sliced ripe olives, optional
2 cups soy milk
1 cup cornmeal
1 tablespoon egg replacement powder (such as Ener-G), dissolved in ¼ cup water
1 tablespoon olive oil
½ teaspoon salt

Heat water or oil in a large skillet. Add onion and garlic. Cook and stir until onion is tender. Stir in burger, beans, tomatoes, tomato sauce, **Chili Powder Substitute**, salt, and olives, if desired. Spoon mixture into a 2-quart casserole dish coated with cooking spray. Heat oven to 350°F. Whisk soy milk, cornmeal, egg replacement, oil, and salt together in a medium saucepan. Cook over medium heat, stirring frequently, until thickened. Spread cornmeal mixture evenly over mixture in casserole dish. Bake 20 minutes, or until hot and bubbling.
Makes 6 servings. 270 calories, 5 g fat, 779 mg sodium.

Lemon Oil Dressing

- ⅓ cup lemon juice
- ⅓ cup olive oil
- ⅓ cup water
- 1 tablespoon honey
- 1 tablespoon minced fresh parsley
- salt, optional

Stir lemon juice, olive oil, water, honey, and parsley together in a small bowl. Season to taste with salt. Refrigerate until chilled. Shake or stir before serving.
Makes about 1 cup; 16 1-tablespoon servings.
40 calories, 4 g fat, 1 mg sodium.

Pineapple Whip

Crust:

- 1 cup graham cracker crumbs
- 3 tablespoons canola or grape-seed oil
- 1 tablespoon honey

Filling:

- 1 cup water
- ½ cup granulated cane sugar
- ¼ cup slivered blanched almonds
- ¼ cup cornstarch
- 1½ tablespoons olive oil
- 2 tablespoons lemon juice
- ½ teaspoon salt
- ½ teaspoon vanilla extract
- 1 14-ounce can crushed pineapple (with juice)

Crust: Heat oven to 350°F. Mix graham cracker crumbs, oil, and honey together. Press into the bottom of a 9-inch square baking dish. Bake about 10 minutes, or until lightly browned.

Filling: Process water, sugar, almonds, cornstarch, oil, lemon juice, salt, and vanilla in a blender or food processor until smooth. Pour into a medium saucepan. Stir in crushed pineapple and cook over medium heat, stirring frequently, until thickened.

Spread over graham cracker crust. Refrigerate until chilled and firm. Cut into nine squares.
Makes 9 servings. 189 calories, 10 g fat, 188 mg sodium.

Menu 22

Tex-Mex-Middle East Fusion

Sipping piña colada is a treasured Christmas Eve tradition in my family. Over time, I have managed to make the drink a little healthier and more guilt-free. We find it refreshing to drink the blend of pure coconut milk and pineapple juice. Even though the snow may be falling outside in Alberta, Canada, we can pretend to enjoy the warmth of Mexico.

Most people think that coconut milk is nothing but the watery liquid found in coconuts. Coconut milk is actually a milky-white, sweet liquid that is obtained from the flesh of mature coconuts. The grated coconut meat is squeezed, then soaked in warm water and squeezed a second or third time (for thin coconut milk). Thick milk is used for preparing desserts or sauces, whereas thin coconut milk is used in the preparation of soups. Coconut milk contains a wide range of vitamins and minerals, including potassium, folate, and other vital nutrients.

- **Chili**
- **Corn Bread**
- Tossed Green Salad with **Ranch Dressing**
- **Baked Pita Chips** or Tortilla Chips
- **Mexican Hummus** or **Salsa** (p. 53)
- Fresh Sliced Papaya, Pineapple, and Mango (served with fancy toothpicks)
- **Piña Colada**

Chili

olive oil or water, for frying
1 large onion, chopped
1 cup green bell peppers, chopped
4 cloves garlic, minced
1 12-ounce package meatless burger (such as Yves) or 2 cups **Ground Gluten** (p. 33)
2 cups cooked or 1 15- to 19-ounce can black beans, rinsed
2 cups cooked or 1 15- to 19-ounce can kidney beans, rinsed
1 28-ounce can diced tomatoes, seasoned with herbs
1 15-ounce can tomato sauce (about 2 cups)
1 cup corn
½ teaspoon **Chili Powder Substitute** (p. 52) or chili powder
salt

Heat a little oil or water in a large saucepan. Add onion, bell peppers, and garlic; cook and stir until onion is tender. Stir in meatless burger and cook for 2 minutes. Stir in beans, diced tomatoes, tomato sauce, corn, and **Chili Powder Substitute**. Season to taste with salt. Simmer until heated through.

Makes 14 1-cup servings. 132 calories, 1 g fat, 374 mg sodium.

VARIATIONS:

- Also good served over baked potatoes or brown rice.
- You can replace the beans with a variety of other canned beans.

Corn Bread

1½ cups soft or silken tofu, drained (preferably reduced-fat)
1 tablespoon egg replacement powder (such as Ener-G) dissolved in 3 tablespoons water
1 cup cornmeal
1 cup cream-style corn
¼ cup olive oil
1½ teaspoons baking powder (preferably aluminum-free)
¼ teaspoon salt
cooking spray
Chili, optional

Heat oven to 400°F. Process tofu and egg replacement in a blender or food processor until smooth. Transfer to a mixing bowl and mix in cornmeal, cream-style corn, oil, baking powder, and salt. Pour into a 9-inch square baking dish coated with cooking spray. Bake 30 minutes, or until golden brown. Let cool 10-15 minutes before cutting. Serve topped with **Chili**, if desired.

Makes 9 servings. 137 calories, 7 g fat, 187 mg sodium.

COOK'S HINTS:

- This corn bread has a moist cakelike texture.

Ranch Dressing

1 cup eggless mayonnaise (such as Vegenaise)
½ cup unsweetened soy milk
1 teaspoon dried parsley
¾ teaspoon garlic powder
¾ teaspoon onion powder

½ teaspoon salt-free herb seasoning (such as Spike)
½ teaspoon dried dill

Whisk mayonnaise, soy milk, parsley, garlic powder, onion powder, Salt-free herb seasoning, and dill together in a small bowl until smooth. Refrigerate until chilled.
Makes 2 cups; 32 1-tablespoon servings.
31 calories, 3 g fat, 72 mg sodium.

Baked Pita Chips

¼-⅓ cup olive oil
1 teaspoon herb seasoned salt (such as Spike), or to taste
garlic powder, or to taste
6 whole-wheat pitas

Heat oven to 400°F. Whisk oil, seasoned salt, and garlic powder together. Brush each side of pita bread with seasoned oil using a pastry brush. Cut pita bread into wedges. Place in a single layer on a baking sheet. Bake 5-10 minutes or until golden brown and crisp. Serve with **Mexican Hummus**.
Makes 8 servings. 187 calories, 8 g fat, 400 mg sodium.

COOK'S HINTS:

- Also good served with **Hummus**, **Salsa**, or soup (instead of crackers).

Mexican Hummus

2 cups cooked chickpeas, drained, liquid reserved
⅓ cup sesame tahini
¼ cup lemon juice
2 cloves garlic, peeled
1 teaspoon onion powder
1 4-ounce can green chilies
Salt

Process chickpeas, tahini, lemon juice, garlic, onion powder in a food processor or blender until smooth, adding chickpea liquid or water, if needed, for processing. Transfer to a bowl. Stir in green chilies. Season to taste with salt. Season with additional lemon juice, garlic, or onion powder, if desired. Serve with **Baked Pita Chips**.
Makes 2½ cups; 40 1-tablespoon servings.
27 calories, 1 g fat, 37 mg sodium.

COOK'S HINTS:

- Other serving ideas: Serve with **Pita Bread**, tortilla chips, crackers, or bread.

Piña Colada

4 cups unsweetened pineapple juice
2 cups ice cubes
1 cup coconut milk
1 tablespoon fructose, granulated cane sugar or honey, or to taste, optional
2-4 cups sparkling water
pineapple wedges, for garnish, optional

Process pineapple juice, ice cubes, coconut milk, and fructose, if desired, in a blender until smooth. Pour into a pitcher. Stir in sparkling water. Garnish with a wedge of fresh pineapple on the edge of each glass, if desired.
Makes 8 servings. 134 calories, 6 g fat, 7 mg sodium.

Veggie Scallops

Menu 23

Picnic Favorites

Choosing a healthful diet does not mean having to give up your favorite foods—it just means making a few recipe adjustments. There is nothing like a picnic with family and friends.

- **Vegeburgers** on Whole-Wheat Buns
- **Baked Beans**
- Corn on the Cob
- **Potato Salad**
- Carrot and Celery Sticks
- **Cherry Pie** with Nondairy Ice Cream
- **Lemonade**

Vegeburgers

½ cup millet cooked in 2 cups water until tender
1 16-ounce package medium or firm water-packed tofu
2 cups quick-cooking oats
1 medium onion, finely chopped
½ cup pecans, ground fine
2 tablespoons nutritional yeast flakes
2 tablespoons unfermented soy sauce substitute or reduced-sodium soy sauce
2 teaspoons to 2 tablespoons beef-style seasoning,* or to taste
2 teaspoons garlic powder
1 teaspoon poultry seasoning
½ teaspoon salt
lettuce, to taste
tomatoes, to taste
toppings and condiments, to taste

Prepare millet. Process tofu in a blender or food processor until smooth. Transfer to a mixing bowl. Mix in oats, onion, cooked millet, pecans, nutritional yeast flakes, soy sauce substitute, beef-style seasoning, garlic powder, poultry seasoning, and salt. Let stand about 10 minutes. Heat a nonstick skillet over medium heat. Form mixture into burgers with hands and place in skillet. Cook both sides of burgers until golden brown. Serve warm on whole-wheat burger buns with lettuce, tomatoes, favorite toppings, and condiments.

Makes 12 servings. 137 calories, 5 g fat, 244 mg sodium.

*see glossary

Baked Beans

6 cups water
2 cups navy beans, rinsed and sorted
1 5.5-ounce can tomato paste
2 tablespoons dried onion
1-2 tablespoons pure maple syrup
1 tablespoon prepared mustard or **Homemade Mustard** (p. 103)
1 tablespoon molasses
1 tablespoon unfermented soy sauce substitute or reduced-sodium soy sauce
1 teaspoon garlic powder
Salt

Heat water to boiling in a large saucepan and add beans; reduce heat and simmer 1½ hours or until beans are tender. Stir in tomato paste, dried onion, maple syrup, mustard, molasses, soy sauce substitute, and garlic powder. Simmer 10 minutes or longer, to allow flavors to blend. Season to taste with salt.
Makes 8 servings. 213 calories, 1 g fat, 258 mg sodium.

COOK'S HINTS:

- These beans are also good served with toast and fresh tomatoes for breakfast.
- These freeze well.
- To cook in a slow cooker, reduce water to 4 cups and cook beans on low for 8 hours or overnight. Stir in remaining ingredients. Cook another 30 minutes (or longer).
- To decrease intestinal reactions, soak beans for 12 hours before cooking. Drain and rinse. Add a pinch of ginger to beans when cooking, if desired.
- Add sliced meatless frankfurters if desired.

Potato Salad

6 large potatoes, peeled and cut into 1-inch cubes
3 green onions, sliced
6 radishes, sliced
1 teaspoon dried dill
3 dill pickles, sliced, optional
1 cup eggless mayonnaise (such as Nasoya), or to taste
salt
paprika, for garnish, optional
parsley sprigs, for garnish, optional

Place potatoes in a large saucepan and cover with water. Add a little salt, and heat to boiling; reduce heat and simmer 15-20 minutes or until tender. Drain and rinse with cold water. Place in a large salad bowl. Stir in green onions, radishes, dill, and pickles, if desired. Stir in eggless mayonnaise. Season to taste with salt. Refrigerate several hours before serving. Garnish with paprika and parsley, if desired.
Makes 8 servings. 207 calories, 10 g fat, 245 mg sodium.

Cherry Pie

4 cups pitted fresh or frozen (thawed and drained) cherries (about 2½ pounds with pits)
⅔ cup granulated cane sugar, or to taste
⅓ cup cornstarch
2 tablespoons lemon juice
½ teaspoon vanilla extract
1 **Whole-Wheat Piecrust** (p. 26)
cooking spray

Heat oven to 400°F. Mix cherries, sugar, cornstarch, lemon juice, and vanilla together in a bowl. Prepare **Whole-Wheat Piecrust** dough. Roll out half of pie dough between two sheets of wax paper and line a 9-inch pie plate coated with cooking spray. Spoon cherry filling into pie crust. (If there is an abundance of juice, pour off some of the liquid.) Roll the remaining dough between two sheets of wax paper into a 12-inch circle. Drape dough over filling and trim, leaving a 1-inch overhang. Fold the edges under the bottom crust, pressing and then crimping

them to seal. Cut slits in the top crust with a sharp knife, forming steam vents. Bake for 25 minutes, then reduce the temperature to 350°F and bake for another 25-30 minutes, or until the crust is golden brown. Cool pie on a rack. It is delicious served with nondairy ice cream.

Makes 8 servings. 351 calories, 14 g fat, 270 mg sodium.

COOK'S HINTS:

- Replace sweet cherries with tart cherries and sweeten to taste.

Lemonade

1 large or 2 small lemons
6 cups cold water
½ cup pure maple syrup or honey, or to taste
12 ice cubes

Squeeze juice from lemons. Pour into a pitcher. Add water. Stir in maple syrup until dissolved. Taste for sweetness, adding more sweetener if desired. Add ice cubes and serve immediately.

Makes 6 servings. 73 calories, 0 g fat, 10 mg sodium.

Menu 24

Comfort Food, Vegan Style

My mom made the best macaroni and cheese casserole. But when I changed my diet, I thought it meant saying good-bye to comfort food. Through trial and error we've found ways to enjoy comfort food dishes made with natural ingredients that both taste good and support good health.

- **Macaroni and Cheeze Casserole**
- **Bean Salad**
- Green Salad with Salad Dressing
- Whole-Grain Buns with Margarine
- **Carob Puffed-Wheat Squares**
- Fresh Strawberries

Macaroni and Cheeze Casserole

1 cup peeled, cubed, cooked potato
6 cups brown rice elbow macaroni or other small whole-grain pasta
salt and oil, for cooking pasta, optional
cooking spray
30 whole-wheat soda crackers
2 tablespoons olive oil
2 cups water
1 12-ounce package silken tofu (preferably reduced-fat)
¾ cup slivered almonds
⅓ cup nutritional yeast flakes
¼ cup pimento or **Roasted Red Bell Peppers** (p. 52)
¼ cup lemon juice
2 teaspoons salt
2 teaspoons onion powder
1 clove garlic, peeled
¼ teaspoon ground turmeric
meatless sausages, sliced, optional

Prepare potato. Cook macaroni according to package directions with a little salt and oil, if desired. Drain and place in a 9"x13" baking dish coated with cooking spray. Process soda crackers in a food processor or blender until finely ground. Add oil and process until mixed. Remove from the food processor; set aside.

Heat oven to 350°F. Process cooked potato, water, tofu, almonds, yeast flakes, pimento, lemon juice, salt, onion powder, garlic, and turmeric in a blender or food processor until very smooth. Pour over cooked macaroni; mix well. Stir in sliced meatless sausages, if desired. Sprinkle macaroni with cracker crumbs. Bake 20-30 minutes, or until hot and bubbling and crumbs are golden brown.

Makes 12 servings. 289 calories, 8 g fat, 477 mg sodium.

Bean Salad

1 14- to 16-ounce can wax beans, drained and rinsed (about 1¾ cups)
1 14- to 16-ounce can green beans, drained and rinsed (about 1¾ cups)
1 14- to 16-ounce can kidney beans, drained and rinsed (about 1¾ cups)
1 14- to 16-ounce can chickpeas, drained and rinsed (about 1¾ cups)
½ cup finely chopped green bell pepper
½ cup finely chopped red bell pepper
½ cup finely chopped celery
½ cup finely chopped onion
⅓ cup lemon juice
3 tablespoons olive oil
½ teaspoon salt
minced fresh parsley for garnish, optional

Stir wax beans, green beans, kidney beans, chickpeas, bell peppers, celery, onion, lemon juice, oil, and salt together in a salad bowl; mix well. Cover and refrigerate for several hours. Garnish with minced fresh parsley, if desired.

Makes 8 ¾-cup servings. 128 calories, 5 g fat, 104 mg sodium.

Carob Puffed-Wheat Squares

¾ cup brown sugar
½ cup pure cane syrup (such as Roger's) or honey
½ cup carob chips
⅓ cup non-hydrogenated margarine (such as Earth Balance)
8 cups puffed wheat
Cooking spray

Heat brown sugar, cane syrup, carob chips, and margarine in a large saucepan over medium heat until mixture starts to bubble and carob chips melt. Remove from heat. Mix in puffed wheat all at once. Press mixture into a 9"x13" baking dish coated with cooking spray. Refrigerate until firm. Cut into squares and serve.

Makes 20 servings. 109 calories, 4 g fat, 51 mg sodium.

COOK'S HINTS:

- You can replace puffed wheat with other puffed grains such as kamut, spelt, rice, or corn (or a combination).

Menu 25

Family-style Vegan

*The **Un-Pizza Buns** are so simple to make, and yet delicious. Focusing on flavor from herbs and garlic, you don't miss the cheese.*

*The **Carob Mayonnaise Cake** was a family favorite recipe with a few of the ingredients changed to make it totally vegetarian. This is the cake my children request Grandma to make for their birthdays. It is a rich, moist, dark cake.*

- **Creamy Carrot Leek Soup**
- **Un-Pizza Buns**
- Raw Vegetable Platter (Zucchini Sticks, Jicama Sticks, Sliced Cucumber, Cherry Tomatoes, Cauliflower Florets, Broccoli Florets, and Assorted Bell Peppers)
- **Dill Dip**
- **Carob Mayonnaise Cake**

Creamy Carrot Leek Soup

water or olive oil, for cooking leek
1 large leek, thinly sliced (white part only)
4 cups water
8 cups sliced carrots
4 cups peeled and chopped potatoes
1 teaspoon crushed dried tarragon
1 teaspoon dried thyme leaves
2 teaspoons to 2 tablespoons chicken-style seasoning,* or to taste
1 teaspoon salt
3-4 cups water

*see glossary

Heat a small amount of water or oil in a 6-quart saucepan. Add leek; cook and stir until tender. Stir in water, carrots, potatoes, tarragon, thyme, chicken-style seasoning, and salt. Heat to boiling; reduce heat and simmer 20 minutes, or until potatoes and carrots are tender. Working in batches, process soup in a blender or food processor until smooth. Return to the saucepan. Stir in enough water to achieve desired thickness. Heat over medium-high heat until heated through.
Makes 20 1-cup servings. 60 calories, 0 fat, 181 mg sodium.

Un-Pizza Buns

1 28-ounce can diced tomatoes with herbs
2 tablespoons cornstarch
¼ cup nutritional yeast flakes
2 tablespoons olive oil
4 cloves garlic, minced
½ teaspoon dried basil
½ teaspoon dried oregano leaves
½ teaspoon salt
18 whole-wheat burger buns

Topping suggestions:

sliced onions
sliced bell peppers
sliced mushrooms
sliced olives
pineapple tidbits

Heat oven to 350°F. Stir tomatoes and cornstarch together in a saucepan. Cook, stirring constantly, until thickened. Stir in nutritional yeast, oil, garlic, basil, oregano, and salt; mix well. Place burger bun halves, cut side up, on baking sheets. Spread about 2 tablespoons tomato mixture on each bun half. Arrange toppings as desired on each bun. Bake about 10 minutes, or until buns begin to brown around edges. Serve hot.
Makes 36 servings. 82 calories, 2 g fat, 208 mg sodium. (Analysis does not include toppings.)

Dill Dip

1 cup nondairy sour cream (such as Tofutti)
1 cup eggless mayonnaise (such as Nayonaise)
1 24-gram package natural dill dip mix (such as Simply Organic)

Whisk sour cream, mayonnaise, and dill dip mix together in a small bowl until smooth. Refrigerate 1-2 hours before serving. Keeps about 2 weeks in the refrigerator.
Makes 2 cups; 32 1-tablespoon servings. 36 calories, 3 g fat, 108 mg sodium.

VARIATION:

- Serve as a salad dressing, adding soy milk to thin, if desired.

Carob Mayonnaise Cake

2 cups unbleached all-purpose flour
⅔ cup granulated cane sugar
¼ cup roasted carob powder
1½ teaspoons baking powder (preferably aluminum-free)
1½ teaspoons baking soda
1 cup eggless mayonnaise (such as Nayonaise)
1 cup water
1 teaspoon vanilla extract
cooking spray

Frosting:

½ cup granulated cane sugar
2 tablespoons carob powder
2 tablespoons soy milk
1 tablespoon nonhydrogenated margarine (such as Earth Balance)
1 teaspoon vanilla extract

Cake: Heat oven to 350°F. Mix flour, sugar, carob powder, baking powder, and baking soda together in a mixing bowl. Mix in mayonnaise, water, and

vanilla just until dry ingredients are moistened. (Do not overmix.) Spread in a 9-inch square glass baking dish coated with cooking spray. Bake 40 minutes or until a toothpick inserted near the center comes out clean. (Cake will be dark and moist.) Let cake cool before frosting.

Frosting: Stir sugar, carob powder, soy milk, margarine, and vanilla together in a small saucepan. Heat to boiling, then whisk constantly for 1 minute. Remove from heat and whisk for 1 minute. Spread frosting evenly over cake. Refrigerate for 2 hours, or until chilled.

Makes 9 servings. 312 calories, 10 g fat, 430 mg sodium.

Menu 26

Down-home Cooking

***Sweet Potato Sticks** are a hit in our family. Any child, big or small, who enjoys french fries will enjoy this healthy alternative.*

- **Black Bean Burgers**
- **Sweet Potato Sticks**
- **Squash Slaw**
- Vegetable Platter
- **Dill Dip** (p. 77)
- **Date Squares**

Black Bean Burgers

Olive oil or water, for cooking onion
1 medium onion, finely chopped
3-4 cloves garlic, minced
3 cups cooked black beans or 2 15-ounce cans, drained
1½ cups soft bread crumbs, or more, as needed
1 teaspoon **Chili Powder Substitute** (p. 52) or chili powder, or to taste
½ teaspoon ground cumin
½ teaspoon salt
cooking spray
Salsa (p. 53), optional
lettuce, optional
eggless mayonnaise, optional
tomatoes, optional
nondairy cheese, optional
gravy, optional

Heat a little oil or water in a nonstick skillet. Add onion and garlic; cook and stir until onion is tender. Mash black beans in a mixing bowl. Mix in bread crumbs, **Chili Powder Substitute**, cumin, and salt. Stir in cooked onion and garlic and mix well. (If mixture is too moist, add more bread crumbs.) Coat with a large nonstick skillet with cooking spray. Heat over medium heat. Drop bean mixture by heaping spoonfuls (about ⅓ cup at a time) into skillet and flatten into burgers. Cook until browned on both sides. Serve on whole-wheat burger buns with salsa, lettuce, eggless mayonnaise, tomatoes, and nondairy cheese, if desired. They can be also served with gravy.

Makes 10 servings. 141 calories, 1 g fat, 239 mg sodium.

COOK'S HINTS:

- To make soft bread crumbs, grind several slices of bread at a time in a blender or food processor.

Sweet Potato Sticks

2 large sweet potatoes
4 tablespoons olive oil
1 tablespoon herb-seasoned salt (such as Spike), or to taste
2 teaspoons garlic powder
cooking spray
ketchup, optional

Heat oven to 400°F. Wash and peel the sweet potatoes. Cut into ½-inch-thick strips about 3 inches in length and place in a bowl. Drizzle with oil. Mix until sweet potatoes are coated. Sprinkle with seasoned salt and garlic powder. Mix well. Transfer to a baking sheet coated with cooking spray. Bake about 20 minutes, or until potato sticks are crisp and lightly browned. Serve with ketchup for dipping, if desired.

Makes 8 servings. 90 calories, 7 g fat, 600 mg sodium.

Squash Slaw

1 spaghetti squash
½ cup shredded fresh carrot
¼ cup finely chopped red pepper
3 tablespoons olive oil
1 teaspoon lemon juice
1 teaspoon pure maple syrup
¼ teaspoon herb-seasoned salt (such as Spike)
¼ teaspoon garlic powder
⅛ teaspoon ground ginger

Peel spaghetti squash and shred with a fork (or use a food processor with a shredding blade). Mix 4 cups shredded squash, carrot, and pepper together in a bowl. Refrigerate. Stir oil, lemon juice, maple syrup, seasoned salt, garlic, and ginger together with a fork in a small glass or measuring cup. Stir dressing into salad just before serving.

Makes 8 ½-cup servings. 68 calories, 5 g fat, 14 mg sodium.

Date Squares

1¼ cups dates
¾ cup water
1 teaspoon vanilla extract
1½ cups whole-wheat pastry flour or unbleached all-purpose flour
1½ cups quick-cooking oats
1 cup brown sugar
2 teaspoons baking powder (preferably aluminum-free)
¼ teaspoon salt
1 cup nonhydrogenated margarine (such as Earth Balance), softened
cooking spray

Heat oven to 350°F. Heat dates and water together in a small saucepan and simmer 5 minutes or until dates are softened. Stir in vanilla. Remove from heat and mash into a paste. Mix flour, oats, sugar, baking powder, and salt together in a mixing bowl. Mix in margarine with a pastry blender (or two table knives), until mixture resembles coarse crumbs. Press half of crumb mixture in the bottom of a 9-inch square baking dish coated with cooking spray. Spread date filling over crumb base. Sprinkle remaining crumb mixture over date filling and press down slightly. Bake 30 minutes or until golden brown. Cool to room temperature. Refrigerate until chilled. Cut into squares.

Makes 16 servings. 289 calories, 12 g fat, 280 mg sodium.

About Sweet Potatoes and Yams

Yam

Many people get confused as to what is a sweet potato and what is a yam. In the United States most people use both terms to refer to a sweet potato, when really these two vegetables are in no way related.

The sweet potato is found in tropical America and is a part of the morning-glory family. The yam is a tuber (a bulb) of a tropical vine found in Central and South America, as well as the West Indies, Africa, and Asia.

There are two main varieties of sweet potato. The pale sweet potato has a very thin yellow skin with bright-yellow flesh. This variety is neither sweet nor moist, but more like the texture of a white baking potato. The darker-skinned sweet potato has a thicker orange skin with sweet, moist flesh.

The true yam is not marketed or grown widely in the United States. It is usually marketed in the Latin American markets. A yam can be as small as a potato or can grow as large as 7 feet and weigh more than 120 pounds. The skin color can be from off-white to dark brown, and the flesh can range in color from off-white to yellow to pink to purple. Sweet potatoes are high in vitamins A and C, and yams have a higher sugar content. Both sweet potatoes and yams can be prepared like a potato—baked, boiled, steamed, or fried.

Sweet potato

Menu 27

Flavors of Native North America

It's a challenge to find a plant-based food that resembles fish. But these "fish" sticks are fun to make and enjoyable to eat!

Tip: Add a little kelp powder to your recipes when you want a "fishy" flavor.

- **Fishy Sticks** with **Tartar Sauce**
- Baked Potatoes
- Corn on the Cob
- Steamed Broccoli with **Cheeze Sauce** (p. 61)
- **Bannock** with Margarine
- Nondairy Ice Cream with Berries
- **Hot Fruit Cider**

Fishy Sticks

¾ cup **Flax-seed Gel**
1 recipe **Tofu Cottage Cheese** (4 cups)
1 cup quick-cooking or rolled oats, cooked in 2 cups of water
1 cup whole-grain cracker crumbs
1 cup onion, chopped
1 tablespoon nutritional yeast flakes
2 teaspoons to 2 tablespoons chicken-style seasoning,* or to taste
½ teaspoon salt
cooking spray
1 cup cornflake crumbs
1 teaspoon onion powder
¼ teaspoon garlic powder
½ teaspoon salt (do not add if crackers are salted)
soy milk
oil, for frying
fresh parsley sprigs, for garnish
lemon wedges, for garnish
Tartar Sauce

*see glossary

Heat oven to 300°F. Prepare **Flaxseed Gel**. Prepare **Tofu Cottage Cheese** in a large bowl. Add **Flaxseed Gel**, cooked oats, cracker crumbs, onion, nutritional yeast, chicken-style seasoning, and salt. Spread mixture evenly to cover the bottom of a 10"x16" baking sheet coated with cooking spray. Bake 45 minutes or until golden brown and set. Cool to room temperature. Cover and refrigerate 8 hours or overnight. Slice into 2"x4" pieces.

Mix cornflake crumbs, onion powder, garlic powder, and salt, if desired, together in a pie pan or flat dish. Place ¼ cup soy milk in a bowl. Dip each stick into soy milk, then into crumb mixture, thoroughly coating each side and edge. Heat a small amount of oil in a large skillet over medium heat. Fry sticks until golden brown on both sides. Garnish with fresh parsley and lemon wedges, if desired. Serve with tartar sauce.
Makes 20 sticks. 199 calories, 8 g fat, 350 mg sodium.

Flaxseed Gel

2 cups water
6 tablespoons flaxseeds

Heat water to boiling in a small saucepan and stir in flaxseeds; reduce heat and simmer 5 minutes. Remove from heat and immediately pour through a fine-mesh strainer with a bowl underneath. Discard the flaxseeds or use in bread recipes. Cover and refrigerate the gel for up to 1 week.
Makes 1½ cups (equivalent to 6 eggs). 48 calories, 3 g fat, 6 mg sodium.

COOK'S HINTS:

- Flaxseed Gel works as a binder in recipes such as patties and meatless meatloaves. Use ¼ cup Flaxseed Gel as a substitute for each egg.

Tofu Cottage Cheese

1 16-ounce package medium or firm water-packed tofu
¾ cup raw cashews
¼ cup water
1½ tablespoons lemon juice
¾ teaspoon garlic salt
½ teaspoon onion powder

Mash tofu with a fork until it resembles cottage cheese. Process cashews, water, lemon juice, garlic salt, and onion powder in a blender or food processor until very smooth. Stir into mashed tofu. Refrigerate or use to replace cottage cheese in recipes such as lasagna.

Makes 4 cups; 64 1-tablespoon servings.
26 calories, 2 g fat, 25 mg sodium.

Tartar Sauce

1 cup eggless mayonnaise (such as Nayonaise)
1-2 pickles, finely chopped
2 tablespoons lemon juice
1 tablespoon pickle relish
1 tablespoon minced fresh parsley
1 tablespoon mustard, ½ teaspoon dry mustard, or **Homemade Mustard** (p. 103)

Stir mayonnaise, pickles, lemon juice, pickle relish, parsley, and mustard together in a small bowl. Cover and refrigerate 1 hour. Serve with Fishy Sticks, or use on sandwiches or Vegeburgers (p. 73). Keeps 1 week in the refrigerator.

Makes 1½ cups; 24 1-tablespoon servings.
35 calories, 3 g fat, 162 mg sodium.

Bannock

1½ cups whole-wheat flour
1½ cups unbleached all-purpose flour
1½ tablespoons baking powder (preferably aluminum-free)
½ teaspoon salt
½ cup nonhydrogenated margarine (such as Earth Balance), softened
1¾ cups water
cooking spray
margarine

Heat oven to 425°F. Mix whole-wheat flour, all-purpose flour, baking powder, and salt together in a mixing bowl. Cut margarine into flour mixture with a pastry blender (or two table knives). Mix in water. Press dough evenly into a 9-inch square glass baking dish coated with cooking spray. Bake 20 minutes, or until top of bread is golden brown. Serve warm with margarine.

Makes 9 servings. 221 calories, 9 g fat, 214 mg sodium.

COOK'S HINTS:

- This bread, similar to baking powder biscuits, is a popular recipe of the Native American Cree of the Canadian North.
- You can make bannock the Native American way by cooking it over a campfire. Divide the dough into four lumps and firmly wrap each lump around the end of a 4-foot stick and prop securely over the fire until browned. (Or melt a little margarine in a deep cast-iron skillet. Spread the dough evenly in the pan. Cook over a bed of hot coals or a wire grill for about 15 minutes, turning every 5 minutes or until both sides are golden brown and it becomes firm throughout.)
- Tastes good with pure maple syrup.
- For a different taste, add ¾ cup currants or raisins.

Hot Fruit Cider

8 cups (2 liters) unsweetened apple juice
8 cups (2 liters) unsweetened orange juice
4 cups (1 liter) unsweetened cranberry juice
4 whole cinnamon sticks
8-10 whole cloves
1-2 mandarin oranges peeled and divided into sections

Stir apple juice, orange juice, cranberry juice, cinnamon sticks, cloves, and mandarin oranges together in a 5- to 6-quart saucepan. Heat to boiling over medium heat; reduce heat and simmer 30 minutes (or more) to blend flavors. Strain out cloves and remove cinnamon sticks. Garnish each serving with a piece of mandarin orange.

Makes 16 1-cup servings. 129 calories, 0 g fat, 7 mg sodium.

- You can also heat cider in a slow cooker on low for 4-5 hours, or on high for 2-3 hours, or until heated through.
- Leftover juice can be frozen or refrigerated for up to one week.

Menu 28

Native Feast

Corn bread is one of the few dishes that have traveled to all corners of the country, beginning with Native Americans, who ground a coarse meal from corn kernels we might not find palatable today. The breads have been baked in all manner of skillets and pans, over open fires, in beehive ovens tucked into the chimney, and in ordinary home ovens. Corn bread is inexpensive and easy to make, and is nutritious when made from whole-grain cornmeal.

- **Veggie Scallops** with **Tartar Sauce** (p. 81)
- **Baked Sweet Potatoes**
- **Wild Rice**
- Wild Greens Salad with **Lemon Oil Dressing** (p. 69)
- Assorted Greens, Shredded Carrots, Green Onions, Sunflower Seeds, and Dried Cranberries
- **Native Corn Bread**
- Red Clover or Wintergreen Herbal Tea
- **Blueberry Crisp** with Nondairy Ice Cream

Veggie Scallops

- 4 cups **Homemade Gluten** (p. 32) or frozen meatless scallops (such as Cedar Lake), thawed
- 2 cups unbleached all-purpose or whole-wheat flour
- ½ cup cornmeal
- 2 tablespoons nutritional yeast flakes
- 2 teaspoons to 2 tablespoons chicken-style seasoning,* or to taste
- ½ teaspoon sweet paprika or spicy paprika
- ½ teaspoon onion powder
- ½ teaspoon garlic powder
- 1 teaspoon kelp powder, optional
- 2 tablespoons olive oil, for frying, as needed
- **Tartar Sauce**

Cut gluten into 2-inch chunks. Mix flour, cornmeal, nutritional yeast, chicken-style seasoning, paprika, onion powder, and garlic powder in a bowl. Stir in kelp powder, if desired. Heat oil in a large skillet over medium heat. Dip gluten chunks in breading mixture and fry until brown on both sides. Transfer to a serving dish. Serve with Tartar Sauce.

Makes 8 servings. 286 calories, 2g fat, 37 mg sodium. (Analysis does not include oil for frying.)

COOK'S HINTS:

- Kelp powder, available at ethnic and natural food stores, adds a more "fishy" flavor.

Baked Sweet Potatoes

- 2 large (or 4 medium) sweet potatoes, as needed
- cooking spray
- olive oil, optional
- dried herbs, optional
- salt, optional

Heat oven to 350°F. Wash sweet potatoes, and peel, if desired. Cut each sweet potato in half lengthwise, then each half into about four or six wedges. Place potatoes in baking dish coated with cooking spray.

*see glossary

Brush sweet potatoes with oil, if desired. Sprinkle with herbs and salt, if desired. Cover and bake 1 hour, or until sweet potatoes are tender when tested with a fork.

Makes 8 servings. 178 calories, 0 g fat, 14 mg sodium.

Wild Rice

- 1 cup wild rice
- 3 cups water
- ½ teaspoon salt

Rinse and drain wild rice, carefully removing any extraneous material such as hulls. Heat water and salt to a boil in a saucepan and stir in wild rice; reduce heat to low and simmer, covered, 35-45 minutes, or until rice is tender. Drain excess water, if needed.

Makes 3 cups; 8 servings. 71 calories, 0 g fat, 149 mg sodium.

Native Corn Bread

- 1 cup cornmeal
- 1 cup unbleached all-purpose flour
- 2 tablespoons granulated sugar cane
- 1 tablespoon baking powder (preferably aluminum-free)
- ½ teaspoon salt
- ⅓ cup water
- 2 tablespoons flaxseeds
- 1 cup soy milk
- 3 tablespoons olive oil
- cooking spray

Heat oven to 425°F. Mix cornmeal, flour, sugar, baking powder, and salt together in a mixing bowl. Process water and flaxseeds in a blender or food processor until flaxseeds are ground. Stir flaxseed mixture, soy milk, and oil into cornmeal mixture; mix well. Pour into a 9-inch square baking pan coated with cooking spray. Bake 20-25 minutes, or until a toothpick inserted near the center comes out clean.

Makes 9 servings. 189 calories, 8 g fat, 148 mg sodium.

Blueberry Crisp

- 3 cups quick or rolled oats
- 1 cup whole-wheat flour
- 1 cup unbleached all-purpose flour
- ¾ cup nonhydrogenated margarine (such as Earth Balance), softened
- ½ cup pure maple syrup
- 1½ teaspoons baking powder (preferably aluminum-free)
- ½ teaspoon salt
- cooking spray
- 6 cups fresh or frozen blueberries
- ¾ cup water
- ¼ cup cornstarch
- ¼ cup granulated cane sugar or maple syrup
- 1 teaspoon vanilla extract
- nondairy ice cream, optional

Heat oven to 350°F. Mix oats, whole-wheat flour, all-purpose flour, margarine, maple syrup, baking powder, and salt together in a mixing bowl. Press half of the mixture into a 9"x13" glass baking dish coated with cooking spray. Stir blueberries, water, cornstarch, sugar, and vanilla together in a saucepan. Cook, stirring constantly, over medium-high heat until thickened. Spread blueberry mixture over crust in the baking dish. Sprinkle remaining crust mixture over the top of the filling and press gently. Bake 30 minutes or until top is golden brown. Serve warm with nondairy ice cream, if desired.

Makes 12 servings. 476 calories, 15 g fat, 437 mg sodium.

Ukrainian Apple Cake

Menu 29

Culinary Tour of the Ukraine

*When I was growing up, my mom made **Lazy Cabbage Rolls**. Since she suffered from crippling arthritis in her fingers, this recipe proved ideal for her to make. I am excited that my mom has been pain-free for more than 15 years since she converted to a total vegetarian diet!*

- **Cabbage Rolls** or **Lazy Cabbage Rolls**
- **Beets With Dill**
- Steamed Baby Red Potatoes with **Mushroom Sauce**
- **Easy Tomato-Cucumber Salad**
- **Lemon-Poppy Seed Bread** with Margarine
- **Ukrainian Apple Cake**

Cabbage Rolls

1 large green cabbage
water, for cooking onion
1 large onion, chopped
2 cloves garlic, minced
1 cup shredded carrots
4 cups cooked **Perfect Brown Rice** (p. 16)
1 12-ounce package meatless burger (such as Yves) (2 cups)
2 teaspoons to 2 tablespoons beef-style seasoning,* or to taste
2 10-ounce cans condensed tomato soup
1 cup water
cooking spray

Wash cabbage and cut out most of the core, deep enough to allow separation of leaves. Place head of cabbage core side down in 1 inch of water in a large saucepan. Heat to boiling; reduce heat and simmer, covered, until cabbage begins to wilt. Remove from heat. Cool cabbage under cold water. Peel off each cabbage leaf. (Cut excess core out of middle leaves, if needed, to make rolling easier.)

Heat a small amount of water in a large skillet or saucepan. Add onion, garlic, and shredded carrots; cook and stir until vegetables are tender. Stir in cooked rice, burger, and beef-style seasoning. Remove from heat. Stir tomato soup and water together; pour ½ cup into a 9"x13" baking dish coated with cooking spray and spread evenly. Heat oven to 350°F. Place about ⅓ cup of the rice-and-burger mixture in the center of each cabbage leaf. Starting at the core end, roll leaf up tightly, folding in sides as you roll. Place cabbage roll, seam-side down, in the baking dish. Repeat with remaining cabbage leaves and filling. Pour remaining tomato soup over cabbage rolls. Cover and bake 45 minutes or until sauce is bubbling and cabbage is tender.

Makes 20 cabbage rolls. 122 calories, 2 g fat, 175 mg sodium.

*see glossary

Lazy Cabbage Rolls

Instead of rolling cooked cabbage leaves, alternate layers of chopped fresh cabbage with the rice-and-burger mixture in a 9"x13" baking dish coated with cooking spray. Pour the diluted tomato soup over the top. Cover and bake at 350°F for 45 minutes or until sauce is bubbling and cabbage is tender.

Beets With Dill

- 4 cups fresh beets
- 1 cup onion, chopped
- 1 tablespoon chopped fresh dill or 1 teaspoon dried
- salt

Cook beets until tender. Drain. When cool enough to handle, peel beets and slice, shred, or cube. Heat a little water in a nonstick skillet. Add onion; cook and stir until tender. Stir in beets and dill. Simmer until heated through. Season to taste with salt.

Makes 6 ¾-cup servings; 49 calories, 0 g fat, 72 mg sodium.

Mushroom Sauce

- 2 tablespoons nonhydrogenated margarine (such as Earth Balance)
- 1 large onion, chopped
- 2 cups sliced fresh mushrooms
- ⅓ cup unbleached all-purpose flour
- 2 cups soy milk
- 4 cups water
- 1 teaspoon garlic powder
- ½ teaspoon salt

Melt margarine in a large skillet over medium heat. Add onion and mushrooms; cook and stir until slightly browned. Stir in flour using a whisk or fork. Lightly brown flour, stirring often, being careful not to burn it. Gradually whisk in soy milk and water; reduce heat and simmer 10 minutes, or until thickened to a medium-thick consistency. Stir in garlic powder and salt. Cover and keep warm until ready to serve.

Makes 16 ½-cup servings. 37 calories, 2 g fat, 107 mg sodium.

Easy Tomato-Cucumber Salad

- ½ cup eggless mayonnaise (such as Vegenaise)
- 2 tablespoons nondairy sour cream (such as Tofutti) or **Tofu Sour Cream** (p. 67)
- 1 tablespoon chopped fresh dill or 1 teaspoon dried
- 2 large tomatoes, chopped (about 2 cups)
- 1 large cucumber, peeled and chopped (about 2 cups)

Stir mayonnaise, sour cream, and dill together in a salad bowl. Stir in chopped tomatoes and cucumbers. Refrigerate.

Makes 8 servings. 67 calories, 5 g fat, 122 mg sodium.

Lemon-Poppy Seed Bread

2 tablespoons flaxseeds
½ cup warm water
½ cup soy milk
1½ tablespoons stevia powder or ¾ cup granulated cane sugar
1 tablespoon quick-rising yeast
2 cups whole-wheat flour
½ cup raw sunflower seeds
½ cup raisins
⅓ cup grape-seed or olive oil
¼ cup lemon juice
2 tablespoons sesame tahini
½ teaspoon salt
cooking spray
1 tablespoon poppy seeds

Heat oven to 350°F. Process flax seeds and warm water in a blender or food processor for 1 minute. Pour into a mixing bowl. Heat soy milk in a small saucepan until warm, but not hot to the touch (about 110°F). Pour into flax mixture in the bowl. Stir in stevia and yeast. Thoroughly mix in flour, sunflower seeds, raisins, oil, lemon juice, tahini, and salt. Spoon batter into a 5"x9"x3" loaf pan coated with cooking spray. Smooth the top and sprinkle poppy seeds evenly over the top. Bake about 50 minutes or until a toothpick inserted near the center comes out clean. Remove from the oven and cool in the pan for 5-10 minutes. Transfer to a wire rack to cool.

Makes 1 loaf; 16 ½-inch slices. 157 calories, 9 g fat, 78 mg sodium.

COOK'S HINTS:

- Stevia is natural no-calorie sweetener that comes from a plant whose leaves are 300 times sweeter than sugar. It is available in liquid or powdered form.

Ukrainian Apple Cake

¼ cup nonhydrogenated margarine (such as Earth Balance), softened
1 cup granulated cane sugar
1 tablespoon lemon juice
½ cup soy milk
1½ tablespoons egg replacement powder (such as Ener-G) dissolved in ¼ cup water
½ teaspoon salt
1 tablespoon ground cinnamon or substitute
½ teaspoon nutmeg
1½ cups whole-wheat flour
1½ cups unbleached all-purpose flour
1 tablespoon baking powder (preferably aluminum-free)
1 teaspoon baking soda
5 cups thinly sliced, peeled apples (about 5 medium apples)
½ cup chopped walnuts or pecans, optional
cooking spray
confectioners' sugar glaze, optional

Heat oven to 375°F. Beat margarine, sugar, and lemon juice together in a mixing bowl. Mix in soy milk, egg replacement, salt, cinnamon, and nutmeg. Mix in whole-wheat flour, all-purpose flour, baking powder, and baking soda. (Dough will be stiff and dry.) Stir in sliced apples, and walnuts, if desired. (As apples are mixed in, the batter will become more moist and cakelike.) Transfer the batter to a 9"x13" baking dish coated with cooking spray. Bake 45 minutes or until a toothpick inserted near the center comes out clean. Drizzle with a confectioners' sugar glaze, if desired. Serve warm or cold.

Makes 16 servings. 173 calories, 3 g fat, 178 mg sodium.

Menu 30

Hearty Ukrainian Fare

A friend decided to replace his traditional family pierogies served for Christmas dinner with my version using whole grains and healthier fillings. He experienced some trepidation, wondering if he should change years of tradition. Imagine his surprise when family members said, "These were the best pierogies ever!"

As the cook at Foothills Camp, I have many opportunities to try a variety of recipes when I prepare meals for groups of up to 300 people. ***Poppy Seed Cake*** *has become a popular request since I first served it for a banquet featuring Ukrainian fare. For a uniquely delicious strawberry shortcake, replace the shortcake with* ***Poppy Seed Cake****.*

- **Pierogies** with **Soy Sour Cream** (p. 66)
- **Meatless Meatballs** in **Beef-style Gravy** (p. 34) with Mushrooms
- **Cucumber Salad**
- **Dark Rye Bread** with Margarine
- **Poppy Seed Cake**

Pierogies

2 cups soy milk
4 teaspoons egg replacement powder (such as Ener-G) dissolved in ¼ cup water
1 teaspoon salt
3¾-4 cups whole-wheat flour, as needed
8 cups water
1-2 tablespoons olive oil
1 teaspoon salt
chopped onions, optional
Soy Sour Cream

Prepare pierogi filling(s) of choice; set aside.

Mix soy milk, egg replacement, and salt together in a mixing bowl. Mix in 3¾ cups flour. Add additional flour, as needed, to form dough into a ball that is no longer sticky. Roll dough out to ⅛-inch thick on a lightly floured surface. Cut 2-inch circles using a round cutter or drinking glass. Place a scant tablespoon of filling in the center of each circle. Fold dough in half over the filling. Press edges together firmly to seal. Repeat with remaining dough and filling, rerolling dough as needed.

Heat water to boiling in a large saucepan. Add oil and salt. Drop eight to10 pierogies into the water. Boil 8 minutes; remove pierogies with a slotted spoon. Place in a baking dish. Repeat until all pierogies are cooked.

To serve, bake pierogies until heated through (or fry with chopped onions until lightly browned on each side.) Serve with **Soy Sour Cream**.

Makes about 2 dozen pierogies. (Nutritional information included with the fillings).

COOK'S HINTS:

- To make lighter dough, replace some of the whole-wheat flour with spelt or unbleached all-purpose flour.
- Other ideas for pierogi fillings: sauerkraut with minced vegetarian frankfurters, or mashed potatoes with minced onions and vegetarian bacon bits.

Pierogi Fillings

Potato-Cheeze Filling

1½ cups mashed potatoes
½ cup raw cashews
⅓ cup water
2 tablespoons nutritional yeast flakes
2 tablespoons chopped onion
2 teaspoons lemon juice
1½ teaspoons pimento or **Roasted Red Bell Peppers** (p. 52)
1½ teaspoons unfermented soy sauce substitute or reduced-sodium soy sauce
1 small clove garlic, peeled or minced
½ teaspoon salt

Prepare mashed potatoes and place in a mixing bowl. Process cashews, water, nutritional yeast, onion, lemon juice, pimento, soy sauce substitute, garlic, and salt in a blender or food processor until very smooth. Pour into the bowl with mashed potatoes and mix well.
Makes 2 cups filling (enough for about 36 pierogies). Each filled pierogi: 99 calories, 2 g fat, 143 mg sodium.

Potato-Spinach Filling

- 2 cups mashed potatoes
- ¾ cup finely chopped cooked spinach
- 1 tablespoon olive oil
- ⅔ cup chopped onion
- 1 large clove garlic, minced
- 1 teaspoon salt

Prepare mashed potatoes. Prepare spinach. Heat oil in a nonstick skillet. Add onion and garlic; cook and stir until onion is tender. Stir in mashed potatoes, spinach, and salt. Cook and stir until mixture is heated through.
Makes 3 cups filling (enough for about 60 pierogies). Each filled pierogi: 85 calories, 1 g fat, 147 mg sodium.

Potato-Onion Filling

- 2 cups cooked potatoes
- ¼ cup soy milk
- olive oil or water
- ½ cup minced red onion
- ½ teaspoon salt

Prepare potatoes. Mash hot cooked potatoes with soy milk until light and fluffy. Heat a little oil or water in a skillet. Add onion; cook and stir until onion is tender. Stir onion and salt into potatoes.
Makes 2½ cups filling (enough for about 48 pierogies). Each filled pierogi: 84 calories, 1 g fat, 129 mg sodium.

Blueberry Filling

- ½ cup water
- 2 tablespoons cornstarch
- 2 cups fresh or frozen blueberries
- 2 tablespoons honey

Stir water and cornstarch together in a saucepan until cornstarch is dissolved. Stir in blueberries and honey. Heat over medium heat, stirring constantly, until thickened.
Makes 2 cups filling (enough for about 36 pierogies). Each filled pierogie: 86 calories, 1 g fat, 115 mg sodium.

- Serve blueberry pierogies warm, as a dessert with **Soy Whipped Cream** (p. 17), for breakfast, or for a light supper.

Meatless Meatballs

- 2 cups hot mashed potatoes
- 2 cups cooked **Perfect Brown Rice** (p. 16)
- 8 ounces medium or firm water-packed tofu, drained
- 3 cups quick-cooking oats
- 1 cup finely ground pecans
- ¼ cup soy milk
- ¼ cup unfermented soy sauce substitute or reduced-sodium soy sauce
- 3 tablespoons wheat germ
- 2 tablespoons nutritional yeast flakes
- 2 tablespoons chopped onion
- 4 teaspoons to ¼ cup beef-style seasoning,* or to taste
- 1 tablespoon lemon juice
- 2 teaspoons egg replacement powder (such as Ener-G) dissolved in 1 tablespoon water
- ¾ teaspoon garlic powder
- olive oil or cooking spray, for frying, optional

Prepare mashed potatoes and rice. Place tofu in a mixing bowl and mash with a fork. Mix in mashed potatoes, cooked rice, oats, pecans, soy milk, soy sauce substitute, wheat germ, nutritional yeast,

*see glossary

onion, beef-style seasoning, lemon juice, egg replacement, and garlic powder. Form mixture into 1½-inch diameter balls using your hands (or a small scoop).

Heat a little oil in a large skillet. Add meatballs and fry until lightly browned on both sides. (Or place meatballs on a baking sheet coated with cooking spray. Bake at 350°F for 20 minutes; turn balls over and bake 10 minutes or until lightly browned on both sides.)

To serve: Cover meatballs with **Beef-style Gravy**, adding mushrooms if desired. Bake 20-30 minutes or until bubbling.

Makes about 48 meatballs. 92 calories, 3 g fat, 64 mg sodium.

COOK'S HINTS:

- Other serving ideas: Serve meatballs with **Sweet-and-Sour Sauce** (p. 15) or marinara sauce.
- Make extra meatballs and freeze for future use.

Cucumber Salad

1 English cucumber, thinly sliced
1 small sweet onion, thinly sliced
2 tablespoons olive oil
2 tablespoons lemon juice
½ teaspoon herb seasoned salt (such as Spike)
½ teaspoon honey
cherry tomatoes, for garnish, optional
ripe olives, for garnish, optional

Mix cucumber and sweet onion together in a salad bowl. Whisk together oil, lemon juice, seasoned salt, and honey. Pour over cucumber and onion; mix well. Garnish with cherry tomatoes or olives, if desired. Serve immediately.

Makes 8 servings. 46 calories, 3 g fat, 74 mg sodium.

Dark Rye Bread

2½ cups warm water
2 tablespoons molasses (preferably unsulfured blackstrap)
1 tablespoon quick-rising active dry yeast
3 cups rye flour
¼ cup vital wheat gluten
2 tablespoons carob powder
1 tablespoon lemon juice
¾ teaspoon salt
3 cups whole-wheat flour
cooking spray

Stir water, molasses, and yeast together in a mixing bowl. Mix in rye flour, vital wheat gluten, carob powder, lemon juice, and salt. Add enough whole-wheat flour so dough is not sticky. Knead dough by hand for about 8 minutes, or with a stand mixer, using a dough hook, for about 4 minutes. Divide dough in half; shape into two loaves and place in two 5"x9"x3" loaf pans coated with cooking spray. Cover pans with a towel. Let rise in a warm place until doubled in size. Heat oven to 375°F. Bake about 30 minutes or until loaf sounds hollow when tapped.

Makes 2 loaves; 32 ½-inch slices. 84 calories, 0 g fat, 57 mg sodium.

Poppy Seed Cake

1¼ cup granulated cane sugar
¾ cup nonhydrogenated margarine (such as Earth Balance), softened
¾ cup soy milk
½ cup poppy seeds
4 teaspoons egg replacement powder (such as Ener-G) dissolved in ¼ cup water
1 tablespoon lemon juice
1 teaspoon vanilla extract
2 cups unbleached all-purpose flour
2 teaspoons baking powder (preferably aluminum-free)
¼ teaspoon salt
cooking spray
Carob Cream Cheese Frosting (p. 95), optional

Heat oven to 350°F. Mix sugar, margarine, soy milk, poppy seeds, egg replacement, lemon juice and vanilla together in a mixing bowl. Stir in all-purpose flour, baking powder, and salt until just mixed. (Do not overmix.) Spoon into a 9-inch square baking dish coated with cooking spray (or a 9-inch springform pan). Bake 30 minutes or until a toothpick inserted near the center comes out clean. Let cake cool to room temperature. Frost with **Carob Cream Cheese Frosting**, if desired.

Makes 9 servings. 387 calories, 18 g fat, 315 mg sodium.

German

Potato Soup

Menu 31

Oktoberfest

My dad grew up in a German family, so a few of these special German recipes were passed on to my mother, who learned to prepare some tasty dishes. One of our family favorites was ***Apple Strudel****. I remember my mom working and pulling the dough until it was paper-thin. We would all get involved cutting apples and helping out where we could. After a full day of work, we would sit and enjoy a large, delicious piece of fresh apple strudel (with plenty extra to be frozen for future enjoyment). This apple strudel is a simple, quick version, but still has the wonderful flavor and aroma of the all-day recipe.*

- **Sauerkraut and Potato Casserole** with **Soy Sour Cream** (p. 66)
- **Tomato Salad**
- **Yellow Split-pea Puree**
- **Multi-grain Sunflower Bread** with Margarine
- Choice of dessert: **Scrumptious German Carob Cake**, **Apple Strudel**, or **Apple Streusel Cake**

Sauerkraut and Potato Casserole

6 large potatoes, chopped and cooked
1 32-ounce jar naturally fermented sauerkraut, drained (about 4 cups)
cooking spray
olive oil, for frying
1 13-ounce package or 8 meatless frankfurters, sliced diagonally
1 large onion, chopped
1¼ cups **Condensed Mushroom Soup** (p. 145)
shredded nondairy cheese, optional
Soy Sour Cream (p. 66)

Prepare potatoes. Heat oven to 350°F. Spread sauerkraut evenly on the bottom of a 3-quart baking dish coated with cooking spray. Heat a little oil in a skillet. Add meatless frankfurters and onion; cook and stir until onion is tender and frankfurters are lightly browned. Spread on top of sauerkraut. Stir the cooked potatoes and Condensed Mushroom Soup together; spread on top of frankfurters and onion. Sprinkle with cheese, if desired. Bake 30-40 minutes or until heated through. Serve with Soy Sour Cream.

Makes 16 1-cup servings. 123 calories, 2 g fat, 240 mg sodium.

COOK'S HINTS:

- Look for naturally fermented sauerkraut (such as Bubbies), made without vinegar, in the refrigerated section of natural food stores.

Tomato Salad

5 medium tomatoes, chopped into medium-size pieces
1 large onion, chopped into medium-size pieces
⅓ cup olive oil
3 tablespoons lemon juice
1 tablespoon minced fresh basil or 1 teaspoon dried leaves
¾ teaspoon minced fresh thyme or ¼ teaspoon dried leaves
½ teaspoon salt or 1 tablespoon unfermented soy sauce substitute or low-sodium soy sauce
1 teaspoon granulated cane sugar, optional
¼ teaspoon cayenne, optional
lettuce leaves, for garnish

Place chopped tomatoes and onion in a salad bowl. Stir in oil, lemon juice, basil, thyme, and salt. Stir in sugar and cayenne, if desired. Refrigerate 1 hour before serving. Serve on a bed of lettuce leaves.
Makes 8 servings. 97 calories, 9 g fat, 150 mg sodium.

Yellow Split-Pea Puree

6 cups water
2 cups dry yellow split peas, rinsed
1 large onion, chopped
1 large carrot, chopped
1 turnip or large parsnip, chopped
4 teaspoons to ¼ cup beef-style seasoning,* or to taste
⅛ teaspoon dried marjoram
⅛ teaspoon dried thyme leaves
1 teaspoon salt, or to taste
2 tablespoons nonhydrogenated margarine (such as Earth Balance) or olive oil
1 small onion, chopped
2 tablespoons unbleached all-purpose flour

Heat water, split peas, onion, carrot, turnip, beef-style seasoning, marjoram, thyme, and salt to boiling in a 4-quart saucepan; reduce heat and simmer, partly covered, for 1 hour, or until split peas and vegetables are tender. Heat margarine in a large skillet; cook and stir small onion until tender. Stir in flour; set aside. Drain split peas and vegetables in a colander. Working in batches, transfer to a blender or food processor and process until smooth. Transfer pea mixture to onion and flour mixture in the skillet. Whisk until light and fluffy while cooking over medium heat until heated through.
Makes 12 1-cup servings. 151 calories, 2 g fat, 311 mg sodium.

*see glossary

Multigrain Sunflower Bread

- 4 cups warm water
- ¼ cup molasses
- 3 tablespoons quick-rising yeast
- 3 cups whole-wheat flour
- 2 cups finely ground multigrain cereal
- ⅔ cup raw sunflower seeds
- ½ cup ground flaxseeds
- ¼ cup olive oil
- 1 tablespoon salt
- 4 cups unbleached all-purpose flour, as needed
- cooking spray

Stir warm water, molasses, and yeast together in a large mixing bowl. Mix in whole-wheat flour, multigrain cereal, sunflower seeds, ground flaxseeds, oil, and salt. Gradually add unbleached all-purpose flour, 1 cup at a time, until dough is no longer sticky, but soft. Cover dough and let rise about 20 minutes or until doubled in size. Divide dough into four pieces. Knead each piece for about 2 minutes and shape into a loaf. Place in four 5"x9"x3" loaf pans coated with cooking spray. Cover bread pans, and let rise about 20 minutes, or until doubled in size. Heat oven to 350°F. Bake 25 minutes, or until crust is browned and loaf sounds hollow when tapped.

Makes 4 loaves; 64 ½-inch slice servings.
81 calories, 2 g fat, 111 mg sodium.

COOK'S HINTS:

- Grind the multigrain cereal in a blender or food processor until it is very fine, almost like flour. A powerful blender, such as a Vita-Mix, will grind it the best.

Scrumptious German Carob Cake

- 2 cups soy milk
- 1 cup granulated cane sugar
- ⅓ cup grape-seed oil or mild-flavored olive oil
- 3 tablespoons lemon juice
- 2 teaspoons vanilla extract
- 1 cup whole-wheat flour
- 1 cup unbleached all-purpose flour
- ½ cup carob powder
- 2 teaspoons baking powder, preferably aluminum-free
- ½ teaspoon salt
- cooking spray

Coconut Topping

- 1⅓ cups shredded, unsweetened coconut
- ⅔ cup brown sugar
- ½ cup soy milk
- ¼ cup grape-seed oil or mild-flavored olive oil

Carob Cream Cheese Frosting

- ¼ cup nondairy cream cheese (such as Tofutti)
- 2 tablespoons carob powder
- 1 teaspoon vanilla extract
- ½-1 cup confectioners' sugar, as needed

Cake: Heat oven to 350°F. Mix soy milk, sugar, oil, lemon juice, and vanilla together in a mixing bowl. Mix whole-wheat flour, all-purpose flour, carob powder, baking powder, and salt together in a separate bowl. Gently stir flour mixture into liquid mixture. Do not overmix. Pour batter into two 8-inch round cake pans coated with cooking spray. Bake 25 minutes or until a toothpick inserted near the center comes out clean. Transfer to wire racks to cool.

Coconut Topping: Heat coconut, brown sugar, soy milk, and oil to boiling in a small saucepan over medium heat; reduce heat and simmer 1 minute. Cool to room temperature.

Carob Cream Cheese Frosting: Process cream cheese, carob powder, and vanilla in a food processor until smooth. Add ½ cup confectioners' sugar and process until mixed. Add more confectioners' sugar, as needed, to give frosting a spreadable consistency.

Layer cooled cakes on a platter with half of the **Coconut Topping** spread between the cakes and the remaining half on top of the cake. Frost around the side of the cake using **Carob Cream Cheese Frosting**. Refrigerate 1 hour or until frosting is set.

Makes 12 servings. 299 calories, 15 g fat, 136 mg sodium.

COOK'S HINTS:

- German chocolate cake is actually not a traditional German dessert. The original recipe, "German's Chocolate Cake," was sent to a Texas newspaper in 1957 by a homemaker. The cake recipe called for the brand-name ingredient Baker's German's Sweet Chocolate, created by a man named Samuel German.

Apple Strudel

6 cups thinly sliced, peeled apples
½ cup raisins
½ cup pure cane syrup (such as Roger's)
2 teaspoons ground cinnamon or substitute
10 large sheets phyllo dough (about 8 ounces)
⅓ cup olive oil, or as needed
1½ cups dry, unseasoned bread crumbs

Heat oven to 350°F. Mix apples, raisins, cane syrup, and cinnamon together; set aside. Place one phyllo sheet on a towel and brush with oil. Place a second phyllo sheet on top and brush with oil. Repeat until five phyllo sheets have been used. Sprinkle ¾ cup of bread crumbs evenly over the layered phyllo sheets. Spread half of the apple filling in a 3-inch strip along the narrow end of the phyllo, leaving a 2-inch border. Lift towel, using it to roll phyllo up over apples and tucking in the sides in jelly-roll fashion. Brush the top of the strudel with oil. Place strudel on a baking sheet. Repeat the procedure for the second strudel using the remaining ingredients. Bake about 20 minutes or until apples soften slightly and pastry is golden brown. Serve warm or cold.
Makes 2 strudels; 16 servings.
144 calories, 5 g fat, 87 mg sodium.

COOK'S HINTS:

- These freeze well, but should be placed in the oven after thawing to crisp up again.

Apple Streusel Cake

1 cup whole-wheat flour
1 cup unbleached all-purpose flour
1 cup nonhydrogenated margarine (such as Earth Balance)
1 cup granulated cane sugar
1 tablespoon vanilla extract
1 tablespoon baking powder (preferably aluminum-free)
4½ teaspoons egg replacement powder (such as Ener-G) dissolved in 6 tablespoons water
cooking spray
4 medium apples, cored, peeled, and sliced (about 4 cups)
1½ teaspoons ground cinnamon or substitute
¼ teaspoon nutmeg
⅛ teaspoon ground cloves
½ cup sliced almonds

Streusel:

- ¼ cup nonhydrogenated margarine (such as Earth Balance), melted
- 1 cup unbleached all-purpose flour, spelt flour, or whole-wheat pastry flour
- ¼ cup granulated cane sugar
- cooking spray

Cake: Mix whole-wheat flour, all-purpose flour, margarine, sugar, vanilla, baking powder, and egg replacement together in a large mixing bowl. Spread the dough evenly on the bottom of a 9"x13" baking dish coated with cooking spray. Place sliced apples on top of dough in two or three rows, slightly overlapping each other. Sprinkle with cinnamon, nutmeg, cloves, and almonds. Heat oven to 350°F.

Streusel: Mix melted margarine, flour, and sugar together with a fork in a small bowl. Sprinkle streusel over the top of the cake. Bake 1 hour or until a toothpick inserted near the center comes out clean.

Makes 16 servings. 295 calories, 13 g fat, 182 mg sodium.

Menu 32

Flavors of Germany

*A special supper in our home during my growing-up years consisted of bierocks, kuchen, and a hot drink. This meal took a little more work to prepare, but oh, how we savored it. Sometimes we made my dad's favorite — **Carrot Pachingas** — as a special treat.*

- **Potato Soup**
- **Bierocks**
- Fresh Vegetable Platter or Salad Plates
- **Carrot Pachingas**
- **Sweet Tofu Kuchen** or **Blueberry Kuchen**
- Hot Drinks

Potato Soup

- water, for cooking onions
- 2 cups chopped onion
- 5 cloves garlic, minced
- 10 cups water
- 8 cups peeled and cubed potatoes (about 5-6 medium)
- 2-6 tablespoons chicken-style seasoning,* or to taste
- 1 teaspoon dried basil
- ½ teaspoon salt-free herb seasoning (such as Spike)
- ½ teaspoon dried thyme leaves
- salt

Heat a little water in a 6- to 8-quart saucepan. Add onion and garlic; cook and stir until onion is tender. Stir in 10 cups water, cubed potatoes, chicken-style seasoning, basil, salt-free seasoning, and thyme. Heat to boiling over high heat; reduce heat and simmer 20-30 minutes or until potatoes are tender. Working in batches, process soup in a blender or food processor until smooth. Return soup to the saucepan. Season to taste with salt.

Makes 20 1-cup servings. 34 calories, 0 g fat, 29 mg sodium.

Bierocks

Dough:

- 3 cups whole-wheat flour
- 3 cups unbleached all-purpose flour or spelt flour
- 2 cups water
- ¼ cup granulated cane sugar
- ¼ cup olive oil
- 2 tablespoons quick-rising yeast
- 1½ teaspoons egg replacement powder (such as Ener-G) dissolved in 2 tablespoons water
- 2 teaspoons salt

*see glossary

Filling:

- Water, for cooking onion
- 1 medium onion, chopped
- 1 12-ounce package meatless burger (such as Yves) (about 2 cups)
- 2 teaspoons to 2 tablespoons beef-style seasoning,* or to taste
- ½ teaspoon salt
- ½ teaspoon dried basil
- 5 cups cabbage, shredded or thinly sliced
- cooking spray

Dough: Mix whole-wheat flour, all-purpose flour, water, sugar, oil, yeast, egg replacement, and salt together in a large bowl (or the bowl of a stand mixer). Knead briefly to form a soft, pliable dough. (If dough is too dry, add water, 1 tablespoon at a time.)

Filling: Heat a small amount of water in a large skillet. Add onion; cook and stir until tender. Stir in meatless burger and cook until lightly browned. Stir in beef-style seasoning, salt, and basil. Stir in cabbage and cook about 15 minutes or until cabbage is tender. Set aside to cool slightly.

Roll the dough on a lightly floured surface into a 10"x25" rectangle. Cut the dough into 10 5-inch squares. Place 2 tablespoons of filling in the middle of each square. Bring corners of dough into the center and pinch the edges closed. Place seam-side down on a baking sheet coated with cooking spray. Heat oven to 350°F. Let rise 15 minutes. Bake 20-30 minutes or until golden brown. Serve hot.

Makes 10 servings. 391 calories, 7 g fat, 772 mg sodium.

COOK'S HINTS:

- You can make the dough ahead of time and refrigerate until needed.
- Since **Bierocks** and **Carrot Pachingas** use the same dough, double the ingredients and mix at the same time.
- Bierocks freeze well. To reheat, place on a baking sheet and cover with foil. Bake at 350°F for 20-30 minutes or until heated through.

*see glossary

Carrot Pachingas

- 1 recipe **Bierock Dough**
- 2 cups cooked carrots
- 1½ cups soy milk
- 1 cup dates
- 3 tablespoons unbleached all-purpose flour
- 3 tablespoons olive or grape-seed oil
- 2½ tablespoons cornstarch
- 1 teaspoon ground cinnamon or substitute
- 1 teaspoon vanilla extract
- ½ teaspoon salt
- ¼ teaspoon ground cloves
- ¼ teaspoon ground allspice
- cooking spray

Prepare the dough; set aside. Prepare the carrots. Process cooked carrots, soy milk, dates, flour, oil, cornstarch, cinnamon, vanilla, salt, cloves, and allspice in a blender or food processor until very smooth. Pour into a medium saucepan and heat, stirring constantly, until thickened; set aside.

Roll dough into a 9"x15" rectangle on a lightly-floured surface. Cut dough into 15 3-inch squares. Place 1 tablespoon of filling in the middle of each square. Bring corners of dough into the center and pinch the edges closed. Place seam-side down on a baking sheet coated with cooking spray. Heat oven to 350°F. Let rise 15 minutes. Bake 20 minutes, or until golden brown. Serve warm or at room-temperature as a dessert.

Makes 15 servings. 324 calories, 8 g fat, 413 mg sodium.

COOK'S HINTS:

- These freeze well. To reheat, place on a baking sheet and cover with foil. Bake at 350°F for 20-30 minutes or until heated through.

Sweet Tofu Kuchen

Dough:

1 cup whole-wheat flour
½ cup unbleached all-purpose flour
½ cup warm water
¼ cup granulated cane sugar
¼ cup olive oil
1½ teaspoons dry active yeast
1 teaspoon egg replacement powder (such as Ener-G) dissolved in 1 tablespoon water
¼ teaspoon salt
cooking spray

Filling:

1 16-ounce package medium or firm water-packed tofu, drained (preferably reduced-fat)
1 cup granulated cane sugar
1 tablespoon vanilla extract
¾ cup raw cashews
½ cup water
1 tablespoon egg replacement powder (such as Ener-G), dissolved in ¼ cup water
1 tablespoon lemon juice
ground cinnamon or substitute

Dough: Mix whole-wheat flour, all-purpose flour, water, sugar, oil, yeast, egg replacement, and salt together in a mixing bowl. Press dough into a 9-inch square baking dish coated with cooking spray. Cover with a towel and let stand 10 minutes. Heat oven to 350°F.

Filling: Place tofu in a mixing bowl and mash with a fork until it resembles cottage cheese. Mix in sugar and vanilla. Process cashews, water, egg replacement powder, and lemon juice in a blender or food processor until smooth. Pour over mashed tofu mixture; mix well. Spread filling evenly over dough. Sprinkle with cinnamon. Bake 30 minutes or until golden brown around bottom edges of dough and slightly browned on top. Let cool slightly. Serve warm with a hot drink for dessert.

Makes 12 servings. 273 calories, 12 g fat, 57 mg sodium.

Blueberry Kuchen

2 cups unbleached all-purpose flour or spelt flour
½ cup brown sugar
1 teaspoon baking powder (preferably aluminum-free)
½ teaspoon salt
1 cup water
⅔ cup raw cashews
3 tablespoons olive oil
1 teaspoon vanilla extract
cooking spray
1½ cups fresh or frozen blueberries
Creamed Pears (p. 106) or nondairy ice cream, optional

Heat oven to 350°F. Mix flour, brown sugar, baking powder, and salt together in a mixing bowl. Process water, cashews, oil, and vanilla in a blender or food processor until smooth. Pour into flour mixture and mix gently until mixture sticks together when compressed. Press two thirds of the crumb mixture over the bottom of a 9-inch baking dish coated with cooking spray (or a 9-inch springform pan). Arrange blueberries evenly on top. Sprinkle with remaining crumb mixture. Bake 45 minutes or until golden brown. Serve warm or cold with **Creamed Pears** or nondairy ice cream, if desired.

Makes 12 servings. 190 calories, 10 g fat, 100 mg sodium.

COOK'S HINTS:

- *Kuchen* means cake.
- You can replace blueberries with other fruits, such as sliced peaches or apples.

French

Vegetable Crepes

Menu 33

Nouvelle Cuisine

When I cooked at Foothills Camp for an Adventist Development and Relief Agency (ADRA) summit, they asked me to cater a French meal for the banquet. It posed a big challenge for me to create total vegetarian versions of dishes usually rich in cream, butter, eggs, and meat. Enjoy the tasty results. Bon appétit!

- **Vegetable Crepes**
- **Wild Rice Dish**
- Spring Salad Mix with **Honey-Mustard Poppy Seed Dressing**
- **Potato Buns** with Margarine
- **Elegant Lemon Cheesecake**
- Grape Juice

Vegetable Crepes

Filling:

water or olive oil, for cooking vegetables
2 cups soy chicken cut into ¼-inch cubes, optional
2 carrots, shredded
3 cups chopped mixed vegetables (broccoli, cauliflower, celery, bell peppers, corn, peas, etc.)
1 12-ounce can mushrooms, drained, or 6 fresh mushrooms, sliced
4 cups fresh bean sprouts
1 medium onion, chopped
3 tablespoons unfermented soy sauce substitute or reduced-sodium soy sauce, or to taste

Crepes:

1 16-ounce package medium or firm tofu, drained
1 cup whole-wheat flour or unbleached all-purpose flour
½ cup soy milk
¾ teaspoon garlic powder
¼ teaspoon salt
⅔ cup chopped green onions
cooking spray

Topping:

olive oil, for cooking onion
1 medium onion, chopped
shredded nondairy cheese, optional

Filling: Heat a little water or oil in a large skillet or wok. Add soy chicken (if desired), carrots, mixed vegetables, mushrooms, bean sprouts, and onion. Cook and stir until onion is tender. Stir in soy sauce substitute. Cook and stir briefly until most of the liquid has evaporated; set aside.

Crepes: Heat oven to its lowest temperature setting. Process tofu, flour, soy milk, garlic powder, and salt in a blender or food processor until very smooth. Pour into a bowl and stir in chopped green onions. Heat a small nonstick skillet (or crepe pan) coated with cooking spray over medium heat. Pour in ¾ cup batter. (Batter should be spread out evenly to about ¼-inch thick on the bottom of the pan.) Cook until bottom of crepe is lightly browned. Turn crepe over and cook the second side until lightly browned. Transfer to a baking dish in the oven to keep warm. Repeat with remaining crepe batter.

To assemble: Place about ¾-1 cup vegetable filling in the center of each crepe. Tightly roll crepe around the filling and place seam-side down in a large baking dish. Increase oven temperature to 400°F.

Topping: Heat a small amount of oil in a small skillet. Add onion; cook and stir onion until tender. Arrange cooked onion on top of crepes and sprinkle with shredded nondairy cheese, if desired. Bake 20 to 30 minutes, or until heated through.
Makes 10 crepes. 133 calories, 3 g fat, 283 mg sodium.

*see glossary

Wild Rice Dish

- 2 tablespoons olive oil
- 1 large onion, thinly sliced
- 1 cup thinly sliced mushrooms
- 4 cloves garlic, minced
- 7 cups water
- 1 cup wild rice
- 1 cup pearl barley
- 1 cup brown rice
- 1 tablespoon + 2 teaspoons to ⅓ cup chicken-style seasoning,* or to taste
- 1 teaspoon dried thyme leaves
- ½ teaspoon dried oregano leaves
- ½ teaspoon salt

Heat oven to 350°F. Heat oil in a skillet. Add onion, mushrooms, and garlic; cook and stir about 5 minutes, or until onion is tender. Transfer to a 4-quart baking dish. Stir in water, wild rice, barley, brown rice, chicken-style seasoning, thyme, oregano, and salt. Cover and bake 1 hour, or until grains are tender and liquid is absorbed.
Makes 10 1-cup servings. 225 calories, 4 g fat, 275 mg sodium.

Honey-Mustard Poppy Seed Dressing

- ⅔ cup olive oil
- ⅓ cup granulated cane sugar
- ⅓ cup lemon juice
- 2 tablespoons chopped onion
- 1 tablespoon prepared yellow mustard or **Homemade Mustard** or 1 teaspoon dry mustard
- ½ teaspoon salt
- 1 tablespoon poppy seeds

Process oil, sugar, lemon juice, onion, mustard, and salt in a blender or food processor until smooth. Stir in poppy seeds. Cover and refrigerate at least 1 hour.
Makes 1½ cups; 12 1-tablespoon servings. 67 calories, 6 g fat, 56 mg sodium.

Homemade Mustard

½ cup raw cashews
½ cup lemon juice
2 teaspoons ground turmeric
1 teaspoon onion powder
1 teaspoon garlic powder
1 teaspoon salt

Process cashews, lemon juice, turmeric, onion powder, garlic powder, and salt in a blender or food processor until smooth. Refrigerate at least 1 hour.
Makes about 1 cup; 48 1-teaspoon servings. 15 calories, 1 g fat, 49 mg sodium.

Potato Buns

1 cup hot mashed potatoes
2 cups warm soy milk
1 tablespoon active dry yeast
½ cup honey
¼ cup olive oil
1 tablespoon egg replacement powder (such as Ener-G) dissolved in ¼ cup water
1 teaspoon salt
4 cups whole-wheat flour
2 cups unbleached all-purpose flour, as needed
cooking spray

Prepare mashed potatoes. Stir warm milk and yeast together in a mixing bowl and let stand 10 minutes. Whisk in mashed potatoes, honey, oil, egg replacement, and salt. Mix in whole-wheat flour, and enough all-purpose flour to make a soft dough. Knead into a ball. Cover and let rise about 30 minutes, or until doubled. Shape dough into 24 buns and place on baking sheets coated with cooking spray. Let rise 20 minutes, or until doubled. Heat oven to 350°F. Bake 10 minutes, or until lightly browned.
Makes 2 dozen buns. 162 calories, 3 g fat, 107 mg sodium.

Elegant Lemon Cheesecake

Crust:

1 cup unbleached all-purpose flour
2 teaspoons baking powder (preferably aluminum-free)
¼ teaspoon salt
⅔ cup soy milk
½ cup honey
1½ tablespoons lemon juice
2 teaspoons egg replacement powder (such as Ener-G) dissolved in 3 tablespoons water
cooking spray

Lemon Filling:

1 cup water
3 tablespoons agar powder
¼ cup raw cashews
2 12-ounce packages firm silken tofu (preferably reduced-fat)
⅓ cup honey
2 tablespoons lemon juice
2 teaspoons vanilla extract
1 teaspoon grated lemon peel

Lemon Sauce:

2 tablespoons cornstarch
2 cups water
⅓ cup fructose or granulated cane sugar, or to taste
2½ tablespoons lemon juice

Crust: Heat oven to 350°F. Mix flour, baking powder, and salt together in a mixing bowl. Mix soy milk, honey, lemon juice, and egg replacement together in a separate bowl. Stir liquid ingredients into flour mixture. Mix well, but do not overmix. Spread batter evenly over the bottom of a 10- or 12-inch springform pan coated with cooking spray. Bake 30 minutes, or until golden brown. Let cool.

Lemon Filling: Heat water in a saucepan until almost boiling. Stir in agar. Remove from heat. Process cashews in a blender or food processor until finely ground. Add agar mixture, tofu, honey, lemon juice, vanilla, and lemon peel and process until smooth. Pour mixture over cooled cheesecake crust. Cover and refrigerate 3 hours, or until set.

Lemon Sauce: Stir cornstarch and water together in a small saucepan. Stir in fructose and lemon juice. Heat mixture to boiling over medium heat, stirring constantly; reduce heat and simmer until thickened. Cool to room temperature. Refrigerate.

To serve: Remove the sides of the springform pan and cut cheesecake into 12 wedges. Transfer each slice to an individual plate and drizzle with lemon sauce.

Makes 12 servings. 222 calories, 3 g fat, 102 mg sodium.

Menu 34

French du Jour

Our South African friends told us about the tradition of crepe-making contests in their homeland. They fell in love with these crepes and labeled them "first-place winners" (even though they could not believe the crepes did not contain eggs).

- **Butternut Squash Soup**
- Spring Salad Mix with **Lemon Oil Dressing** (p. 69)
- **Croissants**
- **Tofu Crepes** with **Berry Filling** and **Creamed Pears**

Butternut Squash Soup

- 2 cups mashed, cooked butternut squash
- water or olive oil, for cooking onion
- 1 cup chopped onion
- 2 cups water
- 1 large potato, peeled and chopped (about 2 cups)
- 2 teaspoons to 2 tablespoons chicken-style seasoning,* or to taste
- ½ teaspoon salt
- ¼ teaspoon dried thyme leaves
- 2 cups water
- 1 cup raw cashews

Prepare squash; set aside. Heat a little water or oil in a large saucepan over medium heat. Add onion; cook and stir until tender. Stir in water, potato, chicken-style seasoning, salt, and thyme; cook until potato is tender. Working in batches, transfer to a blender or food processor; process until smooth. Return to the saucepan.

Process water and cashews in a blender or food processor until smooth. Add cooked squash and process until mixed. Stir into potato mixture in the saucepan. Heat over low heat, stirring occasionally, until heated through.

Makes 10 1-cup servings. 165 calories, 11 g fat, 140 mg sodium.

COOK'S HINTS:

- Replace butternut squash with other types of winter squash.

*see glossary

Croissants

- 1 cup hot water
- ⅓ cup honey
- ¾ cup soy milk
- 1 tablespoon dry active yeast
- 3 cups whole-wheat flour
- 2 teaspoons egg replacement powder (such as Ener-G) dissolved in 2 tablespoons water
- 1½ teaspoons salt
- 2 cups unbleached all-purpose flour
- 1 cup nonhydrogenated margarine (such as Earth Balance)
- 1 cup unbleached all-purpose flour
- 1 recipe **Flaxseed Gel** (p. 80)

Stir hot water and honey together in a large mixing bowl until honey is dissolved. Stir in soy milk. Sprinkle in yeast. Let stand 10 minutes, or until yeast bubbles. Stir in whole-wheat flour, egg replacement, and salt.

Pulse 2 cups all-purpose flour and margarine in a food processor 15-20 times, or until mixture resembles coarse meal. Stir into flour mixture. Mix in 1 cup all-purpose flour. (Do not knead.) Cover the bowl with plastic wrap and refrigerate at least 4 hours, or until dough is completely chilled.

Turn chilled dough out onto a lightly floured surface. Divide into four equal portions and return all but one to the refrigerator. Working with one portion at a time, roll dough out on a lightly floured surface into a 16-inch circle. Cut into eight equal wedges. Starting at the wide end, roll up each wedge towards the point. Place, point-side down, on ungreased baking sheets. Curve ends toward the middle to form a crescent shape. Repeat with remaining dough, spacing each croissant 2 inches apart on the baking sheets. Cover with a towel. Let rise in a warm place for about 1 hour, or until doubled. Heat oven to 325°F. Prepare **Flaxseed Gel** and lightly brush over croissants. Bake 20 minutes, or until lightly browned. Serve warm or cold.
Makes 32 croissants. 142 calories, 6 g fat, 202 mg sodium.

Tofu Crepes

- 1½ cups soft water-packed or firm silken tofu, drained (preferably reduced-fat)
- 1½ cups soy milk
- 1½ cups unbleached all-purpose flour or whole-wheat pastry flour
- 2 tablespoons honey
- 1 tablespoon baking powder (preferably aluminum-free)
- ½ teaspoon vanilla extract
- cooking spray

Process tofu, soy milk, flour, honey, baking powder, and vanilla in a food processor or blender until very smooth. Heat a small nonstick skillet (or crepe pan) coated with cooking spray over medium heat. Pour in ⅓ cup batter and tilt the pan until batter is evenly distributed. Cook until bottom of crepe is lightly browned. Turn crepe over and cook the second side until lightly browned. Transfer crepe to a plate. Repeat with remaining batter. (Crepes may be stacked.)
Makes 10 crepes. 107 calories, 1 g fat, 42 mg sodium.

- To serve, place ½ cup **Berry Filling** in the middle of each crepe and roll up. Place seam-side down in a baking dish. Top with **Creamed Pears**.
- Crepes are delicious for dessert, breakfast, or a light supper.

Berry Filling

4 cups frozen mixed berries, partly thawed
1½ cups unsweetened apple juice
3 tablespoons cornstarch

Place berries in a medium saucepan. Stir apple juice and cornstarch together and pour over the berries. Heat over medium-high heat, stirring constantly, until fruit is thickened and cornstarch turns translucent.
Makes 10 servings. 58 calories, 0 g fat, 2 mg sodium.

COOK'S HINTS:

- Replace berries with other fresh or frozen fruit, such as peaches or strawberries.
- Also good on waffles or pancakes.

Creamed Pears

2 14-ounce cans pears (in natural fruit juice)
¾ cup raw cashews
1 teaspoon vanilla extract
1 tablespoon honey, optional

Drain juice from one can of pears. Process pears, cashews, vanilla, and honey, if desired, in a blender or food processor until very smooth. Refrigerate until chilled. Use as a topping on crepes, waffles, pancakes, fruit salad, or strawberry shortcake.
Makes 4¼ cups; 68 1-tablespoon servings. 20 calories, 1 g fat, 1 mg sodium.

Menu 35

Bon Appétit

Although quiche is now a classic dish of French cuisine, it originated in Germany, in a region that the French later renamed Lorraine. The word quiche *is from the German* kuchen*, meaning cake.*

The original quiche lorraine was an open pie with a filling consisting of an egg custard with cream and smoked bacon. Later cheese was added. The bottom crust was originally made from bread dough, but has evolved into a pie or puff pastry crust.

Because the main ingredient is eggs, total vegetarians do not often think about making quiche. Tofu is a wonderful, versatile food that can replace eggs, such as has been fabulously done in this recipe. Quiche can be served as an entrée for any meal of the day.

- **Mini Quiches**
- **Pecan-Rice Croquettes** with **Chicken-style Gravy** (p. 34)
- **Roasted Vegetables**
- **Green Bean Amandine**
- **Baguettes** with Margarine
- **Apple Upside-Down Cake** with **Soy Whipped Cream** (p. 17)

Mini Quiches

1½ recipes **Whole-wheat Piecrust** (p. 26) made into 36 2-inch tart shells
1 14-ounce package medium or firm tofu, drained
2 tablespoons unbleached all-purpose flour
1 tablespoon egg replacement powder (such as Ener-G) dissolved in ¼ cup water
2 teaspoons herb seasoned salt (such as Spike)
1 cup shredded nondairy cheese
½ cup sliced mushrooms
½ cup finely chopped green bell pepper
¼ cup finely chopped celery
¼ cup finely chopped onion
¼ cup minced fresh parsley

Heat oven to 350°F. Place tart shells on two baking sheets. Process tofu, flour, egg replacement, and seasoned salt in a food processor or blender until smooth. Add nondairy cheese, mushrooms, bell pepper, celery, onion, and parsley. Pulse to mix. Spoon about 2 tablespoons filling into each tart shell. Bake 20 minutes, or until golden brown.
Makes 36 servings. 103 calories, 6 g fat, 77 mg sodium.

- These can be frozen for future use.
- To make one large quiche, pour filling into a 9-inch unbaked pie shell. Bake 40 minutes, or until golden brown.

Pecan-Rice Croquettes

1 cup finely ground pecans
1 cup cooked **Perfect Brown Rice** (p. 16)
1 cup soft whole-wheat bread crumbs
1 cup soy milk
1 small onion, finely chopped
1 tablespoon unbleached all-purpose flour
1 tablespoon dried parsley
½ teaspoon salt
cooking spray

Heat oven to 350°F. Mix pecans, rice, bread crumbs, soy milk, onion, flour, parsley, and salt together in a bowl. Shape mixture into croquettes (little square patties) on a baking sheet coated with cooking spray. Bake about 40 minutes, or until golden brown. Serve with **Chicken-style Gravy**, if desired.
Makes 8 servings. 195 calories, 11 g fat, 257 mg sodium.

Roasted Vegetables

6 medium or large potatoes, peeled and cut into 1-inch pieces
1 medium sweet potato, peeled and cut into 1-inch pieces
2 parsnips, peeled and cut into 1-inch pieces
4 carrots, peeled and cut into 1-inch pieces
1 large onion, peeled and cut into 1-inch pieces
¼ cup olive oil
¼ cup water
1 teaspoon dried thyme leaves or rosemary
1 teaspoon salt

Heat oven to 400°F. Mix potatoes, sweet potato, parsnips, carrots, and onion together in a large baking dish. Stir oil, water, thyme, and salt together in a small bowl. Pour over

vegetables and mix well. Bake, covered, for 30 minutes, or until vegetables are tender.
Makes 10 servings. 202 calories, 6 g fat, 272 mg sodium.

Green Bean Amandine

½ cup slivered almonds
4 cups fresh (or frozen) green beans, trimmed
1 cup finely chopped red bell pepper
1 teaspoon thyme

Toast slivered almonds in the oven (or a toaster oven) at 300°F for about 20-30 minutes, stirring occasionally, or until lightly browned. Heat a small amount of water in a 2-quart saucepan. Add green beans; simmer about 5 minutes, or until crisp-tender. Drain. Stir in red pepper and thyme. Cover and let steam for 2 minutes. Transfer to a serving bowl. Sprinkle with almonds.
Makes 8 servings. 75 calories, 5 g fat, 6 mg sodium.

VARIATION:

- Omit thyme and cook green beans with a little onion and garlic.

Baguettes (French Bread)

2½ cups warm water
2 tablespoons granulated cane sugar
1 tablespoon dry active yeast
1 tablespoon salt
4 cups whole-wheat flour
2 cups unbleached all-purpose flour, as needed
olive oil, for brushing loaves, optional

Stir water, sugar, and yeast together in a mixing bowl. Let stand 10 minutes, or until yeast bubbles. Mix in salt and whole-wheat flour. Gradually mix in all-purpose flour until dough is no longer sticky. Knead on a lightly floured surface for 4 minutes. Return dough to the mixing bowl and cover with a towel; let rise in a warm place for 30 minutes, or until doubled in size.

Knead dough a little. Divide into four equal portions. Form each portion into a long loaf, about 2"x14" in size. Slash the top diagonally every few inches with a sharp knife. Let rise 30 minutes in a warm place. Heat oven to 400°F. Bake loaves for 10 minutes. Lower heat to 350°F and bake 10 minutes, or until golden brown. Remove from oven. Lightly brush each loaf with oil, if desired. Cool to room temperature.
Makes 4 baguettes; 56 1-inch slices. 51 calories, 0 g fat, 125 mg sodium.

Apple Upside-Down Cake

6 large (or 8 medium) apples, peeled, cored, and sliced (about 8 cups)
cooking spray
2 cups unbleached all-purpose flour or spelt flour
1 cup soy milk
½ cup honey
⅓ cup mild-flavored olive oil
1 tablespoon baking powder (preferably aluminum-free)
1 tablespoon egg replacement powder (such as Ener-G) dissolved in ¼ cup water
1 teaspoon vanilla extract
¼ teaspoon salt

Heat oven to 350°F. Place sliced apples in a 9"x13" glass baking dish coated with cooking spray. Mix together in a mixing bowl flour, soy milk, honey, oil, baking powder, egg replacement, vanilla, and salt. Drop the dough by spoonfuls over the sliced apples, and spread until evenly distributed. Bake 25-30 minutes, or until golden brown. Serve, at room temperature or chilled, with **Soy Whipped Cream** (p. 17).

Makes 12 servings. 223 calories, 7 g fat, 59 mg sodium.

COOK'S HINTS:

- The French call this style of dessert a *clafouti*, in which a batter is poured over and through the fruit.

Honey Greek Cake (*Karithopita*)

Menu 36

Mediterranean Panache

The Mediterranean diet has been studied extensively in recent years because of the notably low incidence of chronic diseases and the notably high life-expectancy rates attributed to the diet. The traditional Mediterranean diet delivers as much as 40 percent of its total daily calories from fat, yet the associated incidence of cardiovascular disease is significantly decreased.

Mediterranean people tend to eat red meat sparingly and they consume large amounts of omega-3 fatty acids — something that the rest of the developed societies don't get enough of. Health professionals agree that the Mediterranean diet is healthier than the Northern European and American diets because of the higher consumption of fruits, vegetables, legumes, nuts, and olive oil. Olive oil is a good source of antioxidants, and as a monounsaturated fat it does not have the same cholesterol-raising effect as saturated fats.

Option 1

- **Okra in Tomato Sauce**
- **Tomato-Lentil Couscous**
- **Root Vegetables in Olive Oil**
- Green Salad with Salad Dressing
- **Focaccia**
- **Apple Torte**

Option 2

- **Rice Stacks**
- **Cooked Lentils (*Mazidra*)**
- **Apple Torte**

Okra in Tomato Sauce

2 tablespoons olive oil
1 medium onion, cut in half and sliced
2 cloves garlic, minced
2 cups okra, trimmed (about 1 pound, preferably smaller-sized okra)
4 medium tomatoes, peeled and chopped
2 tablespoons lemon juice
1-2 teaspoons fructose or granulated cane sugar
½ teaspoon salt, or to taste
¼ cup minced fresh cilantro or parsley

Heat oil in a skillet over medium heat. Add onion; cook and stir until tender. Add garlic and cook for 1 minute. Stir in okra and cook for about 5 minutes, turning the okra pods over as they cook. Stir in tomatoes, lemon juice, fructose, and salt; cook for 15 minutes. Remove from heat. Stir in cilantro or parsley. Serve immediately.
Makes 6 ½-cup servings. 102 calories, 5 g fat, 207 mg sodium.

Tomato-Lentil Couscous

½ cup cooked small brown lentils (such as Eston or French)
1½ cups water
2 tablespoons olive oil
1 teaspoon onion powder
1 teaspoon dried parsley
1 teaspoon nutritional yeast flakes
¾ teaspoon salt
¼ teaspoon celery seeds
¼ teaspoon garlic powder
1 cup whole-wheat couscous
3 tablespoons oil-packed sun-dried tomatoes, drained and chopped
fresh parsley, for garnish, optional
chopped fresh tomatoes, for garnish, optional

Prepare lentils. Stir water, oil, onion powder, parsley, nutritional yeast, salt, celery seeds, and garlic powder together in a medium saucepan. Heat to boiling; stir in couscous. Reduce heat and simmer, covered, 1-2 minutes, or until water is absorbed. Remove from heat; let stand 5 minutes. Fluff with a fork. Gently stir in cooked lentils and sun-dried tomatoes. Garnish with fresh parsley and chopped fresh tomatoes, if desired.

Makes 6 ½-cup servings. 174 calories, 5 g fat, 331 mg sodium

Root Vegetables in Olive Oil

3 tablespoons olive oil
2 large carrots, cut into ¾-inch slices
1 medium celeriac (celery root) (about 1 pound), peeled and cut into ¾-inch cubes
1 medium sweet potato, peeled and cut into ¾-inch cubes
2 tablespoons lemon juice
½ teaspoon salt, or to taste
1-2 teaspoons fructose or granulated cane sugar, or to taste
2 tablespoons minced fresh dill, or 2 teaspoons dried

Heat oil in a large saucepan over low heat. Add carrots, celeriac, and sweet potato; cook and stir 5 minutes. Stir in lemon juice, salt, and fructose. Add just enough water to cover vegetables. Simmer, covered, 20-25 minutes or until vegetables are tender. Uncover and simmer 5 minutes to reduce liquid. Remove from heat. Stir in dill.

Makes 6 servings. 106 calories, 7 g fat, 251 mg sodium.

- Also good served cold, as a salad.

Focaccia

1 teaspoon honey
½ cup warm water
1 tablespoon active dry yeast
2 teaspoons salt
2 tablespoons olive oil
4 cups spelt flour (or a combination of whole-wheat and unbleached all-purpose flour), or as needed
cooking spray
olive oil, for topping
coarse sea salt

Stir honey and warm water together in a large mixing bowl until honey dissolves. Sprinkle in yeast. Let stand 10 minutes. Stir in salt, oil, and enough flour to make a soft dough. Turn dough out onto a lightly floured surface and knead about 10 minutes, or until smooth and elastic. Return to the bowl, cover with a cloth, and let rise in a warm place, or until doubled in size. Knead dough a few minutes. Press into a 10-inch tart pan or pie plate coated with cooking spray. Cover with a damp cloth and let rise 30 minutes, or until doubled in size. Heat oven to 400°F. Poke the dough all over with your fingers (or the handle of a wooden spoon) to make dimples in the surface. Drizzle oil over the dough and use a pastry brush to spread the oil to the edges. Sprinkle with coarse sea salt. Bake 20-25 minutes or until lightly browned. Remove from the pan and cool on a rack. Best if eaten the same day.

Makes 8 servings. 239 calories, 5 g fat, 586 mg sodium.

COOK'S HINTS:

- Focaccia freezes well.

Rice Stacks

cooked brown rice or **Perfect Brown Rice** (p. 16)
Cooked lentils (***Mazidra***)
chopped lettuce
chopped tomatoes
chopped cucumber
chopped bell peppers
sprouts of your choice
chopped green onions
sliced ripe olives
shredded carrots
Guacamole (p. 66)
Tofu Sour Cream (p. 67)

Prepare each ingredient in quantities according to the number of people you plan to serve. Serve each ingredient in separate bowls or as a large salad plate. Begin to assemble by stacking each item in the order given to form a "haystack." Good served with garlic toast.

Cooked Lentils (*Mazidra*)

3 cups water
1 cup small brown lentils (such as Eston)
1 medium onion, chopped
½ teaspoon garlic powder
1 10.75-ounce can milk-free tomato soup
salt
taco seasoning, optional

Stir water, lentils, onion, and garlic powder together in a medium saucepan. Bring to boiling over high heat. Reduce heat and simmer about 30 minutes, or until lentils are slightly tender. Stir in tomato soup. Season to taste with salt and taco seasoning. Continue to simmer about 10 minutes, or until lentils are cooked but not mushy. Serve on rice or on **Rice Stacks**.
Makes 8 ½-cup servings. 112 calories, 1 g fat, 214 mg sodium.

COOK'S HINTS:

- For a richer flavor, replace the tomato soup with puréed tomatoes.

Apple Torte

½ cup nonhydrogenated margarine (such as Earth Balance), softened
¼ cup granulated cane sugar
1 cup spelt or unbleached all-purpose flour
cooking spray
⅓ cup raspberry jam

Filling:

1 8-ounce container nondairy cream cheese (such as Tofutti)
¼ cup granulated cane sugar
2 teaspoons egg replacement powder (such as Ener-G) dissolved in 2 tablespoons water
1 teaspoon vanilla extract

Topping:

3 cups peeled and thinly sliced apples
¼ cup granulated cane sugar
½ teaspoon ground cinnamon or substitute
½ cup sliced almonds

Heat oven to 450°F. Beat margarine and sugar together in a mixing bowl. Mix in flour. Press evenly on the bottom and slightly up the sides of a 9-inch springform pan coated with cooking spray. Spread jam evenly over the crust.

Filling: Process cream cheese, sugar, egg replacement, and vanilla in a food processor until smooth. Spread over jam layer.

Topping: Mix apples, sugar, and cinnamon together. Spoon into the pan. Sprinkle with sliced almonds. Bake 25-30 minutes, or until set and apples are tender. Cool. Transfer to a serving platter and remove sides of springform pan before serving.
Makes 12 servings. 264 calories, 13 g fat, 181 mg sodium.

About Lentils

The lentil plant (*Lens culinaris*) belongs to the family *Leguminosae* (legume) and is a cousin to peas. The plants are grown for their seeds, which are contained in pods. The botanical name derives from their resemblance in shape to the lens of the eye. Often left to dry on the plant before they are harvested, they can be cooked in many ways as well as being ground into flour. Although there are two types of lentil, the large-seeded *macrosperm* and the Persian *microsperma*, which has small to medium-sized seed, there are many varieties within these two groups. They are used in countless cuisines worldwide and are a staple in many Middle Eastern countries, as well as India.

Types of Lentils

The three most common types used in cooking are brown, red, and green.

Brown lentils, also known as continental or Egyptian lentils, are generally the least expensive and most easily obtained. They are mild in flavor and hold their shape well after cooking, but easily turn mushy if overcooked. They are ready in about 35 minutes, although if you want to ensure they remain firm, add oil to the cooking water and cook for a shorter period, about 20 minutes.

Red lentils are less common than brown lentils and have a slightly sweeter taste than the brown variety. They take a little less time to cook, although they tend to become somewhat mushy and are therefore more suitable for soups and stews.

Green lentils, also known as Puy or French lentils, are the finest but most expensive lentils. They are the meatiest and richest tasting, and remain quite firm after cooking, making them an excellent choice for salads. Originally grown in the volcanic soils of Puy in France, they are now also grown in North America and Italy.

There are two less common but still interesting lentils that you may not have seen. **Beluga lentils** are black and glisten when cooked, making them look like beluga caviar. **White lentils** (skinned and split black lentils) have a very smooth texture and are suitable for chilled vegetable salads and stuffing mixes.

Preparing Lentils

One advantage of lentils over other legumes is that they do not require soaking. (You can soak them for a few hours if you wish, this will reduce the cooking time by about half.) Before cooking lentils, you should rinse them in cold water and pick through them for any dirt or gravel that may be present. When cooking lentils by themselves, in preparation for adding to a recipe or as an accompaniment, use three times the amount of water to lentils and avoid cooking with anything acidic, such as vinegar, as that retards the cooking process. It is possible to substitute one type of lentil for another, although you may need to adjust the cooking time. Cooking times for the main three types of lentils are:

- Brown lentils: 35 minutes
- Red lentils: 10-15 minutes
- French (green) lentils: 20 minutes

Lentils can be frozen, but make sure you only partly cook them beforehand, so that when they are defrosted and added to a recipe they retain some texture.

Lentil Sprouts

A garden-in-a-jar can give you, in four or five days, crisp lentil sprouts for your veggie burgers or a salad of almost any kind. All you need is: a 1-quart (1.25-liter) widemouthed fruit jar, a square of cheesecloth or a nylon stocking, a rubber band, and 1 pound (500 g) of lentils from the grocery store. You will use ¼ cup (50 ml) of lentils for each jar.

1. Wash in a colander or strainer ¼ cup lentils for each quart jar. Add 2 cups lukewarm water. Fasten the cheesecloth over the top with the rubber band. Let stand overnight.
2. Drain off water. Turn jar upside-down until all the water is drained out.
3. Hold jar on its side. Shake it so that the lentils are scattered along one side of the jar. Lay the jar on its side in a dark place. (It is ideal to place it slightly tilted in a drain rack with a towel over it.) The light-colored sprouts will give you sprouts used in chop suey.
4. Each morning, put the jar under the faucet and let lukewarm water run into it. Leave the cloth cover on it. Stand the jar upside-down until every bit of the water is drained out. Shake so that the sprouting lentils lie along one side. Return the jar to the spot you have selected.
5. In about four days your sprouts will be about 1-1¼ inches long and will nearly fill the jar. If you want the sprouts to have little green leaves, put the jar in a sunny window.
6. Take off the cheesecloth. Put on the jar's cap and screw ring. Keep in the refrigerator. The sprouts taste better when they are eaten within a week.

Menu 37

Tuscany and Beyond

Ribollita is a traditional hearty Tuscan soup, and a popular next-day leftover Italian bean soup that literally means "reboiled." You can make ribollita with any leftover Italian-style bean soup. Kale is a popular component of this soup. Black kale, called toscano in Tuscany, is not actually black, but dark green. It is a natural accompaniment to the substantial texture of the other vegetables, beans, and herbs.

- **Ribollita**
- **Mediterranean Salad** on a Bed of Lettuce
- **Whole-Wheat Pita Bread**
- Platter of Assorted Nuts and Dried Fruit
- Almonds, Walnuts, Hazelnuts, Pine Nuts, Figs, Raisins, Dates
- Red Grape Juice

Ribollita

2 tablespoons **Pesto Sauce** (p. 147)
3 tablespoons olive oil
2 onions, chopped
2 carrots, sliced
2 stalks celery, thinly sliced
1 fennel bulb, trimmed and chopped
4 cloves garlic, minced
3¾ cups vegetable broth
1 14-ounce can great northern or cannellini beans, drained
1 14-ounce can diced tomatoes
½ teaspoon salt, or to taste
1 tablespoon olive oil
1 pound kale, stems removed and coarsely chopped
8-10 slices whole-wheat **French Bread** (p. 108), cubed

Prepare **Pesto Sauce**. Heat oil in a large saucepan. Add onions, carrots, celery, fennel, and garlic; cook and stir 10 minutes. Stir in vegetable broth, beans, tomatoes, and **Pesto Sauce**. Heat to boiling; reduce heat and simmer, covered, 25-30 minutes, or until vegetables are tender. Stir in salt. Heat oil in a skillet. Fry kale 5 minutes, or until wilted. Place cubed bread in soup bowls. Spoon kale over the bread. Ladle soup over kale.

Makes 16 1-cup servings. 125 calories, 5 g fat, 198 mg sodium.

COOK'S HINTS:

- You can substitute spinach for the kale. Because it wilts quickly, cook only 2 minutes.

Mediterranean Salad

2 cups water
1 cup small lentils (such as Eston or French), rinsed
2 teaspoons to 2 tablespoons beef-style seasoning,* or to taste
2 medium potatoes, peeled, cubed, cooked
⅓ cup sun-dried tomatoes (not oil-packed)
1 14-ounce can baby corn, drained, cut into bite-size pieces
½ onion, chopped
1 large carrot, shredded
½ cup thinly sliced celery
½ cup chopped cucumber
½ cup sliced mushrooms

Dressing:

½ cup olive oil
3 tablespoons lemon juice
2 teaspoons minced fresh dill or 1 teaspoon dried
2 fresh cloves garlic, minced
1 teaspoon extra-spicy salt-free seasoning (such as Mrs. Dash)
1 teaspoon celery salt
Whole-Wheat Pita Bread, optional

*see glossary

Heat water, lentils, and beef-style seasoning to boiling in a saucepan; reduce heat and simmer, covered, 30 minutes, or until lentils are tender. Drain; let cool. Prepare potatoes. Cover dried tomatoes with boiling water; let stand 2 minutes; drain and slice into thin pieces. Stir baby corn, onion, carrot, celery, cucumber, and mushrooms together in a bowl. Stir in cooked lentils and potatoes.

Dressing: Process oil, lemon juice, dill, garlic, salt-free seasoning, and celery salt in a blender or food processor until mixed. Pour over salad and mix well. Serve with **Whole-Wheat Pita Bread** or on a bed of lettuce.
Makes 12 servings. 187 calories, 9 g fat, 237 mg sodium.

COOK'S HINTS:

- Eston or French lentils work the best in this recipe because they retain their shape when cooked.

Whole-Wheat Pita Bread

1½ cups warm water
¼ cup unsweetened applesauce
1 tablespoon quick-rising yeast
1 tablespoon honey
1 teaspoon salt
2 cups whole-wheat flour
3-4 cups spelt or unbleached all-purpose flour, as needed

Heat oven to 550°F. Stir water, applesauce, yeast, honey, and salt together in a large mixing bowl. Stir in whole-wheat flour. Stir in spelt flour, 1 cup at a time. Knead in enough flour so that dough is no longer sticky. (You may need a little more or less flour.) Form dough into golf ball-sized portions. Roll each ball on a lightly floured surface into a 4-inch circle about ¼-inch thick. Place on an ungreased baking sheet and let rise 10 minutes. Bake 3-5 minutes, or until puffed up and golden brown. Let bread cool.

To serve: Cut with a sharp knife halfway around the side (or cut in half) to create a pocket. Stuff each pocket with your favorite fillings, such as chili, fresh vegetables, mock tuna, or tofu-egg salad, or serve with **Hummus** (p. 120) for dipping.
Makes about 20 pita breads. 115 calories, 0 g fat, 118 mg sodium.

Menu 38
Mediterranean Medley

*This **Hearty Mediterranean Soup** recipe is one of the most requested soups when I cater for functions. Although unique compared to basic vegetable soup, it is quick and simple to make, yet filling and nutritious. And it hits the spot on a cold day.*

- **Hearty Mediterranean Soup**
- Tossed Salad with **Mediterranean Salad Dressing**
- Toasted **French Bread** (p. 131) with **Bruschetta**
- Pita Bread with **Baba Ghanoush**
- **Strawberry Cheesecake Tarts**

Hearty Mediterranean Soup

2 tablespoons olive oil
2 onions, chopped
1-2 cloves garlic, minced
¼-½ teaspoon ground ginger
½ teaspoon paprika
3 cups water
1 28-ounce can diced tomatoes
1 cup red lentils, rinsed
1-3 tablespoons beef-style seasoning,* or to taste

*see glossary

1 15- to 19-ounce can chickpeas, drained
½ teaspoon dried oregano leaves
¾-1 teaspoon dried basil, crushed
salt

Heat oil in a large saucepan. Add onions and garlic; cook and stir 2 minutes. Add ginger and paprika; cook and stir 1 minute, stirring constantly. Stir in water, tomatoes, lentils, and beef-style seasoning and heat to boiling over high heat; reduce heat to medium low and simmer, covered, 30-40 minutes, or until lentils are tender. Stir in chickpeas, oregano, and basil. Season to taste with salt. Simmer, uncovered, 10 minutes.

Makes 12 1-cup servings. 172 calories, 4 g fat, 104 mg sodium.

Mediterranean Salad Dressing

⅓ cup olive oil
2 tablespoons lemon juice
1 tablespoon minced fresh basil
1 teaspoon Dijon mustard
1 clove garlic, peeled
¼ teaspoon salt

Process oil, lemon juice, basil, mustard, garlic, and salt in a blender or food processor until smooth. Refrigerate until chilled.

Makes about ½ cup; 8 1-tablespoon servings. 73 calories, 8 g fat, 72 mg sodium.

Bruschetta

2 large tomatoes, chopped
1 tablespoon olive oil
1-2 cloves garlic, minced
1 tablespoon minced fresh basil or
1 teaspoon dried, crushed
¼ teaspoon salt, or to taste

Mix tomatoes, oil, garlic, basil, and salt together. Cover and refrigerate 1 hour. Spoon onto toasted **French Bread** just before serving. (Or place **Bruschetta** in a bowl beside hot toasted **French Bread** and let people serve themselves.)

Makes about 2 cups; 16 1-tablespoon servings. 6 calories, 0 g fat, 19 mg sodium.

Baba Ghanoush

1 large eggplant
3 tablespoons sesame tahini
3 tablespoons fresh lemon juice, or to taste
2-3 cloves garlic
½ teaspoon salt, or to taste
¼ cup minced onion
minced fresh flat-leaf parsley, for garnish
¼ red bell pepper, cut into thin slices, for garnish

Heat the oven to broil. Pierce the eggplant all over, using a fork. Place the eggplant on a baking sheet and roast 45 minutes, turning every 15 minutes, or until the outer shell is blackened and charred, and the inside is tender. Let cool 5 minutes (or use cold water to cool). Cut the eggplant open lengthwise with a knife, and scoop out the pulp with a spoon. Place the pulp in a food processor or blender. Add tahini, lemon juice, garlic, and salt; process until smooth. Stir in minced onion. Transfer to a serving bowl, and garnish with parsley and red bell pepper. Refrigerate until chilled.

Makes about 4 cups; 64 1-tablespoon servings. 6 calories, 0 g fat, 18 mg sodium.

Strawberry Cheesecake Tarts

1 recipe **Whole-wheat Piecrust** (p. 26) or 1½ dozen tart shells
2 cups frozen, sliced strawberries, thawed
¼ cup water
2 tablespoons cornstarch
1 tablespoon honey

Filling:

1 8-ounce container nondairy cream cheese (such as Tofutti)
¼ cup granulated cane sugar
1 tablespoon cornstarch

2 teaspoons egg replacement powder (such as Ener-G) dissolved in 2 tablespoons water
¼ teaspoon vanilla extract

Prepare pie dough using the **Whole-Wheat Piecrust** recipe. Make dough into 18 ready-to-bake tart shells. Heat strawberries, water, cornstarch, and honey in a medium saucepan, stirring constantly, until thickened and cornstarch turns translucent. Remove half of the thickened strawberry mixture; set aside. Heat oven to 425°F. Mash remaining strawberry mixture and spoon into the tart shells. Bake tarts for 10 minutes. Remove from oven. Reduce oven temperature to 350°F.

Filling: Process cream cheese, sugar, cornstarch, egg replacement, and vanilla in a food processor or blender until smooth. Spoon filling into tarts. Bake 10 minutes, or until filling is set. Remove from oven and let cool. Top each tart with reserved strawberry mixture. Refrigerate at least 2 hours before serving.

Makes 18 servings. 158 calories, 8 g fat, 136 mg sodium.

Menu 39

Middle East Feast

When a friend shared an abundance of kale from her garden, my sister Diana (Clarke) inspired us to try this soup recipe. Because of its hardiness, kale holds up well in soup, yet it has a pleasant mild flavor. Kale is a dark green leafy vegetable high in calcium.

- **Hearty Kale-Quinoa Soup**
- **Falafels**
- **Whole-Wheat Pita Bread** (p. 117)
- Shredded Lettuce
- **Hummus** or **Tahini Sauce**
- **Tabbouleh**
- **Baklava**

Hearty Kale-Quinoa Soup

olive oil, for cooking onions
2 onions, chopped
3 cups celery, chopped
2 cloves garlic, minced
10 cups hot water
6 cups carrots, chopped
¾ cup red lentils
¾ cup quinoa, thoroughly rinsed in a fine-mesh strainer and drained
1-3 tablespoons chicken-style seasoning,* or to taste
¼ cup unfermented soy sauce substitute or reduced-sodium soy sauce
6 cups kale, stems removed, and coarsely chopped
2 tablespoons minced fresh dill or 1 tablespoon dried

Heat a small amount of oil in a 9-quart stockpot. Add onions, celery, and garlic; cook and stir until onions are tender. Stir in water, carrots, red lentils, quinoa, chicken-style seasoning, and soy sauce substitute; heat to boiling. Reduce heat and simmer 1 hour. Stir in kale and dill; simmer 10 minutes. Serve immediately to maintain the bright-green color of the kale.

Makes 25 1-cup servings. 68 calories, 1 g fat, 140 mg sodium.

COOK'S HINTS:

- Recipe may be cut in half.

Falafels

1 cup cooked yellow split peas
1 cup dry bread crumbs, as needed
2 15-ounce cans chickpeas (3½ cups)
⅓ cup sesame seeds
¼ cup wheat germ

*see glossary

3 tablespoons unfermented soy sauce substitute or reduced-sodium soy sauce
2 tablespoons dried onion
2 tablespoons lemon juice
1 tablespoon dried parsley
2 cloves garlic, peeled
2 teaspoons ground cumin
1 teaspoon salt
cooking spray

Prepare yellow split peas. Prepare dry bread crumbs. Heat oven to 400°F. Drain chickpeas, reserving ½ cup liquid. Process chickpeas, ½ cup chickpea liquid, split peas, and sesame seeds in a food processor or blender until smooth. Add wheat germ, soy sauce substitute, onion, lemon juice, parsley, garlic, cumin, and salt; process until smooth. Transfer mixture to a bowl. Mix in bread crumbs as needed, until mixture holds together. Roll mixture with hands into 1½-inch balls. Place balls on a baking sheet coated with cooking spray and gently flatten each ball to form a thick disk. Bake 20-30 minutes, turning after 15 minutes, until evenly browned on both sides. Serve in **Whole-Wheat Pita Bread** with **Hummus** or **Tahini Sauce** and shredded lettuce.

Makes 25-30 falafels. 70 calories, 2 g fat, 141 mg sodium.

COOK'S HINTS:

- Cook yellow split peas, with at least 2 cups of water for every cup of split peas, for 20-30 minutes until tender, adding more water if needed.
- To make dry bread crumbs, process two or three slices of bread in a food processor or blender. Dry out in the oven at 250°F for about 10-15 minutes.
- These freeze well. Make ahead and reheat as needed.
- For an appetizer, serve with fancy toothpicks and **Tahini Sauce** for dipping.

Hummus

2 cups cooked chickpeas
⅓ cup sesame tahini
¼ cup lemon juice, or to taste
2 cloves garlic, peeled, or to taste
½ teaspoon onion powder, or to taste
½ teaspoon salt, or to taste
minced fresh parsley or olives, for garnish, optional

Process chickpeas, tahini, lemon juice, garlic, onion powder, and salt in a food processor or blender until very smooth. Season to taste with additional salt, lemon juice, onion powder, or garlic, if desired. Refrigerate until chilled. Serve as a dip for **Whole-Wheat Pita Bread**, crackers, or vegetables. Garnish with minced fresh parsley or olives, if desired.

Makes 2 ½ cups; 40 1-tablespoon servings. 26 calories, 1 g fat, 65 mg sodium.

Tahini Sauce

1 cup sesame tahini
¼ cup lemon juice
¼ cup water
2-3 cloves garlic, peeled
½ teaspoon salt

Process tahini, lemon juice, water, garlic, and salt in a blender or food processor until very smooth. Serve over **Falafels**. For an appetizer, serve with fancy toothpicks and **Tahini Sauce** for dipping.

Makes 1½ cups; 24 1-tablespoon servings. 58 calories, 5 g fat, 49 mg sodium.

Tabbouleh

1½ cups boiling water
1¼ cups fine-grain bulgur wheat
½ teaspoon salt
¼ cup minced fresh mint leaves, or 2 tablespoons dried leaves

3 tablespoons olive oil
3 tablespoons lemon juice
2 cloves garlic, minced
2 cups chopped tomato
2 cups English cucumber, finely chopped
1 cup green bell pepper, finely chopped
1 cup minced fresh parsley
⅓ cup chopped green onions
1 cup pitted ripe olives, optional

Pour boiling water over bulgur wheat and salt in a bowl. Let stand 20 minutes. Whisk mint, oil, lemon juice, and garlic together and pour over bulgur wheat; mix well. Refrigerate 2 hours, or until ready to serve. Just before serving, stir in tomato, cucumber, bell pepper, parsley, green onions, and olives, if desired.

Makes 8 servings. 142 calories, 6 g fat, 159 mg sodium.

- Lebanese cooks traditionally make this salad with lots of parsley combined with bulgur wheat, tomatoes, green onions, olive oil, lemon juice, mint, and salt.
- For a different taste, replace mint with ½ teaspoon dried oregano leaves.

Baklava

¾ cup granulated cane sugar
1½ tablespoons ground cinnamon or substitute
½ cup olive oil, as needed
¾ cup honey, or as needed
1 16-ounce package phyllo dough (about 20-25 large sheets)
cooking spray
1 cup ground walnuts

Heat oven to 350°F. Stir sugar and cinnamon together in a small bowl. Pour oil in a separate bowl. Heat honey in a small saucepan until warm and runny. Cut phyllo dough in half crosswise. Place two sheets of phyllo dough on the bottom of a 9"x13" baking dish coated with cooking spray. Brush lightly with oil. Sprinkle with cinnamon sugar. Place two more sheets of phyllo on top. Drizzle with honey. Repeat layers until half of phyllo is used. Brush top layer of phyllo with oil. Sprinkle with half of the walnuts. Generously drizzle honey over walnuts. Repeat layers until remaining phyllo is used. Brush top layer of phyllo with oil. Sprinkle remaining walnuts over the top. Generously drizzle honey over walnuts. Bake about 15 minutes, or until golden brown and slightly crispy. (Watch carefully to avoid overbrowning.) Cut into squares. Refrigerate until chilled.

Makes 40 servings. 139 calories, 6 g fat, 69 mg sodium.

Menu 40
Flavors of the Middle East

*When my two oldest boys, Nathan and Reuben, were preschoolers, we watched a children's television program that featured a man making chocolate candy with tahini. The boys thought it looked yummy and asked, "Mom, can we make candy like that with carob?" The three of us went to the kitchen and created our own **Tahini Candy**. Since then I have taught this recipe in dozens of cooking classes. It has become a favorite recipe for many people, but for me I think it will always be one of those favorite memories.*

- **Quinoa** with **Black-eyed Pea Topping**
- **Whole-wheat Pita Bread** (p. 117)
- **Green Beans with Tomatoes**
- **Lebanese Salad**
- **Tahini Candy**

Quinoa

5 cups water
3 cups quinoa, thoroughly rinsed in a fine-mesh strainer
¾ teaspoon salt

Heat water to boiling in a medium saucepan. Stir in rinsed quinoa and salt; reduce heat and simmer, covered, for 15 minutes, or until quinoa is tender and water is absorbed.
Makes 10 servings. 191 calories, 3 g fat, 188 mg sodium.

Black-eyed Pea Topping

4 cups water
1 cup black-eyed peas, sorted and rinsed
1 28-ounce can diced tomatoes
2 cups chopped onion
2 cloves garlic, minced
2 cups shredded carrots
1 cup chopped zucchini
1 8-ounce can tomato sauce (1 cup)
1 teaspoon dried basil
½ teaspoon ground cumin
½ teaspoon ground ginger
½ teaspoon salt, or to taste

Heat water and black-eyed peas to boiling in a medium saucepan; reduce heat and simmer 1 hour, or until beans are tender. Drain; set aside. Heat tomatoes, onion, and garlic in a large nonstick skillet; simmer about 10 minutes. Stir in carrots, zucchini, tomato sauce, basil, cumin, ginger, and salt; simmer until vegetables are tender. Stir in cooked black-eyed peas and simmer for 2 minutes, or until heated through. Serve over cooked Quinoa, Perfect Brown Rice (p. 16), or baked potatoes.
Makes 8 servings. 78 calories, 0 g fat, 459 mg sodium.

Green Beans With Tomatoes

1 tablespoon olive oil
2 onions, finely chopped
2-3 cloves garlic, minced
2 pounds fresh green beans, trimmed (whole or cut into bite-size pieces)
2 cups peeled and chopped tomatoes
1 green bell pepper, thinly sliced
¼-½ cup minced fresh parsley
¼ cup water
½ teaspoon salt, or to taste

Heat oil in a large saucepan. Add onions and garlic; cook and stir until onions are tender. Stir in green beans, tomatoes, bell pepper, parsley, water, and salt. Simmer, covered, for 15 minutes, or until beans are crisp-tender.
Makes 8 servings. 88 calories, 2 g fat, 172 mg sodium.

Lebanese Salad

2 large **Whole-Wheat Pita Bread** (p. 117)
olive oil spray
garlic powder
1 15-ounce can chickpeas, drained and rinsed
2 cups grape or cherry tomatoes, cut in half
2 small cucumbers, peeled, cut in half lengthwise, then sliced
1 medium red bell pepper, finely chopped
6 green onions, thinly sliced
¼ cup minced fresh parsley
½ cup small fresh mint leaves (chopped, if large)
2 tablespoons lemon juice
2 tablespoons olive oil

Heat oven to 300°F. Place pita bread on a baking sheet. Lightly spray both sides of pita bread with oil and sprinkle with garlic powder. Bake 10 minutes, turning bread once, or until it is crisp. Let bread cool. Break into bite-size pieces.

Stir chickpeas, tomatoes, cucumbers, bell pepper, green onions, parsley, and mint leaves together in a salad bowl. Whisk together lemon juice and oil; pour over salad. Stir in bread pieces and mix well. Serve immediately.
Makes 8 servings. 181 calories, 5 g fat, 100 mg sodium.

COOK'S HINTS:

- A combination of red and yellow tomatoes is especially attractive.

Tahini Candy

½ cup sesame tahini
¼ cup pure maple syrup
1 teaspoon vanilla extract
⅓ cup carob powder, sifted
¼ cup unsweetened shredded coconut

Stir tahini, maple syrup, and vanilla together in a small mixing bowl. Stir in sifted carob powder with a fork and mix well. Shape mixture into a 1-inch round log. Roll in coconut (including the ends). Place on a plate or piece of waxed paper. Refrigerate or freeze until firm. Cut into 1-inch pieces. Serve chilled (candy softens quickly at room temperature). Store in a container in the refrigerator or freezer.

Makes about 32 pieces. 42 calories, 3 g fat, 1 mg sodium.

Menu 41

Simply Greek

*The **Honey Greek Cake** has the flavors of more complex, time-consuming Greek desserts such as baklava, but is easier to make. A little goes a long way, so be sure to cut it into small pieces. It is quite elegant when cut into diamond-shaped pieces and served with a hot drink.*

- **Greek Lentil Stew**
- **Vegetarian Gyros**
- **Greek Salad**
- **Honey Greek Cake (*Karithopita*)**

Greek Lentil Stew

2 tablespoons olive oil
1 medium onion, chopped
1 large leek, chopped
4 cloves garlic, minced
6 cups vegetable broth
2 cups small brown lentils
2 cups fresh or frozen corn
3 fresh tomatoes, chopped (about 2 cups)
1 cup sliced carrots
1 teaspoon salt, or to taste
minced fresh parsley, for garnish, optional
fresh lemon wedges, for garnish, optional

Heat oil in a 6-quart saucepan. Add onion, leek, and garlic; cook and stir 3 minutes. Stir in vegetable broth, lentils, corn, tomatoes, carrots, and salt. Heat to boiling; reduce heat and simmer 30 minutes, or until lentils are tender. Garnish with fresh parsley and lemon wedges, if desired. (This allows each person to add lemon juice to their taste.)

Makes 16 1-cup servings. 129 calories, 2 g fat, 158 mg sodium.

COOK'S HINTS:

- You can replace the vegetable broth with powdered vegetable broth and water. Or use leftover vegetable cooking water. Or use 6 cups water and 2-6 tablespoons chicken-style or beef-style seasoning. (The amount of seasoning varies by brand. See the glossary.)

Vegetarian Gyros

- ½ cup finely chopped cucumber, peeled, if desired
- ½ cup nondairy sour cream (such as Tofutti) or **Soy Sour Cream** (p. 66)
- ¼ cup eggless mayonnaise (such as Vegenaise)
- 1 tablespoon lemon juice
- 10-12 cups shredded lettuce
- 1 cup thinly sliced red onion
- 1 cup thinly sliced green bell pepper
- 1 tablespoon olive oil
- 4 cloves garlic, minced
- 1 12-ounce package meatless burger (such as Yves) (about 2 cups)
- 1 teaspoon dried oregano leaves
- ¼ teaspoon dried thyme leaves
- 6 6-inch **Whole-Wheat Pita Bread** (p. 117), cut in half

Mix cucumber, sour cream, mayonnaise, and lemon juice together in a small bowl. Refrigerate. Prepare lettuce, red onion, and bell pepper and place in separate bowls.

Heat oil in a skillet. Add garlic; cook and stir until just beginning to brown. Add meatless burger, oregano, and thyme; cook and stir until heated through. Transfer to a serving bowl.

To serve: Spread the cucumber cream mixture on the inside of each pita bread half. Add about 2½ tablespoons burger mixture. Top with shredded lettuce, sliced red onion, and green bell pepper. Serve immediately.

Makes 12 servings. 177 calories, 6 g fat, 349 mg sodium.

COOK'S HINTS:

- You can also let each person assemble his or her own gyro.

Greek Salad

- ¼ cup lemon juice
- 3 tablespoons olive oil
- 2 tablespoons water
- ½ teaspoon dried oregano leaves
- ½ teaspoon garlic powder
- ¼ teaspoon dried thyme leaves
- 1 16-ounce package extra-firm water-packed tofu, drained, cut into ½-inch cubes
- 3 large tomatoes, chopped
- 1 large English cucumber, cut into ½-inch pieces
- ½ red bell pepper, cut into ½-inch pieces
- ½ yellow bell pepper, cut into ½-inch pieces
- ½ orange bell pepper, cut into ½-inch pieces
- 1 6-ounce can pitted ripe olives, drained

1 medium red onion, sliced into thin rings

Stir lemon juice, oil, water, oregano, garlic, and thyme together in a 1-quart bowl. Mix in tofu. Cover and refrigerate to marinate 2-3 hours, stirring occasionally.

Stir tomatoes, cucumber, bell peppers, olives, and onion together in a salad bowl. Add marinated tofu and stir gently. Refrigerate 30 minutes before serving. Serve with a slotted spoon to remove excess liquid.

Makes 10 servings. 147 calories, 10 g fat, 308 mg sodium.

COOK'S HINTS:

- Replace tofu with herbed tofu for additional flavor.

Honey Greek Cake *(Karithopita)*

- 1¼ cups unbleached all-purpose flour
- ½ cup granulated cane sugar
- 1 teaspoon baking powder (preferably aluminum-free)
- 1 teaspoon ground cinnamon or substitute
- ½ teaspoon salt
- ¼ teaspoon ground cloves
- ¾ cup soy milk
- ¼ cup olive oil
- 1½ teaspoons egg replacement powder (such as Ener-G) dissolved in 2 tablespoons water
- cooking spray
- 3 tablespoons granulated cane sugar
- 3 tablespoons honey
- 3 tablespoons water
- 1 teaspoon lemon juice
- 2 tablespoons ground pistachios or walnuts, for garnish

Heat oven to 350°F. Mix flour, sugar, baking powder, cinnamon, salt, and cloves together in a mixing bowl. Mix in soy milk, oil, and egg replacement. Pour into a 9-inch square glass baking dish coated with cooking spray. Bake 35-40 minutes, or until a toothpick inserted near the center comes out clean. Let cool in pan for 30 minutes.

Heat sugar, honey, water, and lemon juice to boiling in a saucepan; reduce heat and simmer 5 minutes. Make a diamond-shaped cut in the top of cake. Pour hot syrup over cake. Sprinkle with pistachios. Let stand 2 hours before serving.

Makes 18 servings. 108 calories, 4 g fat, 69 mg sodium.

COOK'S HINTS:

- Cut the cake into diamond-shaped pieces for the traditional Greek style of serving.

Vegetable Lasagna

Menu 42

Buon Appetito

Risotto is a rich, creamy, traditional Italian rice dish. It is one of the most common ways of cooking rice in Italy. Risotto can be the ideal, quick, one-dish meal. The hint of coconut milk really makes this dish stand out. Try substituting other steamed vegetables, such as broccoli or green beans, in place of the asparagus for a completely different dish.

- **Mock Chicken-Asparagus Risotto**
- Spring Salad Mix with **Italian Salad Dressing** and Olives
- Medley of Steamed Baby Carrots, Yellow Beans, and Green Beans
- Whole-Grain Bread with Margarine
- **Blueberry-Peach Crisp** with Nondairy Ice Cream

Mock Chicken-Asparagus Risotto

1 bunch fresh asparagus spears, trimmed
1 tablespoon olive oil
2 cups soy chicken, chopped
2 cups sliced mushrooms
1 tablespoon olive oil
1 medium onion, chopped
3 cups brown rice
8 teaspoons to ½ cup chicken-style seasoning,* or to taste
9 cups water
3 tablespoons minced fresh parsley or 1 tablespoon dried parsley
3 tablespoons coconut milk
⅓ cup **Imitation Parmesan Cheese** (p. 130), or nondairy Parmesan, optional
salt

Cut asparagus in half lengthwise, then in half crosswise; set aside. Heat 1 tablespoon of oil in a 4-quart saucepan over medium-high heat. Add soy chicken and mushrooms; cook and stir until soy chicken is lightly browned and mushrooms are tender. Remove from the pan; set aside. Add 1 tablespoon oil to the saucepan. Add onion; cook and stir 2 minutes. Add rice; cook 2 minutes, stirring constantly. Stir chicken-style seasoning into water to make broth. Stir 2 cups of broth into rice. When the rice absorbs the broth, stir in 2 more cups of broth. Repeat with remaining broth, about every 5 minutes. Continue to cook about 30 minutes, or until rice is tender. Add remaining 1 cup broth if needed. Stir in asparagus, soy chicken, and mushrooms. Cover and cook 5 minutes. Stir in parsley, coconut milk, and Imitation Parmesan Cheese, if desired. Season to taste with salt.

Makes 14 1-cup servings. 236 calories, 3 g fat, 188 mg sodium.

COOK'S HINTS:

- I like to use thin asparagus spears in this dish.

*see glossary

Italian Salad Dressing

- ½ cup extra-virgin olive oil
- ⅓ cup water
- ¼ cup lemon juice
- 1 tablespoon minced fresh parsley or 1 teaspoon dried
- 2 teaspoons granulated cane sugar
- 1 teaspoon garlic salt
- ¾ teaspoon minced fresh basil or ¼ teaspoon dried
- ¾ teaspoon minced fresh oregano or ¼ teaspoon dried leaves
- ¾ teaspoon minced fresh thyme or ¼ teaspoon dried leaves
- ½ teaspoon onion powder

Process all ingredients in a blender or food processor until smooth. Refrigerate in a covered container at least 1 hour before serving.

Makes 1¼ cups; 20 1-tablespoon servings. 51 calories, 5 g fat, 103 mg sodium.

Blueberry-Peach Crisp

- 4 medium peaches, pitted, peeled, and sliced (or 2 cups sliced frozen peaches, thawed)
- 1½ cups fresh or frozen blueberries or Saskatoon berries
- 1 tablespoon lemon juice
- 2 tablespoons cornstarch
- 1 teaspoon ground cinnamon or substitute
- ½ cup quick-cooking oats
- ⅓ cup unbleached all-purpose or spelt or whole-wheat pastry flour
- ¼ cup nonhydrogenated margarine (such as Earth Balance), softened
- 2 tablespoons brown sugar
- ½ teaspoon ground cinnamon or substitute

Heat oven to 375°F. Mix peaches, blueberries, and lemon juice together in a mixing bowl. Mix cornstarch and cinnamon together and stir into peach and blueberry mixture. Transfer to a 9-inch square baking dish. Stir oats, flour, margarine, brown sugar, and cinnamon together until crumbly. Spoon topping evenly over fruit mixture. Bake 30 minutes, or until fruit is bubbling and topping is lightly browned.

Makes 9 servings. 139 calories, 5 g fat, 72 mg sodium.

Menu 43

That's Amore

Caesar salad has always been a favorite of mine, but unfortunately it contained ingredients I chose not to eat. My sister Diana (Clarke), introduced me to the idea of using Vegenaise salad dressing as a base that has become my absolute favorite! Through trial and error I came up with three different recipes. I couldn't choose which one to include in this cookbook, because each is unique in its own way. Depending on what's in your refrigerator, you can choose what works best for you at any given time.

- **Vegetable Lasagna**
- Steamed Broccoli
- Petite Peas
- **Caesar Salad** with **Croutons**
- Assorted Olives
- **French Bread** with **Garlic Toast Spread**
- **Lemon-Pecan Cake**
- Grape Juice

Vegetable Lasagna

- 10 whole-grain lasagna noodles
- 2 tablespoons olive oil or water
- 1 large onion, chopped
- 1 large carrot, finely chopped
- 1 medium zucchini, finely chopped
- 2 cups sliced mushrooms
- 1 12-ounce package Italian-flavored or plain firm tofu, drained
- 1 28-ounce can diced tomatoes
- 1 28-ounce can tomato puree

2 teaspoons Italian seasoning
2 teaspoons garlic powder
1 teaspoon dried basil, crushed
½ teaspoon salt, or to taste
cooking spray
shredded nondairy cheese, optional
minced fresh parsley, optional

Heat oven to 375°F. Cook lasagna noodles according to package directions. Drain in a colander, and rinse with cold water to prevent sticking together; set aside. Heat oil or water in a large skillet or saucepan. Add onion, carrot, zucchini, and mushrooms; cook and stir until onion is tender. Crumble tofu and stir into vegetable mixture. Stir in tomatoes, tomato puree, Italian seasoning, garlic powder, basil, and salt. Simmer for 20-30 minutes. Place a layer of five lasagna noodles, slightly overlapping, to cover the bottom of a 9"x13" glass baking dish coated with cooking spray. Pour half of the tomato sauce over noodles. Repeat layers with remaining noodles and tomato sauce. Sprinkle with nondairy cheese, if desired. Bake uncovered 30 minutes. Let stand about 10 minutes before cutting. Garnish with fresh parsley, if desired.

Makes 12 servings. 192 calories, 3 g fat, 271 mg sodium.

- Brown rice lasagna noodles work well in this recipe.
- If you use plain tofu, you may wish to add ½-1 teaspoon dried oregano leaves.
- For firmer lasagna, prebake the lasagna for 20 minutes the day before serving. Cool to room temperature. Cover and refrigerate. Bake 20 minutes, or until heated through.

*see glossary

Caesar Salad

Caesar Salad Dressing 1, **2**, or **3**
2 cups **Croutons**
1 large head romaine lettuce, chopped
½ small red onion, cut into thin rings
1 tablespoon imitation bacon bits

Prepare Caesar Salad Dressing of choice. Prepare Croutons. Mix romaine, Croutons, red onion, and imitation bacon bits together in a salad bowl. Pour Caesar Salad Dressing over salad and toss well. Serve immediately.

Makes 8 servings. 84 calories, 6 g fat, 132 mg sodium (analysis does not include salad dressing).

COOK'S HINTS:

- For a more traditional Caesar salad, omit the red onion and imitation bacon bits.

Caesar Salad Dressing 1

1 cup eggless mayonnaise (such as Vegenaise)
2 tablespoons nutritional yeast flakes
2 tablespoons sesame seeds
3 cloves garlic, peeled
2 teaspoons lemon juice
¼ teaspoon onion powder
⅛-½ teaspoon chicken-style seasoning,* or to taste
¼ cup soy milk, as needed

Process mayonnaise, nutritional yeast, sesame seeds, garlic, lemon juice, onion powder, and chicken-style seasoning in a blender or food processor until smooth. While processing, gradually drizzle in soy milk until a pourable consistency is reached. Refrigerate.

Makes 8 servings. 115 calories, 10 g fat, 235 mg sodium.

Caesar Salad Dressing 2

1 cup soy milk
2 tablespoons lemon juice
½ teaspoon onion powder
¾ teaspoon salt
¼ cup grape-seed or canola oil
1 tablespoon powdered precooked cornstarch powder
¼ cup **Imitation Parmesan Cheese** or nondairy Parmesan cheese
2 cloves garlic, peeled

Process soy milk, lemon juice, onion powder, and salt in a blender or food processor. While processing, drizzle in oil. Add precooked cornstarch powder, Imitation Parmesan Cheese, and garlic and process until smooth. Refrigerate.
Makes 8 servings. 94 calories, 8 g fat, 235 mg sodium.

Caesar Salad Dressing 3

⅔ cup raw cashews
⅔ cup water
2-3 tablespoons lemon juice
1½ tablespoons sesame tahini
1-2 cloves garlic, peeled
½ teaspoon onion powder
½ teaspoon salt

Process cashews, water, lemon juice, tahini, garlic, onion powder, and salt in a blender or food processor until smooth. Add more water if a thinner dressing is desired. Refrigerate.
Makes 8 servings. 127 calories, 10 g fat, 148 mg sodium.

Imitation Parmesan Cheese

½ cup sesame seeds
½ cup nutritional yeast flakes
2 teaspoons garlic powder
1 teaspoon onion powder
¾-2 teaspoons chicken-style seasoning,* or to taste
1 tablespoon lemon juice

Process sesame seeds in a food processor or blender until finely ground. Add nutritional yeast, garlic powder, onion powder, and chicken-style seasoning; process until finely ground and well mixed. While processing, drizzle in lemon juice; process until well mixed. Refrigerate up to 4 weeks in an airtight container. Freezes well.
Makes 1 cup; 16 1-tablespoon servings. 28 calories, 2 g fat, 11 mg sodium.

COOK'S HINTS:

- This does not melt like the real thing, but it tastes pretty close if combined in a sauce or added to a recipe.
- Since this cheese browns easily, add during the last few minutes of baking.

Croutons

4 slices whole-grain bread, cut into ½-inch cubes
⅓ cup olive oil
2 teaspoons garlic powder
½ teaspoon onion powder
½ teaspoon dried oregano leaves
1 teaspoon herb seasoned salt (such as Spike)

Heat oven to 450°F. Place bread cubes in a mixing bowl. Stir oil, garlic powder, onion powder, oregano, and herb-seasoned salt together with a fork. Drizzle over bread cubes and toss well to distribute seasonings. Spread out in a single layer on a baking sheet. Bake about 4 minutes, stirring every 2 minutes, or until the bread cubes are evenly browned. Let cool. Store in an airtight container. (Do not seal container until croutons have cooled and they are thoroughly dried out.)
Makes 4 cups; 16 ¼-cup servings. 58 calories, 5 g fat, 110 mg sodium.

*see glossary

French Bread

2½ cups lukewarm water
1 teaspoon granulated cane sugar
1 tablespoon active dry yeast
3 cups whole-wheat flour
¼ cup soy milk powder
1 tablespoon salt
2½ cups unbleached all-purpose flour (or 1½ cups all-purpose flour and 1 cup spelt flour)
cooking spray
cornmeal, for dusting bottom of loaf

Stir water and sugar together in a mixing bowl. Sprinkle with yeast and let stand 10 minutes. Using an electric mixer, gradually beat in whole-wheat flour, milk powder, and salt. Beat about 3 minutes or until smooth. Using a dough hook or spoon, gradually mix in enough of the remaining flour to make a stiff dough. Knead dough until smooth and elastic, about 10 minutes by hand or about 5 minutes with a dough hook. Place dough in a bowl coated with cooking spray and turn dough over to grease top. Cover with a towel.

Let rise 1½ hours, or until dough is tripled in size. Punch dough down; cover, and let rise 1 hour, or until doubled in size. Punch dough down. Divide in half and form each half into a 12-inch loaf. Dust the bottom of each loaf with cornmeal. Place each loaf on a baking sheet coated with cooking spray. Using a serrated knife, cut three ½-inch-deep diagonal slashes along the top of each loaf. Cover loaves with a dish towel and let rise one hour, or until doubled in size.

Heat oven to 425°F. Place a metal cake pan or pie plate on the bottom rack in the oven. Pour 1 cup water into the pan just before baking. Bake 20-25 minutes, or until golden brown. Repeat with remaining loaf, replenishing the 1 cup of water in the baking dish before baking the second loaf.

Makes 2 loaves; 40 ½-inch slices. 63 calories, 0 g fat, 178 mg sodium.

Garlic Toast Spread

1 loaf whole-grain **French Bread**
⅓ cup olive oil
1½ teaspoons garlic powder, or to taste
½ teaspoon herb seasoned salt (such as Spike)
1 tablespoon minced fresh parsley or 1 teaspoon dried

Heat oven to 350°F. Slice bread diagonally into ½-inch thick slices. Whisk oil, garlic powder, herb-seasoned salt, and parsley together in a small bowl. Brush oil mixture evenly over each slice of bread with a pastry brush. Wrap bread in foil and bake about 20 minutes, or until heated through. (Or place bread on a baking sheet and bake about 10 minutes, or until lightly browned, but not dried out.)

Makes 20 servings. 97 calories, 4 g fat, 207 mg sodium.

Lemon-Pecan Cake

¼ cup pure maple syrup
Cooking spray
½ cup chopped pecans
¼ cup granulated cane or brown sugar
1 tablespoon finely grated lemon peel
1 cup raw cashews
1 cup water
½ cup honey
1 tablespoon lemon juice
2 teaspoons egg replacement powder (such as Ener-G)
¼ teaspoon salt
1 cup unbleached all-purpose flour
2 teaspoons baking powder (preferably aluminum-free)

Heat oven to 350°F. Pour maple syrup into the bottom of a 9-inch round cake pan coated with cooking spray. Mix pecans, sugar, and lemon peel together in a small bowl; sprinkle over maple syrup.

Process cashews, water, honey, lemon juice, egg replacement powder, and salt in a blender or food processor until smooth. Pour into a mixing bowl. Mix in flour and baking powder. Spoon batter on top of pecan mixture. Bake 30 minutes, or until lightly browned on top. Let cake stand 5 minutes. Gently turn cake out of pan onto a plate and let cool.

Makes 9 servings. 340 calories, 16 g fat, 71 mg sodium.

Menu 44

Vegan Dinner in Italy

*The **Almond-Cream Fruit Squares** recipe is one of my favorites. My friend Pam Vanpetten shared it with me one year when our families spent Christmas together. We added raspberries for a festive look. Seasonal fruits can be substituted for an attractive change.*

- **Eggplant "Parmesan"**
- Angel Hair Pasta with Almond Cheese and **Homemade Spaghetti Sauce**
- Steamed Asparagus
- **Mandarin Romaine Salad**
- **Herbed Focaccia**
- **Almond Cream Fruit Squares**

Eggplant "Parmesan"

2 cups dry unseasoned whole-wheat bread crumbs
2 tablespoons nutritional yeast flakes
2 tablespoons **Imitation Parmesan Cheese** (p. 130)
1 tablespoon dried parsley
1 teaspoon salt
1 teaspoon garlic powder
1 teaspoon onion powder
1 cup soy milk, as needed
1 medium or large eggplant, sliced into ¼-inch thick rounds
olive oil, for frying, as needed
3 cups Italian-seasoned tomato sauce
1 cup shredded nondairy cheese, optional

Stir bread crumbs, nutritional yeast, **Imitation Parmesan Cheese**, parsley, salt, garlic powder, and onion powder together in a bowl. Stir in soy milk as needed to make a thick paste. Dip eggplant slices in breading mixture, coating both sides and along edges. Heat oil in a large skillet. Add breaded eggplant and fry until lightly browned on both sides.

Adjust oven rack to top position. Heat oven to broil. Place fried eggplant, slightly overlapping, in a large baking dish. Spoon tomato sauce over center of each slice. Sprinkle with nondairy cheese, if desired. Broil about 3 minutes, or until hot and cheese is melted.

Makes 8 servings. 213 calories, 6 g fat, 987 mg sodium.

COOK'S HINTS:

- To decrease the amount of sodium, choose an unsalted tomato sauce and/or reduce the salt by half.

Almond Cheese

1 cup water
2 tablespoons agar powder
1 cup slivered almonds
¼ cup chopped red bell pepper
2 tablespoons nutritional yeast flakes
1½ tablespoons lemon juice
1 teaspoon salt
1 teaspoon onion powder
½ teaspoon garlic powder
cooking spray

Heat water to almost boiling. Stir in agar. Process almonds in a blender or food processor until finely ground. Add agar mixture, bell pepper, nutritional yeast, lemon juice, salt, onion powder, and garlic powder; process until smooth. Pour into a small mold or container coated with cooking spray. Cover and refrigerate 2-3 hours, or until firm.

Makes 2¼ cups; 36 1-tablespoon servings. 28 calories, 2 g fat, 57 mg sodium.

COOK'S HINTS:

- Increase the amount of agar for a firmer cheese.
- This will melt when spread on hot toast or bagels.
- Freezes well. It can usually shred when frozen.

Homemade Spaghetti Sauce

- 2 tablespoons olive oil
- 1 medium onion, chopped
- 2 cups ground **Homemade Gluten** (p. 32) or meatless burger
- 1 cup sliced fresh mushrooms
- 2 cloves garlic, minced
- 4 cups chopped fresh tomatoes or 1 32-ounce can diced tomatoes
- 1 8-ounce can tomato sauce (about 1 cup)
- 1 6-ounce can tomato paste
- 1 tablespoon dried parsley
- ½ teaspoon salt, or to taste
- ½ green bell pepper, chopped, optional

Heat oil in a large saucepan. Add onion, ground Homemade Gluten, mushrooms, and garlic; cook and stir until onion is tender and slightly browned. Stir in tomatoes, tomato sauce, tomato paste, parsley, salt, and bell pepper, if desired. Simmer for about 10 minutes. Serve hot over pasta.

Makes about 10 cups; 20 ½-cup servings. 84 calories, 3 g fat, 284 mg sodium.

COOK'S HINTS:

- For plain **Spaghetti Sauce**, omit the gluten.

Mandarin Romaine Salad

- 1 large head romaine lettuce, chopped
- 3 green onions, chopped
- ¼ cup olive oil
- 3 tablespoons lemon juice
- 2 teaspoons honey
- ¼ teaspoon salt
- 1 tablespoon minced fresh parsley or 1 teaspoon dried parsley
- 1 8-ounce can mandarin orange sections, drained
- ½ cup slivered almonds, lightly toasted

Mix lettuce and green onions together in a large salad bowl. Stir oil, lemon juice, honey, salt, and parsley together and pour over salad. Toss well. Sprinkle oranges and almonds on top. Mix slightly, keeping most of the oranges and almonds on top of the salad.

Makes 8 servings. 146 calories, 12 g fat, 85 mg sodium.

Herbed Focaccia

1½ cups whole-wheat flour
1¼ cups unbleached all-purpose flour
1 tablespoon active dry yeast
1 teaspoon salt
1 teaspoon granulated cane sugar
1 teaspoon garlic powder
1 teaspoon dried oregano leaves
1 teaspoon dried thyme leaves
½ teaspoon dried basil
1 tablespoon olive oil
1 cup warm water
olive oil, for coating bowl
cooking spray
2 tablespoons olive oil, optional
1 tablespoon **Imitation Parmesan Cheese** (p. 130), optional

Mix whole-wheat flour, all-purpose flour, yeast, salt, sugar, garlic powder, oregano, thyme, and basil together in a large bowl. Mix in oil and water. Knead 5-10 minutes, or until dough is smooth and elastic. Lightly coat a large bowl with oil. Place the dough in the bowl and turn, to coat with oil. Cover with a damp cloth, and let rise in a warm place for 20 minutes. Heat oven to 450°F. Punch dough down and transfer to a pizza pan coated with cooking spray. Pat dough into a ½-inch thick round or rectangular shape. Bake 15 minutes, or until golden brown. Brush with oil and sprinkle with **Imitation Parmesan Cheese**, if desired. Serve warm.

Makes 8 servings. 171 calories, 2 g fat, 294 mg sodium.

Almond Cream Fruit Squares

Crust:

2 cups unbleached all-purpose flour
¾ cup nonhydrogenated margarine (such as Earth Balance), softened
½ cup brown sugar

Almond Cream Filling:

2 cups water
1 cup granulated cane sugar
½ cup blanched almonds
¼ cup cornstarch
¼ cup lemon juice
3 tablespoons mild-flavored olive oil
1 teaspoon salt
1 teaspoon almond extract

Fruit Topping:

1 28-ounce can sliced peaches in fruit juice
1 cup raspberries, fresh or frozen
3 tablespoons cornstarch
2 tablespoons granulated cane sugar

Crumb Topping:

¾ cup all-purpose flour
½ cup brown sugar
¼ cup nonhydrogenated margarine (such as Earth Balance), softened
¾ cup sliced almonds

Crust: Heat oven to 375°F. Mix flour, margarine, and brown sugar together with a fork. Press into the bottom of a 9"x13" baking dish. Bake 5 minutes, or until edges just begin to turn golden brown.

Almond Cream: Process water, sugar, almonds, cornstarch, lemon juice, oil, salt, and almond extract in a blender or food processor until smooth. Pour mixture into a saucepan over medium heat; cook, stirring constantly, until thick and bubbling. Remove from heat; spread filling evenly over crust.

Fruit Topping: Stir peaches, raspberries, cornstarch, and sugar together in a saucepan over medium heat; cook, stirring constantly, until thickened. Remove from heat and spread over almond cream.

Crumb Topping: Mix flour, brown sugar, and margarine together until it resembles coarse crumbs. Stir in sliced almonds. Sprinkle crumb topping over fruit topping. Bake 25-35 minutes, or until edges are golden brown. Cool to room temperature. Refrigerate 2-3 hours, or until set. Cut into squares.

Makes 16 servings. 328 calories, 19 g fat, 327 mg sodium.

How to Eat Spaghetti

Many non-Italians don't know how to eat spaghetti. Here are a few very simple Italian table manners to follow when eating a dish of spaghetti:

1. As a general rule, keep your hands on the table throughout the meal (but no elbows). Wait for everyone to be served before starting to eat.
2. Spaghetti is best eaten from a *piatto fondo*, a shallow soup bowl with a rim. Make room at the front of the bowl by pushing the spaghetti a little toward the center. Take a little bunch of the spaghetti with the prongs of the fork. Push it against the front side. Working with the fork in a vertical position and the prongs against the rim of the bowl, twirl the fork clockwise with your fingers to roll the spaghetti around your fork. Raise the fork with the spaghetti wrapped around it above the bowl, and measure the length with your eyes. The most common mistake is to overload the fork with pasta. If you decide you picked up too much (or the spaghetti is too long), drop it and pick up a smaller amount. Roll it again until you form a precise bundle, just the right size to go into your mouth.
3. Spaghetti should be eaten with a fork only. Don't use the spoon to help you wrap the spaghetti around the fork. It is considered bad form.
4. Never cut the threads of pasta with a knife or a fork. Spaghetti is sold in the right length, about 10 inches long, and that is just the right size.
5. Don't slurp. Make absolutely no sounds of any kind.
6. Don't splatter. Spaghetti can sometimes splatter the sauce, so be careful, but do not wear a napkin as a bib unless you are a small child.
7. Avoid serving spaghetti for large or formal parties. Short pasta shapes, such as rigatoni and penne, make it easier to serve and to eat.
8. A delicious pasta sauce may tempt you to eat every drop by wiping the plate with a piece of bread. If you are in an informal setting, compliment the cook and ask your guests for permission to do this. They will most likely all agree with you with big smiles. The Italian term for this is *scarpetta*, meaning "little shoe." However, it is not proper to do this at a formal dinner.

Menu 45

Pastabilities

If you ask for pasta alfredo in a restaurant in Italy, all you will get from your waiter is a stare. In Italy, pasta alfredo does not exist. Italians make a dish of fettuccine pasta dressed with nothing else than aged Parmigiano cheese and a lot of butter, but it is such a simple preparation to them that Italians don't even consider it a recipe.

- Fettucine with **Alfredo Sauce**
- Steamed Broccoli
- Green Salad with **Avocado Dressing**
- **Cornmeal Breadsticks With Garlic Oil Topping**
- **Carob-Mint Tofu Cheesecake**

Alfredo Sauce

2 cups water
1 cup raw cashews
2 tablespoons unbleached all-purpose flour
2 tablespoons nutritional yeast flakes
2 large cloves garlic, peeled
1 teaspoon salt
1 tablespoon nonhydrogenated margarine (such as Earth Balance)
minced fresh parsley or dried, optional

Process water, cashews, flour, nutritional yeast, garlic, and salt in a blender or food processor until smooth. Melt margarine in a saucepan over medium-high heat. Stir in cashew mixture. Heat to boiling, stirring frequently; reduce heat and simmer 2-3 minutes, or until sauce is thickened. Garnish with parsley, if desired. Serve with cooked fettuccine or pasta of choice.

Makes about 3¼ cups; 13 ¼ cup servings.
112 calories, 8 g fat, 196 mg sodium.

COOK'S HINTS:

- For **Fettuccine Alfredo**: Serve **Alfredo Sauce** over cooked fettuccine (preferably whole-grain). Brown rice pasta is often a favorite, but be careful not to overcook it. It can be substituted for white pasta, and your dinner guests won't know the difference.

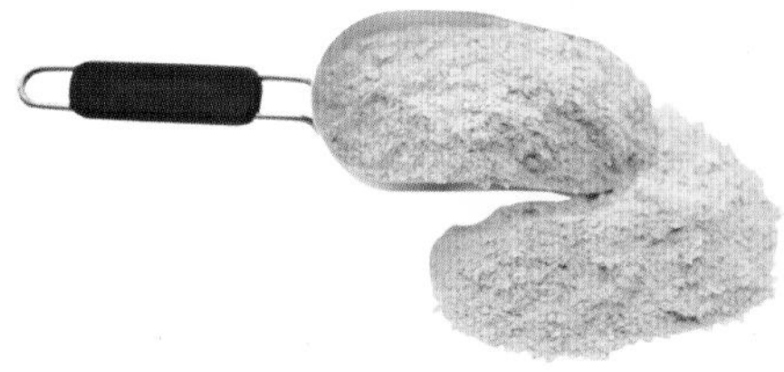

Avocado Dressing

1 ripe avocado, peeled and pitted
⅓ cup water
¼ cup lemon juice
3 tablespoons chopped red onion
½ teaspoon salt
2 tablespoons olive oil

Process avocado, water, lemon juice, onion, and salt in a food processor or blender until smooth. While processing, drizzle in oil. Refrigerate up to 3-4 days in an airtight container.

Makes 1¼ cups; 20 1-tablespoon servings;
28 calories, 3 g fat, 59 mg sodium.

COOK'S HINTS:

- Place an avocado pit in the dressing to help prevent it from turning brown. Remove the pit before serving.
- Serving Idea: Cover a large platter with butter or Bibb lettuce. Next, arrange a layer of sliced tomatoes, and top with red onion rings. Pour **Avocado Dressing** over salad. Garnish with pitted ripe olives.

Cornmeal Bread-sticks With Garlic Oil Topping

- 4 cups water
- 1 cup cornmeal (preferably whole-grain)
- 2 teaspoons salt
- ¾ cup olive oil
- ½ cup honey
- 1 cup warm water
- 1 teaspoon honey
- 2 tablespoons active dry yeast
- 5 cups whole-wheat flour
- 5 cups spelt or unbleached all-purpose flour, or as needed

Garlic Oil Topping:

- ¼ cup olive oil
- 1½ teaspoons garlic powder, or to taste
- ½ teaspoon herb seasoned salt (such as Spike)

Heat 4 cups water to boiling in a large saucepan. Stir in cornmeal and salt; reduce heat and simmer, stirring frequently, 5-7 minutes, or until thickened. Remove from heat. Stir in oil and ½ cup honey; allow to cool to room temperature. Stir 1 cup warm water and 1 teaspoon honey together in a small bowl. Stir in yeast; let stand until yeast bubbles. Stir yeast mixture into cooked cornmeal. Mix in whole-wheat flour. Add spelt flour 1 cup at a time, kneading in until dough is no longer sticky. Place dough in a warm place and cover with a towel. Let rise about 1 hour.

Roll 1 piece of dough (about ½ cup) into a ball, then roll between hands to form into a 6-inch-long breadstick about ½ inch in diameter. Place on a baking sheet coated with cooking spray. Repeat with remaining dough. Heat oven to 400°F. Let breadsticks rise 20 minutes. Bake 15 minutes, or until golden brown.

Garlic Oil Topping: Whisk oil, garlic powder, and seasoned salt together in a small bowl. With a pastry brush, brush the garlic oil topping on the tops of hot breadsticks (or just before serving).

Makes 6 dozen breadsticks. 90 calories, 2 g fat, 66 mg sodium.

COOK'S HINTS:

- This recipe can easily be cut in half.
- For **Cornmeal Buns**: Roll dough out to ½-inch-thick on a lightly floured surface. Cut dough with a round cutter (or shape into buns). Let rise about 20 minutes, or until doubled in size. Bake at 400°F for 20 minutes, or until golden brown. Makes 6 dozen buns.

Carob-Mint Tofu Cheesecake

Crust:

- 1½ cups graham cracker crumbs
- 2 tablespoons carob powder
- 1 tablespoon unbleached all-purpose flour
- ⅓ cup grape-seed or canola oil
- ⅓ cup pure maple syrup
- cooking spray

Filling:

- ½ cup boiling water
- 2 tablespoons agar powder
- 1 12-ounce package firm silken tofu, preferably reduced-fat
- 1 8-ounce package nondairy cream cheese (such as Tofutti)
- ½ cup honey
- 1 tablespoon lemon juice
- 1 teaspoon peppermint extract

Topping:

- 1 cup water
- ¼ cup granulated cane sugar
- 2 tablespoons carob powder
- 2 tablespoons cornstarch
- 1 teaspoon vanilla extract
- ½ teaspoon peppermint extract
- mint leaves for garnish, optional

Crust: Heat oven to 350°F. Mix graham cracker crumbs, carob powder, and flour together in a mixing bowl. Stir in oil and maple syrup with a fork. Press into a 9-inch springform pan coated with cooking spray. Bake 10 minutes. Remove from oven and cool on a wire rack.

Filling: Process boiling water and agar in a blender or food processor 15 seconds. Add tofu, cream cheese, honey, lemon juice, and peppermint extract; process until very smooth. Spread mixture over the cooled graham cracker crust. Refrigerate 2-3 hours, or until firm.

Topping: Stir water, sugar, carob powder, cornstarch, vanilla, and peppermint together in a small saucepan. Cook, stirring constantly, over medium-high heat, until slightly thickened. Remove from heat and spread evenly over the cheesecake. Refrigerate 2-3 hours, or until set. Place cheesecake on a serving platter. Remove the sides of the springform pan. Cut cake into 12 wedges. Garnish with fresh mint leaves, if desired.
Makes 12 servings. 249 calories, 11 g fat, 145 mg sodium.

Menu 46

Lunch in Florence

The artichoke is a perennial in the thistle group of the sunflower family and is believed to be a native of the Mediterranean and the Canary Islands. What we eat as a vegetable is the plant's flower bud. Baby artichokes are smaller versions of larger artichokes that grow on the lower parts of the artichoke plant, where fronds protect them from the sun, in effect stunting their growth. Artichokes are available year-round with the peak seasons in the spring and fall. There are more than 140 artichoke varieties, but less than 40 are grown commercially. Most artichokes grown worldwide are cultivated in France, Italy, and Spain. California provides nearly all of the artichokes eaten in the United States.

- **Minestrone Soup**
- **Artichoke Salad**
- **Potato Focaccia**
- **Carob Potato Cake**
- **Polenta** or **Polenta Pasticciata**

*see glossary

Minestrone Soup

10 cups water
1 28-ounce can diced tomatoes
2 cups cooked navy or kidney beans
1 medium onion, chopped
1 cup chopped potatoes
2 carrots, chopped
¾ cup chopped celery
1 cup peas
1 cup cut green beans
1 cup shredded cabbage
2-6 tablespoons beef-style seasoning,* or to taste
2 teaspoons salt, or to taste
1½ teaspoons dried basil
1 teaspoon dried parsley
1 clove garlic, minced
1 bay leaf
1 cup pasta (elbows or small shells)

Heat water, tomatoes, navy beans, onion, potatoes, carrots, celery, peas, green beans, cabbage, beef-style seasoning, salt, basil, parsley, garlic, and bay leaf to boiling in an 8- or 9-quart stockpot; reduce heat and simmer for 20 minutes. Stir in pasta and simmer 20 minutes, or until pasta is tender. Remove bay leaf.
Makes 24 1-cup servings. 60 calories, 0 g fat, 277 mg sodium.

Artichoke Salad

1 13-ounce package multicolored rotini pasta (about 4 cups)
1 cup nondairy sour cream (such as Tofutti) or **Tofu Sour Cream** (p. 67)
3 tablespoons lemon juice
1 teaspoon Italian seasoning
1 teaspoon dried basil
½ red bell pepper, chopped
1 14-ounce can water-packed artichoke hearts, cut into fourths
1 6-ounce can pitted ripe olives, drained and sliced
¼ cup minced red onion
2 cups broccoli florets, optional
5-8 lettuce leaves, as desired, for garnish

Cook pasta according to package directions. Drain; rinse with cold water. Refrigerate until chilled. Stir nondairy sour cream, lemon juice, Italian seasoning, and basil together in a medium bowl. Mix in bell pepper, artichoke hearts, olives, onion, and broccoli, if desired. Stir in cooked pasta. Line a salad bowl with lettuce leaves standing up around the edges. Transfer salad to the bowl. Serve immediately.

Makes 10 servings. 212 calories, 6 g fat, 250 mg sodium.

Potato Focaccia

1 small potato, peeled and cubed
½ cup warm water
1 teaspoon honey
1 tablespoon dry active yeast
4 cups spelt flour, or a combination of whole-wheat flour and unbleached all-purpose flour
1½ cups whole-wheat flour
1 teaspoon salt
cooking spray

Optional Toppings:

sliced ripe olives, sun-dried tomatoes, sliced cherry tomatoes, minced fresh garlic, minced fresh onion, **Imitation Parmesan Cheese** (p. 130)
mMinced fresh or dried herbs, such as oregano, basil, or rosemary
½ teaspoon salt or herb-seasoned salt (such as Spike)
olive oil, for topping
2 tablespoons olive oil, for dipping

Cook potato in water until tender; drain, reserving liquid. Mash potato and set aside. Place warm water and honey in a mixing bowl; stir until honey dissolves. Sprinkle in yeast. Let stand 10 minutes. Mix in spelt flour, whole-wheat flour, mashed potatoes, and salt. Gradually mix in about ½ cup reserved potato water (or more) until mixture forms a slightly sticky ball of dough. Place in a bowl coated with cooking spray and cover with a clean towel. Let rise 45 minutes, or until doubled in size. Punch dough down and form into a round ball. Flatten into a 12-inch circle, about 1 inch thick, on a pizza pan coated with cooking spray. Press choice of toppings gently into the dough. Sprinkle with salt, if desired. Drizzle with oil over the top. Let rise in a warm place 20 minutes. Heat oven to 375°F. Bake 20 minutes, or until golden brown. Cut into wedges. Serve warm with oil in small bowls for dipping, if desired.

Makes 10 servings. 242 calories, 2 g fat, 238 mg sodium.

Carob Potato Cake

1 cup mashed potatoes
1 cup brown sugar
¾ cup soy milk
¼ cup nonhydrogenated margarine (such as Earth Balance), softened
1½ tablespoons egg replacement powder (such as Ener-G) dissolved in ¼ cup water
1 tablespoon lemon juice
1 teaspoon vanilla extract
2 cups unbleached all-purpose flour
¼ cup carob powder
1 teaspoon baking powder (preferably aluminum-free)
1 teaspoon baking soda
cooking spray

Carob Frosting:

⅓ cup carob chips, melted
2¼ cups confectioners' sugar
⅓ cup mashed potatoes
1 teaspoon vanilla extract
shredded coconut, for garnish, optional

Heat oven to 350°F. Place mashed potatoes, brown sugar, soy milk, margarine, egg replacement, lemon juice, and vanilla in a medium mixing bowl. Beat with an electric mixer on medium speed 1-2 minutes, until smooth and fluffy. Add flour, carob powder, baking powder, and baking soda; beat on low speed 30 seconds, scraping bowl frequently. Increase speed to medium-high and beat until all ingredients are combined. Scrape batter into a 9"x13" baking pan coated with cooking spray. Bake 40 minutes, or until a toothpick inserted near the center comes out clean. Let cool on a wire rack to room temperature.

Carob Frosting: Melt carob chips over low heat (or in a double boiler). Transfer to a food processor. Add confectioners' sugar, mashed potatoes, and vanilla. Process until very smooth. Spread over cooled cake. Sprinkle with coconut, if desired. Makes 16 servings. 123 calories, 4 g fat, 131 mg sodium.

Polenta

7 cups water
2 teaspoons salt
2¼ cups polenta (coarsely ground cornmeal)

Heat water and salt to boiling in a large saucepan. Gradually mix in the polenta while whisking constantly to prevent lumping; reduce heat to low and simmer, covered, 30 minutes, stirring frequently (about every 5 minutes) until polenta becomes thick and soft. (The polenta is ready when it resists the spoon and starts pulling away from the sides of the pan.) While the polenta is still hot, transfer directly to serving dishes or pour onto a lightly oiled wooden board. When the polenta is cold, it can be easily sliced with a string or knife.

COOK'S HINTS:

- Look for polenta in the natural food section of supermarkets, in natural food stores, or in specialty stores.
- The absorption of water depends on the quality of the cornmeal. If the polenta becomes too hard and doesn't pull away from the sides of the pan, add some warm water to adjust the consistency, until it is like a dense paste.
- Polenta is an extremely versatile dish that can be fried, grilled, baked, or eaten on its own topped with tomato sauce.

About Polenta: A Northern Italian Staple

Corn was introduced to Italy in 1494 by a Venetian diplomat who received a few seeds as a present, soon after Columbus's return from his travels to the Indies.

Because corn could produce a large yield gradually, corn cultivation developed over the Veneto area. Soon polenta made from corn replaced all other grains, mainly sorghum and millet. It became the staple of peasants too poor to afford bread, especially in the mountains and valleys of the Alps. For a long time corn was considered a food of inferior quality because of this.

Corn (maize) was also a very convenient crop for the owners of large estates to feed their workers economically. Consequently, in large areas of northern Italy corn polenta became a unique staple. But this led to disastrous consequences, because maize does not contain niacin, an indispensable vitamin for the body. The resulting niacin deficiency caused pellagra, a fatal disease. This illness was unknown to the populations of the Americas, who ate corn with other food, therefore integrating the missing niacin. In northern Italy the phenomenon reached epidemic proportions. After a few decades and thousands of fatalities, the cause was finally understood at the beginning of the 1800s. Adding vegetables to the diet was the easy cure.

Polenta is generally used in northern Italy as a substitute for bread. It is unmolded from the saucepan directly onto a wooden board in the shape of a semicircle; then, when cold, it is sliced with a string. In central Italy it is mostly used as a first course by itself. The polenta is poured onto a wooden board and spread in a thin layer, then topped with different sauces.

Polenta Pasticciata

Leftover polenta, sliced
Tomato sauce
Meatless burger or **Homemade Gluten** (p. 32)
Nondairy cheese
Imitation Parmesan Cheese (p. 130), optional

Heat oven 350 °F. Spread 2-3 tablespoons of tomato sauce on the bottom of a baking pan. Place the polenta slices in the pan and cover evenly with tomato sauce. Top with the meatless burger and nondairy cheese. If desired, sprinkle with Imitation Parmesan Cheese. Repeat with an additional layer if desired. Bake about 15-20 minutes or until hot and bubbling.

COOK'S HINTS:

- In Italy leftover polenta is never wasted. ***Polenta Pasticciata*** resembles the lasagna technique and is a wonderful way to serve polenta.

Menu 47

Innovative Italian

Don't be intimidated if you're not a baker. This Italian bread recipe is extremely easy, and will come out looking like you are experienced. The braided style is fun to make and is very attractive when finished. Dress it up according to the season, following some of the options listed.

- **Chicken Cacciatore**
- Whole-Grain Fettuccine Noodles
- Steamed Brussels Sprouts
- **Carrot Salad**
- **Braided Bread**
- **Orange Cake**

Chicken Cacciatore

2 tablespoons olive oil
1 pound frozen soy chicken, thawed and chopped (about 3 cups)
1 28-ounce can diced tomatoes
1 large onion, chopped
1 green bell pepper, sliced
2 cups sliced mushrooms
1 cup water
½ cup apple juice or white grape juice
1 6-ounce can tomato paste
2 teaspoons to 2 tablespoons chicken-style seasoning,* or to taste
1 clove garlic
½ teaspoon dried basil
½ teaspoon rosemary
½ teaspoon dried oregano leaves

Heat oil in a large skillet. Add soy chicken; cook and stir until golden brown. Stir in tomatoes, onion, bell pepper, mushrooms, water, apple juice, tomato paste, chicken-style seasoning, garlic, basil, rosemary, and oregano. Heat to boiling; reduce heat and simmer 15 minutes, or until vegetables are tender. Serve over cooked pasta or brown rice.
Makes 12 servings. 120 calories, 5 g fat, 463 mg sodium.

Carrot Salad

6 carrots, peeled and shredded (about 6 cups)
½ cup minced fresh parsley
1-2 cloves garlic, minced
¼ cup olive oil
juice from 1 lemon (about 3 tablespoons)

Mix carrots, parsley, and garlic together in a salad bowl. Stir oil and lemon juice together and pour over carrot mixture. Mix well. Refrigerate 30 minutes before serving.
Makes 12 ½-cup servings. 69 calories, 5 g fat, 46 mg sodium.

*see glossary

Braided Bread

1½ cups whole-wheat flour
¼ cup granulated cane sugar
1 tablespoon quick-rising yeast
1 teaspoon salt
¼ cup nonhydrogenated margarine (such as Earth Balance), softened
2 teaspoons egg replacement powder (such as Ener-G) dissolved in 2 tablespoons water
½ cup soy milk
½ cup hot water
1½ cups unbleached all-purpose flour, as needed
cooking spray
sesame seeds, optional

Mix whole-wheat flour, sugar, yeast, and salt together in a mixing bowl. Mix in margarine and egg replacement. Mix soy milk and hot water together; stir into flour mixture. Add all-purpose flour until dough is no longer sticky. Knead dough on a lightly floured surface about 5 minutes, until smooth and elastic. Divide dough into three equal portions. Roll each portion into a long strand about 16 inches long and about 1 inch in diameter. (The length and width are not that important, but they should all be the same length and width.) Place each strand side by side. Pinch all three strands together at one end and slightly fold the end under. Braid the three strands together. Pinch the strands together at the end of the loaf and slightly fold the end under. Place loaf on a baking sheet coated with cooking spray. Lightly spray the top of loaf with cooking spray. Sprinkle with sesame seeds, if desired. Place in a warm place and let rise 30 minutes or until doubled in size. Heat oven to 375°F. Bake 15-20 minutes, or until golden brown. Serve warm, allowing each person to pull his or her own piece of bread from the loaf. Makes 1 loaf; 12 servings. 162 calories, 4 g fat, 259 mg sodium.

VARIATIONS:

- Omit sesame seeds. Coat the top of hot bread with cooking spray, then sprinkle with cinnamon sugar.
- For festive occasions, such as Christmas, add ½ cup dried fruit, such as cranberries, raisins, apples, papaya, or mango.

Orange Cake

2 cups unbleached all-purpose flour
¾ cup fructose or granulated cane sugar
1½ tablespoons egg replacement powder (such as Ener-G) dissolved in 5 tablespoons water
2 teaspoons baking powder (preferably aluminum-free)
½ teaspoon salt
1 cup freshly squeezed orange juice (about 4 oranges)
⅓ cup olive or grape-seed oil
1 tablespoon freshly grated orange peel
cooking spray

Heat oven to 350°F. Mix flour, sugar, egg replacement, baking powder, and salt together in a mixing bowl. Make a well in the center. Pour in orange juice, oil, and grated orange peel and mix together. Spoon into a 9-inch square baking dish (or a fluted tube pan) coated with cooking spray. Bake 30 minutes or until a toothpick inserted near the center comes out clean. Let cool before slicing. Drizzle with a confectioners' sugar glaze, if desired. Makes 9 servings. 250 calories, 8 g fat, 131 mg sodium.

COOK'S HINTS:

- Confectioners' sugar, soy milk, and orange extract make a nice glaze to drizzle over this cake.

Menu 48

Vegan Italiano

Most people can't imagine eating pizza without cheese. But, surprisingly enough, the original Italian pizza did not have cheese. It was originally made similar to flat bread with olive oil and herbs as a topping. In time, tomatoes were introduced (after they lost their reputation as a poisonous fruit). The popular Pizza Margherita owes its name to Italy's Queen Margherita, who visited the Pizzeria Brandi in Naples in 1889. The pizzaioli (pizza maker) on duty that day, Rafaele Esposito, created a pizza for the queen that contained the three colors of the new Italian flag. The red from the tomato, white from the mozzarella, and fresh green basil were a hit with the queen (and the rest of the world). Neapolitan-style pizza then spread throughout Italy, and each region started designing their own versions based on the Italian culinary rule of fresh local ingredients.

- **Cream of Asparagus Soup**
- **Italian Pizza**
- Spring Salad Mix with **Italian Salad Dressing** (p. 128)
- Fresh Red and Green Grapes
- **Carob-Almond Fudge**

Cream of Asparagus Soup

2 tablespoons olive oil
1 small onion, chopped
3 cups water
2 cups fresh (or frozen) asparagus, trimmed and chopped
¼ cup soy milk powder
2 tablespoons unbleached all-purpose flour
1½ teaspoons to 1½ tablespoons chicken-style seasoning,* or to taste
½ teaspoon salt, or to taste

Heat oil in a large saucepan. Add onion; cook and stir until tender. Stir in water and asparagus. Cook until asparagus is tender. Process in a blender or food processor until smooth. Return to saucepan. Whisk in soy milk powder, flour, chicken-style seasoning, and salt. Heat to boiling over medium heat; reduce heat and simmer several minutes, until thickened.

Makes 6 1-cup servings. 77 calories, 5 g fat, 206 mg sodium.

COOK'S HINTS:

- You can replace the water and milk powder with 3 cups unsweetened soy milk.

Italian Pizza

Crust:

1 cup whole-wheat flour
¾ cup water
1 tablespoon quick-rising yeast
1 tablespoon honey
½ teaspoon salt
1 cup whole-wheat flour, as needed
cooking spray

Topping:

2 tablespoons olive oil
2 cloves garlic, thinly sliced
1 cup chopped ripe tomatoes
1 cup thinly sliced yellow or red onion
1 cup thinly sliced fresh mushrooms
½ cup sliced ripe olives
½-1 teaspoon dried oregano leaves
½ teaspoon salt, optional
2 tablespoons olive oil

Crust: Mix 1 cup flour, water, yeast, honey and salt together in a mixing bowl. Stir in remaining 1 cup flour and mix until dough forms a nice ball. (If dough is too sticky, add a little more flour, or if dough is too dry, add a little water.) Place dough

*see glossary

in the center of a 12-inch pizza pan coated with cooking spray. Cover with a towel and let stand 10-15 minutes. Heat oven to 350°F. Press the dough evenly to cover the pizza pan and about ½ inch up the sides to form a crust.

Topping: Brush 2 tablespoons oil on crust. Arrange garlic, tomatoes, onion, mushrooms, and olives over crust. Sprinkle with oregano and salt, if desired. Drizzle 2 tablespoons oil over pizza. Bake 15-20 minutes, or until crust is lightly browned. Cut into wedges. Serve immediately.
Makes 1 12-inch pizza; 12 servings. 132 calories, 6 g fat, 246 mg sodium.

Carob-Almond Fudge

- 1 cup carob chips
- ¾ cup almond butter
- ⅓ cup pure maple syrup
- ½ cup slivered almonds
- cooking spray
- ¼ cup sliced almonds

Mix carob chips, almond butter, maple syrup, and slivered almonds together in a saucepan. Heat over medium heat, stirring frequently, until carob chips melt. Spread evenly in a 5"x9"x3" pan coated with cooking spray. Sprinkle sliced almonds over fudge and press down gently. Refrigerate (or freeze) until firm. Cut into 1-inch pieces. Serve chilled (it becomes soft at room temperature).
Makes 24 servings. 121 calories, 9 g fat, 38 mg sodium.

Menu 49

Nuovo Neapolitan Cuisine

This lasagna recipe is a switch from the traditional tomato-based lasagna, and the peach pie tastes delectable, especially when made with fresh peaches during peak season.

- **Soy Chicken Lasagna**
- **Baked Carrots**
- Steamed Asparagus
- Spring Salad Mix with **Sun-dried Tomato Dressing**
- Warm Whole-Wheat Buns with Margarine
- **Peach Pie** with **Soy Whipped Cream** (p. 17)
- White Grape Juice

Soy Chicken Lasagna

- 10 whole-grain lasagna noodles (such as brown rice pasta)
- 1 16-ounce package medium or firm water-packed tofu, drained
- ¾ cup raw cashews
- ¼ cup water
- 1 tablespoon lemon juice
- ½ teaspoon onion powder
- ½ teaspoon garlic salt
- 2 tablespoons olive oil
- 1½ cups sliced fresh mushrooms
- 1 medium onion, chopped
- 1 20-ounce can soy chicken (such as Cedar Lake), drained and cut into ½-inch cubes
- 2½ cups **Condensed Mushroom Soup**
- cooking spray
- nondairy mozzarella cheese, optional

Cook lasagna noodles according to package directions. Drain; set aside. Place tofu in a medium bowl and mash with a fork until it resembles cottage cheese. Set aside. Process cashews, water, lemon juice, onion powder, and garlic salt in a blender or food processor until smooth. Stir into mashed tofu.

Heat oven to 350°F. Heat oil in a large skillet. Add mushrooms and onion; cook and stir until onion is tender. Stir in soy chicken cubes and **Condensed Mushroom Soup**. Stir in tofu mixture; heat until simmering. Remove from heat.

Place a layer of five lasagna noodles, slightly overlapping, to cover the bottom of a 9"x13" glass baking dish coated with cooking spray. Cover with half of the soy chicken mixture, and sprinkle with nondairy mozzarella cheese (again, if desired). Repeat layers with remaining noodles and soy chicken mixture, ending with the nondairy cheese (again, if desired). Bake 30-45 minutes, or until heated through. Let stand 10 minutes before cutting into squares.
Makes 12 servings. 328 calories, 14 g fat, 323 mg sodium.

COOK'S HINTS:

- This lasagna is more firm when prepared ahead and reheated.

Condensed Mushroom Soup

1½ cups soy milk
1 cup water
1 10-ounce can sliced mushrooms, drained
½ cup finely chopped onion
¼ cup whole-wheat, spelt, or unbleached all-purpose flour
3 tablespoons cornstarch
¾ teaspoon to 2 teaspoons chicken-style seasoning,* or to taste
½ teaspoon dried basil
½ teaspoon salt

Process soy milk, water, two-thirds of the mushrooms, onion, flour, cornstarch, chicken-style seasoning, basil, and salt in a blender or food processor until smooth. Add remaining mushrooms and pulse quickly to chop the mushrooms. Pour into a saucepan over medium heat and cook until thickened, stirring frequently. Let cool to room temperature. Divide into three freezerproof containers (about 1¼ cups each) and refrigerate up to one week or freeze 3-6 months. Use one container to replace one can of condensed mushroom soup in recipes.
Makes 3 1¼-cups containers of condensed soup; per container: 145 calories, 3 g fat, 830 mg sodium.

- To prepare **mushroom soup**, heat 1¼ cups of **Condensed Mushroom Soup** in a saucepan with 1¼ cups soy milk (or water). Cook over medium heat, stirring occasionally, until heated through. (Add additional milk or water if a thinner consistency is desired.)
Makes 2½ cups; 2½ 1-cup servings.
80 calories, 2 g fat, 383 mg sodium.

Baked Carrots

6 cups sliced, peeled carrots (⅛-inch diagonal slices)
½ cup thinly sliced onion
¼ cup water, as needed
2 tablespoons dried parsley
½ teaspoon salt

Heat oven to 350°F. Place carrots, onion, water, parsley, and salt in a 2-quart baking dish. (Add more water if necessary to cover the bottom of the dish). Cover and bake about 30 minutes, or until carrots are tender.
Makes 8 servings. 44 calories, 0 g fat, 35 mg sodium.

* see glossary

Sun-dried Tomato Dressing

- ⅔ cup water
- ⅓ cup extra-virgin olive oil
- ¼ cup oil-packed sun-dried tomatoes, drained
- 1-2 tablespoons lemon juice, or to taste
- 1 large clove garlic
- 1 tablespoon minced fresh oregano or 1 teaspoon dried leaves
- ½ teaspoon granulated cane sugar
- ¼ teaspoon salt

Process all ingredients in a blender or food processor until smooth. Refrigerate at least 1 hour before serving.

Makes 1 ⅓ cups; 21 1-tablespoon servings. 33 calories, 3 g fat, 30 mg sodium.

Peach Pie

- 1 single **Whole-Wheat Piecrust** or **Spelt Piecrust**, baked and cooled (p. 26)
- 6 large fresh peaches, peeled and sliced
- ¼ cup water, or as needed
- ½ cup honey
- 2 tablespoons pure cane syrup (such as Roger's), or corn syrup, or honey
- 2 tablespoons cornstarch
- 2 tablespoons agar powder
- ½ cup **Soy Whipped Cream**

Prepare piecrust. Arrange the slices from four peaches in the baked piecrust. Process remaining peach slices and water in a blender or food processor until smooth. Pour into a 4-cup liquid measure and add water to make 2½ cups. Pour peach puree into a saucepan and stir in honey, cane syrup, cornstarch, and agar. Heat to boiling; reduce heat and simmer 5 minutes, or until mixture is thickened and cornstarch turns translucent. Pour over peach slices in piecrust. Cool to room temperature. Refrigerate 2 hours, or until set. Serve with Soy Whipped Cream.

Makes 1 pie; 8 servings. 449 calories, 14 g fat, 120 mg sodium.

Menu 50

Milano Verde

***Fusilli With Pesto Sauce** is my son Reuben's absolute favorite dish. Replacing the fresh parsley with basil gives it a completely different taste.*

*The **Carob-Tofu Cream Dessert** comes from my friend Sheila Beaudoin. Her husband, Pastor David, considers this to be his favorite dessert. When you try it, I think you'll see why.*

- **Fusilli With Pesto Sauce**
- **Pecan Meatballs** with Marinara Sauce
- Cooked Baby Carrots with Dill
- Green Salad with Dressing
- **Garlic Toast Spread** (p. 131)
- **Carob Candies** or **Carob-Tofu Cream Dessert**

Fusilli With Pesto Sauce

- 1 recipe **Pesto Sauce**
- 1 16-ounce package fusilli

Prepare Pesto Sauce. Cook fusilli according to package directions. Drain and rinse with hot water. Pour pesto sauce over pasta and mix well. Serve immediately.

Makes 10 servings. 289 calories, 14 g fat, 185 mg sodium.

COOK'S HINTS:

- *Fusilli* means "little springs." This shape of pasta works especially well to trap flavorful sauces.

Pesto Sauce

- 2 tablespoons **Imitation Parmesan Cheese** (p. 130)
- 2 packed cups fresh parsley sprigs
- ½ cup pine nuts, walnuts, or almonds
- ⅓ cup olive oil
- ¼ cup water
- 2 cloves garlic, peeled
- ¾ teaspoon salt, or to taste

Prepare Imitation Parmesan Cheese and place 2 tablespoons of it in a blender or food processor. Add parsley sprigs, pine nuts, olive oil, water, garlic, and salt, and process until smooth.

Makes 10 servings. 122 calories, 13 g fat, 182 mg sodium.

COOK'S HINTS:

- Pesto sauce can be frozen up to 4 months. For best results when freezing, omit the **Imitation Parmesan Cheese**. Stir it in before serving.
- Pesto is also tasty as a spread on bread.
- Replace parsley with fresh basil or try a combination of the two herbs.

Pecan Meatballs

- 1 cup finely ground pecans
- 1 16-ounce package medium or firm water-packed tofu, drained
- 2½ cups unseasoned, dry, whole-grain bread crumbs
- 1 medium onion, minced
- 2 tablespoons nutritional yeast flakes
- 1 tablespoon dried parsley
- 2 teaspoons to 2 tablespoons chicken-style seasoning,* or to taste
- 1 teaspoon poultry seasoning
- ½ teaspoon salt
- cooking spray

Heat oven to 375°F. Process pecans in a blender or food processor until ground. Transfer to a mixing bowl. Process tofu in a blender or food processor until smooth, then add to ground pecans. Mix in bread crumbs, onion, nutritional yeast, parsley, chicken-style seasoning, poultry seasoning, and salt. Form into golf ball-sized balls using hands (or a small scoop). Place on two baking sheets coated with cooking spray. Bake 20 minutes; turn balls over and bake another 10 minutes, or until lightly browned.

Makes 3 dozen meatballs; 36 servings. 71 calories, 4 g fat, 93 mg sodium.

COOK'S HINTS:

- To make dry bread crumbs, grind whole-grain bread in a blender or food processor. Spread out on a baking sheet and bake at a low temperature, until dried.
- To serve: cover meatballs with marinara sauce. Bake 20-30 minutes, until bubbling.
- Make extra and freeze for future use.

Carob Candies

- 1½ cups carob chips
- ¾ cup unsweetened shredded coconut
- ½ cup natural peanut butter
- ¼ cup soy milk powder
- ¼ cup water
- 1 teaspoon vanilla extract

Stir carob chips, coconut, peanut butter, soy milk powder, water, and vanilla together in a medium saucepan. Heat over medium heat, stirring frequently, until carob chips melt. Drop by tablespoonfuls onto a baking sheet lined with waxed paper (or use to fill candy molds.) Freeze. Serve frozen.

Makes 2 dozen. 130 calories, 10 g fat, 30 mg sodium.

*see glossary

Carob-Tofu Cream Dessert

Crust:

1 cup graham cracker crumbs
3 tablespoons canola or grape-seed oil
1 tablespoon honey

Filling:

12 ounces medium or firm tofu, drained (about 1½ cups)
⅔ cup brown sugar
¼ cup oil
¼ cup carob powder
1 teaspoon vanilla extract
¼ teaspoon salt

Crust: Heat oven to 350°F. Mix graham cracker crumbs, oil, and honey together. Press into a 9-inch square baking dish. Bake about 10 minutes, or until lightly browned. Let cool.

Filling: Process tofu, brown sugar, oil, carob powder, vanilla, and salt in a blender or food processor until smooth. Pour into baked graham cracker crust. Refrigerate 8 hours or overnight. Serve with a dollop of Soy Whippped Cream (p. 17).

Makes 9 servings. 162 calories, 12 g fat, 155 mg sodium.

- A double recipe will fill a 9"x13" pan.

Menu 51

Pomodoro Italiano

Ratatouille stars as a way to enjoy abundant summer vegetables. It can be served as a side dish or appetizer along with crunchy bread. Ratatouille derives its superb flavor from the freshest of vegetables. The best results will come from your own garden-fresh vegetables or fresh, seasonal produce from your local farmer's market.

- **Stuffed Pasta Shells**
- **Ratatouille**
- Steamed Broccoli
- **Italian Buns**
- **No-Bake Cookies**
- **Sparkling Apple Punch**

Stuffed Pasta Shells

1 16-ounce package medium or firm water-packed tofu, drained
½ cup cashews
⅓ cup water
1 tablespoon nutritional yeast flakes
1 tablespoon lemon juice
1 teaspoon garlic powder
½ teaspoon onion powder
½ teaspoon salt
½ cup shredded carrots
1 10-ounce package frozen, chopped spinach, thawed and squeezed dry
salt, for cooking pasta
1 tablespoon olive oil, optional
1 12-ounce box large pasta shells
2 24-ounce cans Italian tomato sauce
shredded nondairy cheese, optional

Place tofu in a mixing bowl; mash with a fork until it resembles cottage cheese. Process cashews, water, nutritional yeast, lemon juice, garlic powder, onion powder, and salt in a blender or food processor until smooth. Stir into mashed tofu. Mix in carrots and spinach. Refrigerate 1 hour.

Heat a large saucepan of water to boiling. Add a little salt and 1 tablespoon of oil, if desired, to prevent pasta from sticking together. Stir in pasta shells. Cook until pasta is almost tender but not completely cooked (*al dente*). Drain shells in a colander.

Heat oven to 350°F. Pour tomato sauce into a 13×9-inch glass baking dish. Fill each shell with tofu mixture. Place pasta shells in sauce with open side up. Sprinkle with nondairy cheese, if desired. Cover and bake 20-30 minutes, or until hot and bubbling.
Makes 8 servings. 366 calories, 13 g fat, 652 mg sodium.

Ratatouille

- 1 medium eggplant, unpeeled and cut into ¾-inch cubes
- 1 large zucchini, cut into ¾-inch cubes
- ½ large red bell pepper, cut into ½-inch cubes
- 1 medium red onion, cut in half vertically and into ¼-inch thick strips
- cooking spray
- 1 14½-ounce can diced tomatoes
- ¾ teaspoon garlic powder
- ½ teaspoon dried oregano leaves
- ½ teaspoon dried basil
- ½ teaspoon salt
- shredded nondairy cheese, optional

Heat oven to 350°F. Place eggplant, zucchini, bell pepper, and onion in a baking dish coated with cooking spray. Stir in tomatoes, garlic powder, oregano, basil, and salt. Bake, covered, for 30 minutes. Uncover, and sprinkle with nondairy cheese, if desired. Bake an additional 10 minutes, or until vegetables are tender.
Makes 6 servings. 48 calories, 0 g fat, 274 mg sodium.

Italian Buns

- 2½ cups warm water
- 1½ tablespoons dry active yeast
- 2 teaspoons granulated cane sugar
- 1½ cups unbleached all-purpose flour
- 1½ tablespoons egg replacement powder (such as Ener-G) dissolved in 3 tablespoons water
- 2 tablespoons olive oil
- 2 teaspoons salt
- 1½ cups whole-wheat flour, as needed
- oil or cooking spray, for coating bowl
- cooking spray

Stir warm water, yeast, and sugar together in a large mixing bowl. Let stand 10 minutes, or until yeast bubbles. Mix in unbleached flour, egg replacement, oil, and salt. Beat with a stand mixer (or electric mixer) for at least 2 minutes. Gradually mix in whole-wheat flour with a dough hook, adding flour until dough is no longer sticky, forms a ball, and pulls away from the sides. (If mixing by hand, dough should be slightly sticky.) Knead 4-5 minutes with a dough hook (or 8-10 minutes by hand) until dough is smooth and elastic. Lightly coat mixing bowl with oil; place dough in the bowl and turn dough to coat lightly with oil. Cover with a towel and let rise in a warm place until doubled in size, about 1 hour.

Punch dough down, and let rise until doubled, about 45 minutes. Heat oven to 425°F. Punch dough down, and turn out onto a lightly floured surface. Divide dough into 24 equal pieces. Form each piece into an oval roll about 3½ inches long. Place on baking sheets coated with cooking spray. Cover and let rise until doubled in size, about 40 minutes. Place a baking pan half full of water on the bottom rack of the oven and immediately place the baking sheets with rolls in the oven. Bake 20 minutes, or until the tops are golden brown. Cool on a wire rack.
Makes 24 rolls. 67 calories, 1 g fat, 195 mg sodium.

No-Bake Cookies

½ cup soy milk
½ cup honey
1 teaspoon vanilla extract
1¼ cups unsweetened shredded coconut
⅓ cup carob powder
1½ cups quick-cooking oats

Heat soy milk, honey and vanilla to boiling in a saucepan over medium heat. Remove from heat. Mix in coconut and carob powder. Mix in oats and mix well. Drop by tablespoonfuls onto a baking sheet lined with waxed paper. Refrigerate until firm.
Makes 2 dozen. 109 calories, 7 g fat, 6 mg sodium.

Sparkling Apple Punch

6 cups apple juice
2 cups white grape juice
1 cup unsweetened pineapple juice
2 cups lemon-lime flavored carbonated water

Stir apple juice, white grape juice, and pineapple juice together in a punch bowl. Refrigerate until chilled. Stir in carbonated water just before serving.
Makes 11 1-cup servings. 104 calories, 0 g fat, 7 mg sodium.

*see glossary

Menu 52

Vegetarian Cucina

A calzone, sometimes referred to as an Italian sac, is a turnover made from pizza dough stuffed with cheese, meat, and vegetables. The dough is folded over, sealed, salted, and deep-fried. Calzone are typically served with marinara sauce on the side for dipping, or topped with garlic and parsley-infused olive oil. My boys LOVE these baked vegan calzone, even more than homemade pizza!

- **Bean Soup**
- **Calzone** with Marinara Sauce
- **Caesar Salad** (p. 129)
- **Carob Balls**

Bean Soup

8 cups water
2 cups navy beans (or small white beans)
1 28-ounce can diced tomatoes
1 large onion, chopped
1 cup chopped celery
1 cup chopped carrots
1 cup whole-wheat elbow or small shell pasta
1 tablespoon dried parsley
1 teaspoon garlic powder
1 teaspoon salt
½ teaspoon dried basil
2 teaspoons to 2 tablespoons beef-style seasoning,* or to taste, optional

Heat water and beans to boiling in a large saucepan; reduce heat and simmer 1½-2 hours, or until beans are tender. Stir in tomatoes, onion, celery, carrots, pasta, parsley, garlic powder, salt, and basil. Stir in beef-style seasoning, if desired. Simmer until vegetables and pasta are tender.
Makes 16 1-cup servings. 130 calories, 1 g fat, 225 mg sodium.

Calzone

Filling:

1 16-ounce package medium or firm water-packed tofu, drained (preferably reduced-fat)
1 tablespoon olive oil
1 medium onion, chopped
4 cloves garlic, minced
1 10-ounce package frozen chopped spinach, thawed and squeezed dry
2 tablespoons nutritional yeast flakes
1 teaspoon dried basil
½ teaspoon salt
½ cup shredded nondairy cheese, optional

Dough:

cooking spray
2 cups whole-wheat flour
1½ cups warm water
2 tablespoons quick-rise dry active yeast
2 tablespoons granulated cane sugar
½ teaspoon salt
2 cups unbleached all-purpose flour

Filling: Mash tofu in a bowl with a fork. Heat oil in a large skillet. Add onion and garlic; cook and stir 4 minutes. Stir in tofu, spinach, nutritional yeast, basil, and salt. Simmer until liquid has evaporated. Stir in nondairy cheese, if desired.

Dough: Heat oven to 400°F. Coat two baking sheets with cooking spray. Mix whole-wheat flour, water, yeast, sugar, and salt together in a mixing bowl. Gradually mix in all-purpose flour until dough forms a soft ball and is no longer sticky. Divide dough into eight portions. Roll each portion of dough on a lightly floured surface into a circle about 6 inches in diameter. Place about ½ cup of filling on the lower half of each circle, leaving about a ½-inch border. Fold the top half of the dough over the filling. Seal and crimp around the edge using your fingers or a fork. Place four calzone on each baking sheet. Bake 15 minutes, or until nicely browned on the top and bottom. Serve warm with marinara or spaghetti sauce for dipping.
Makes 8 servings. 454 calories, 6 g fat, 600 mg sodium.

Carob Balls

1 cup wheat germ
1 cup chopped dates
1 cup soy milk powder
1 cup finely ground almonds
1 cup natural peanut butter
⅓ cup honey
3 tablespoons apple juice
2 cups carob chips

Heat oven to 325°F. Spread the wheat germ in a small baking dish and toast in the oven 8-10 minutes, until lightly browned. Place dates in a bowl and pour very hot tap water over them and let soften for about 5 minutes. Drain. Reserve wheat germ and dates. Process almonds in a food processor or blender until finely ground.

Mix soy milk powder, ground almonds, peanut butter, honey, and apple juice together in a mixing bowl. Mix in toasted wheat germ and softened dates. Mix well, using hands. Form into 1-inch balls. Melt carob chips in a saucepan over low heat (or in a double boiler). Dip balls in melted carob and place on a baking sheet lined with waxed paper. Place balls in freezer. Remove from freezer 5 minutes before serving.
Makes about 3 dozen balls. 134 calories, 8 g fat, 35 mg sodium.

COOK'S HINTS:

- Make these ahead and store in your freezer. They make excellent gifts.

Index